"I loved this book. I often talk to people who ask, 'Why did this happen to me?' or 'Why did God let that happen?' Noel Forlini Burt beautifully guides us through the lives of biblical figures who face wilderness experiences and similar questions. With wisdom, scholarship, an understanding of attachment patterns, and narratives of 'not enough,' the author opens pathways that slowly lead to a healing trust in the God who sees you!"

Adele Ahlberg Calhoun, author of *The Spiritual Disciplines Handbook*, *Invitations from God*, and *Spiritual Rhythms for the Enneagram*

"Noel Forlini Burt takes us on a spiritually rich journey informed by her expertise in both the Old Testament and spiritual formation. She has drunk deeply from the Scriptures themselves as well as from the insights of the desert fathers and mothers and others who have written profoundly about wilderness experiences and their important role in our spiritual formation. Her discussion of attachment theory and our need for attachment to God enriches the rest. This biblically and spiritually rich book is a must-read for all who walk in the desert or are called to minister to those in the wilderness."

Roy E. Ciampa, professor emeritus at Samford University

"In this beautifully written book, Noel Forlini Burt engages in conversation with a wide range of voices, both ancient and modern, as she invites the reader into a rich and compelling reflection on Scripture. Her work, however, is not simply a rehearsal of a biblical theme. More profoundly, it is an invitation to the wilderness, the 'place where we learn that God is the one before whom we are all laid bare.' In this moment when Christianity has been so culturally co-opted, we need a book that calls us back to the places of deep faithful formation. This is that book."

W. Dennis Tucker, Jr., professor of Christian scriptures at Baylor University's George W. Truett Theological Seminary

GOD IN THE DESERT

A SPIRITUAL THEOLOGY OF WILDERNESS IN THE OLD TESTAMENT

NOEL FORLINI BURT

Academic
An imprint of InterVarsity Press
Downers Grove, Illinois

InterVarsity Press
P.O. Box 1400 | Downers Grove, IL 60515-1426
ivpress.com | email@ivpress.com

InterVarsity Press® is the publishing division of InterVarsity Christian Fellowship/USA®. For more information, visit intervarsity.org.

All Scripture quotations, unless otherwise indicated, are translated by the author.

Cover design: Faceout Studio, Tim Green
Interior design: Jeanna Wiggins
Images: © NAN ZHONG / Moment via Getty Images
© abzee via iStock

ISBN 978-1-5140-1030-3 (print) | ISBN 978-1-5140-1031-0 (digital)

Printed in the United States of America ♾

Library of Congress Cataloging-in-Publication Data
A catalog record for this book is available from the Library of Congress.

33 32 31 30 29 28 27 26 | 13 12 11 10 9 8 7 6 5 4 3 2 1

For Dr. J. Norfleete Day,

who has woven together biblical studies

and spiritual formation so seamlessly,

disciplinarily and in her own life,

that it is difficult to pull them apart.

CONTENTS

Introduction

LETTERS FROM THE DESERT

The road of cleansing goes through that desert.
It shall be named the way of holiness.

ISAIAH 35:8 LXX

NOT LONG AGO, I peeked inside an old cabinet where I keep shoeboxes full of cards and letters from friends through the years. On the top of one of those shoeboxes, I had written the words "Letters from the Desert." As I opened the box, about thirty blue and purple envelopes tumbled out, all written by the same person, all addressed to me.

I had completely forgotten about them.

I don't remember how or why we started, but for about two years I exchanged letters with a friend when we lived on opposite sides of the country. Most of the modern conventions of communication existed then—email, texting, even video call—yet we wrote old-fashioned letters with real pens on real stationery, put a stamp on each envelope, and mailed them.

I assume my own letters are tucked away somewhere in the house she shares with her husband and children.

She's probably forgotten about them too.

I don't remember all the events of those two years in her life or even in my own. I do remember, however, that those years were marked by certain intense experiences, different for both of us but that seemed to overlap. Geographically far apart, we shared a similar spiritual geography. For those two years, we walked with each other through our individual wilderness experiences, our epistolary correspondence a record of our inner landscapes at the time. Our old-fashioned letter writing was a form of spiritual friendship in which we both tried to make sense of our lives, and our lives with God.

Through our letters, I learned that desert or wilderness is a spiritually portable image. Both of us used this image in different ways to describe different aspects of our lives. The varied expressions of wilderness I uncovered in our letters suggest what many of us know intuitively from our own lived experiences—there are many different types of wildernesses, and wilderness is not just a spiritual experience; it is also an embodied reality. We experience wilderness *in* bodies and *as* bodies.

Besides the shoebox containing the letters from the desert, I've also kept stacks of my own journals for the past twenty years. Like the letters from the desert, my journals trace my spiritual geography, giving me a vivid picture of my inner landscape in which I have tried to make sense of my life, and my life with God. These journals function as my spiritual autobiography, and they also reveal that Christians may go through multiple wilderness stretches throughout their lives or encounter wilderness at any time. In this way also, wilderness is a spiritually portable image.

As I revisited our letters and my own journals, a single question seemed common to both: "Who is the God I encounter in the desert?"

That is the central question of this book, not because it is *my question* but because it is *the great question* throughout time for people of faith. Like my own journals, the biblical text is also a spiritual autobiography of sorts. In its sacred pages, individuals and whole communities used narrative, poetry, and yes, letters, to make sense of their lives and their lives with God. The Bible raises the question forcefully and at many different points in the story: "Who is the God *we* encounter in the desert?"

Such a question necessitates, conjointly, an exploration of the desert itself. Nowhere in our letters from the desert did my friend and I attempt a *definition* of wilderness. What we did was sketch a *description* through the events in our lives. Likewise, there is no definition of wilderness in the biblical text, merely descriptions of wilderness as people meander their way through it. Words can only get us so far. Similarly, all throughout Scripture, *the God of the desert resists definition*. Like Moses, we see the back of the God of the desert, but not his face. There too, words can only get us so far.

But what we can do is stop.

We can pause, survey the spiritual terrain of the wilderness, examine the tracks made in the desert by biblical characters, figures in church history, and scholars who have also surveyed this landscape. In doing so, we might just make some sense of our own lives and of our lives with the God of the desert.

It is toward a description of desert—and the God of the desert—that we now turn.

Letters from the Biblical Desert

Examination of the biblical text reveals wilderness to be both literal and metaphorical. Wilderness functions as the literal setting for many stories, yet this geographical setting highlights the metaphorical or spiritual nature of struggle in this hard place. In this way, physical geography and spiritual geography often intertwine. Many of the best-known stories in Scripture take place in the desert.

Within the Pentateuch, wilderness is used as the geographical and narrative setting for most of the events that unfold. In Genesis, the biblical writers use wilderness sparingly yet to great rhetorical effect. Several key stories in Genesis highlight wilderness as a place of critical encounter. Hagar receives a promise from the angel of the Lord in wilderness (Gen 16:7-16) as well as provision by Elohim for her son (Gen 21:8-21). Jacob's dream at Bethel also takes place in wilderness, in which Yahweh reminds Jacob of his faithfulness to the patriarchs before him and promises to be with Jacob also (Gen 28:10-22). In these stories, the wilderness takes on a mystical quality, with dreams, darkness, and human drama met by divine provision. The fierce landscape of the wilderness is mirrored in the beleaguered inner landscape of weary travelers, yet God provides solace for both characters.

In Exodus and the remainder of the Pentateuch, the biblical authors foreground wilderness or desert as the primary geographical and spiritual landscape. In Exodus, the narrative takes a definitive turn toward the desert, with the Hebrew writer revealing, "So God *caused* the people to take the roundabout way of the wilderness" (Ex 13:18). Here the grammatical and the spiritual mutually reinforce each other—the writer uses the Hebrew grammar to convey that the Israelites' arrival in the desert is no accident but a divinely choreographed journey.[1] The Israelites remain suspended in the desert through the long stretch of pentateuchal narrative, where Yahweh leads them through a pillar of cloud by day and a pillar of fire by night (Ex 13:20-22; 14:19-20), where they articulate a narrative regarding scarcity of resources (Ex 14:1-14; 15:22-27; 16:1-12; 17:1-7) and receive the law (Ex 20; Deut 5). In the book of Numbers, which Hebrew tradition aptly names *bemidbar* ("in the wilderness"), the Israelites grumble and rebel against the Lord and Moses (Num 11; 14; 16; cf. Ex 32). Set a generation after the initial wilderness sojourn, the book of Deuteronomy seeks to remember and to reframe the wilderness as a key chapter in the spiritual autobiography of the Israelites, in which Yahweh consoled and provided for his people (Deut 8).

Outside the Pentateuch, the prophet Elijah experiences the succor of Yahweh in the wilderness (1 Kings 19). The prophets Isaiah and Jeremiah

[1]Here the Hebrew writer uses the *hiphil* verbal stem of the geminate verb *savav* ("to turn around, to go around," "to encircle") to underscore the causative agency of God: *wayyassev*.

use wilderness as a metaphor for exile (Is 40; Jer 4), while Hosea longs for a return to the desert in which Yahweh first made a marriage covenant with Israel (Hos 2). The psalmists offer poetic prayers both about their own experiences in wilderness (Ps 63) and about the spiritual history of their ancestors in wilderness (Ps 77–78). In the New Testament, both John the Baptist (Mt 3:1-11; Lk 3:1-20) and Jesus (Mt 4:1-11; Mk 1:12-13; Lk 4:1-13) are fortified for ministry in the desert.

Despite its prevalence in the biblical text, there have been few substantive treatments of the theology of the wilderness. Published more than twenty years ago, Robert Barry Leal's *Wilderness in the Bible: Toward a Theology of Wilderness* remains the most robust treatment of the subject. Leal culls together in one place all the biblical texts that mention wilderness, dividing them into categories: wilderness as a place of critical encounter with God in which individuals experienced wonder, silence, limitlessness, or self-knowledge; wilderness as a place of grace where God revealed Godself, or where people were disciplined, purified, or transformed; wilderness as a picture of God's good creation, whereby the wilderness served as a refuge or a moral and spiritual haven; or, perhaps more stereotypically, wilderness as a negative place.[2] Because he examines the whole of the biblical narrative, Leal's *Wilderness in the Bible* is by necessity a shorter treatment of many different texts. While I provide a fuller treatment of fewer biblical texts, Leal's work is a vital point of connection for my own exploration of both the God of the desert and the desert itself.

Letters from the Historical Desert

While the biblical text is replete with stories that take place there, wilderness also functions as a metaphor for people beyond the Bible. Early Christians have left us a correspondence of sorts (letters, if you will) about their experiences in wilderness. What we find is that, whereas

[2]Robert Barry Leal, *Wilderness in the Bible: Toward a Theology of Wilderness*, Studies in Biblical Literature 72 (Peter Lang, 2004).

people in the Bible are frequently cast into the wilderness, for many Christians in church history, wilderness was an intentional sojourn. For these individuals, wilderness functioned as a place of solace and escape.

In the third and fourth centuries, Christians fled to the Egyptian, Syrian, and Arabian deserts to lead simpler, quieter lives of devotion to God. Their flight to the desert was a rejection of the newly Christianized Roman Empire, which they saw as too ensconced with the trappings of the world, with its ornate worship, easy-believism, and broadening of Jesus' narrow way. These believers made the desert their home, choosing lives of asceticism, isolation, and physical and spiritual poverty. As Thomas Merton says, "The Desert Fathers believed that the wilderness had been created as supremely valuable in the eyes of God precisely because it had no value to men. The wasteland was the land that could never be wasted by men because it offered them nothing. There was nothing to attract them. There was nothing to exploit."[3] Strikingly, the nothingness and the unattractive quality of the desert are also characteristics of the nation of Israel in Isaiah's own day (Is 53:2-3) or of Jesus himself in the New Testament (Mt 8:14-17; Lk 22:35-38; Jn 12:37-41; Acts 8:26-35; Rom 10:11-21; 1 Pet 2:19-25). Moreover, the temptation to exploit God for our own ends, making God into whatever image is most useful for us at any given theological or political moment, is a recognizable impulse throughout history and in our own stories too. The God of the desert resists this impulse, even as the desert reveals our temptations to do so.

The desert fathers and desert mothers fought these same temptations, famously doing battle with inner demons they called the eight *logismoi*, or "thoughts." These eight may have a familiar ring to them: gluttony, avarice, fornication, anger, grief, listlessness, vainglory, and pride. Other lists include acedia, a destructive type of thought I will discuss later. Indeed, traditional spirituality regards the whole of the Christian life as a march through the desert in which we do battle with our thoughts. We

[3]Thomas Merton, *Thoughts in Solitude* (Farrar, Straus & Giroux, 1956), 4-5.

left Egypt (the land of sin), crossed the Red Sea (figuring baptism), and then began a spiritual itinerary that lasts throughout life, what Jean-Charles Nault refers to as "a veritable pilgrimage in the desert." In order to enter the Promised Land (eternal life), we must fight these eight enemies of the spiritual life, which are allegorized in Egypt and the seven other nations Israel must fight (Deut 7:1).[4] Through the spiritual practices of *apatheia*, which refers to a cultivated indifference to what happens to oneself, good or bad, and the prayer of rest, called *hesychasm*, desert fathers and desert mothers became known for their quiet wisdom. Other Christians journeyed to the desert, beseeching these desert dwellers, "Abba [or amma], give me a word." It was out of the desert silence that their words were believed to have generative power.

In the medieval period, Christian mystics adopted many of the same spiritual inclinations of the desert fathers and desert mothers: the choice to lead lives of physical and spiritual poverty, the conviction that God could be sought in silence, and the willing of one thing, understood as devotion to God in the desert tradition and union with God by the mystics, who often wrote about the relationship between God and the believer as one of lover and beloved. For the mystics, the desert proved to be a favorite image of the spiritual life and even for God. John of the Cross describes the experience of numbness in the spiritual life both as a dark night and as "solitary places of the wilderness," in which our experiences of aridness create in us a deeper thirst for God.[5] Meister Eckhart draws on Hosea 2 to encourage Christians to go to an inner desert inside themselves, to be "alone one on One."[6] Elsewhere, Eckhart refers to God as the desert, taking on the same stark and barren qualities as the geographical space itself.[7]

---

[4]Jean-Charles Nault, OSB, *The Noonday Devil: Acedia, the Unnamed Evil of Our Times* (Ignatius, 2015), 25.

[5]Paul A. Boer, ed., *The Essential St John of the Cross: Ascent of Mount Carmel, Dark Night of the Soul, A Spiritual Canticle, Twenty Poems* (Wilder, 2008), 392.

[6]Jon M. Sweeney and Mark S. Burrows, eds., *Meister Eckhart's Book of Darkness and Light: Meditations on the Path of the Wayless Way* (Hampton Roads, 2023), 33.

[7]Meister Eckhart, *The Essential Sermons, Commentaries, Treatises, and Defense* (Paulist Press, 1981), 265.

In the modern era, Christians such as Thomas Merton and Henri Nouwen explored spiritual practices of prayer, silence, and solitude, providing Christians with accessible and popular introductions to desert spirituality.[8] Some feminist and womanist scholars view the wilderness as a symbol of their own oppression in worldly systems of exploitation and domination. Indeed, the movements of #metoo and #churchtoo underscore that, for some women, church itself is a wilderness space. Conversely, other feminist and womanist scholars find comfort in the spiritual symbolism of wilderness as a space of solitude in which they encounter the Jesus who is near to them and works to liberate them from oppressive systems of abuse.[9]

Letters from the Contemporary Desert

There is a case to be made that all of life is wilderness in some way. As long as we exist in a world in which those we know and love suffer, in which the least of these are oppressed, in which our inability to see God face-to-face (or the reality of our own faces, for that matter) necessitates our continued maturing in the faith, we walk the desert road. So long as we continue to write letters or send up letters in the form of prayer to the God we hope keeps watch with us, we make tracks in the desert. So long as we grapple with confusion, spiritual malaise, or the deep questions raised by the places of pain in our own lives and in the lives of those we love, we amble through the wilderness. And, as long as we seek out retreats and spaces of respite (intentional and modern flights into the wilderness), wilderness is a present and embodied reality. At best, what we can say is that some aspects of our lives are wilderness while others are not, but I take the words of Walter Brueggemann to express

---

[8]Accessible and spiritually enriching treatments of this topic include Henri Nouwen, *The Way of the Heart: Connecting with God Through Prayer, Wisdom, and Silence* (Ballantine Books, 1981); Thomas Merton, *The Wisdom of the Desert* (New Directions Books, 1960); Thomas Merton, *Thoughts in Solitude* (Farrar, Straus & Giroux, 1956); and Roberta C. Bondi, *To Pray and to Love: Conversations on Prayer with the Early Church* (Fortress, 1991).

[9]For a useful starting place on womanist interpretations of wilderness and its intersection with wilderness, see Delores Williams, *Sisters in the Wilderness: The Challenge of Womanist God-Talk* (Orbis Books, 1993), which I will explore in chapter one.

the reality of life in today's world: "The narrative of faith is characteristically about a journey in and through wilderness."[10]

Written during the Covid-19 pandemic, Brueggemann's work *A Wilderness Zone* is significant for the way it weaves biblical theology with the contemporary sociopolitical concerns of Covid-19, Black Lives Matter protests in the wake of Trumpism, and economic disparity supported by capitalism and the cheap labor that makes that very capitalism possible and sustainable. In some ways, the global pandemic highlighted what was already present among us—an unwillingness at the political level to engage with those different from ourselves, a weariness and xenophobia that drives our policies about immigration or boundary or border crossing of any kind, a mistrust of and even disgust for brown and Black bodies and communities, and a denial of science rooted in mistrust of medical authority. Brueggemann's critique of our current sociopolitical moment is a reminder of at least two things: Sometimes we exist in a desert of our own making, and desert is not a concept relegated to the numinous or the spiritual but is a descriptor of people's actual lives. As I said previously, this means that *wilderness is an embodied reality*—we experience wilderness *in* bodies and *as* bodies.

As a result, wilderness experiences shape and stretch the very faith that Christians proclaim, sometimes because the character and personality of God in such seasons proves confusing and even jarring. It is in the wilderness that sophisticated theological systems undergo a kenosis, an emptying, a bottomless collapse, dismantling the adult and systematized language we have for God. Theologically and spiritually, we become children again, yet this childlike vulnerability awakens in us a curiosity that leads us to explore questions of faith we might not grapple with in other seasons of life with God.

In many ways, wilderness is a school in which we experience an unlearning of all we thought we knew. The theological statements we have turned into dogma and punctuated with an exclamation point—an

[10] Walter Brueggemann, *A Wilderness Zone* (Cascade Books, 2021), 1.

emphatic straight line with a period at the bottom—lose some of their straight edges and bend into the curious curve of a question mark. Paradoxically, this unlearning (a key idea in the Christian mystical tradition) brings two postures into tension with each other—the cultivation of the childlike trust needed for the desert and the maturity to withstand it. In this way, we learn, as Belden C. Lane aptly calls it, the "solace" of this fierce landscape.[11] Whether we find God consoling or fierce in whatever particular wilderness we find ourselves in, Brueggemann rightly reminds us that wilderness is a journey of *faith*. This means that for people of faith like us, wilderness is a journey we take *with God*. Therefore, God and the desert alike teach us both to lament and to praise. For the psalmists, those poets who frequently prayed about their wilderness experiences, lament and doxology are the whole refrain of the spiritual life, all there is. To join them in their poetic chorus is to know the whole of human experience.

In this way, wilderness is a landscape of grace. It is a liminal space, a space that is betwixt and between, space caught on the threshold from one thing to another, a space that teaches us to hold everything we think we know—about God, about ourselves, and about the way the world works—loosely, with self-reflection, and on occasion with repentant care. Wilderness, more than any other spiritual space, teaches us to let go, to come and die. And it is a space that teaches us to be reborn. For whatever is reborn in this space, in order for it to remain, it must remain *in* God. This is one of the gifts we receive in the desert, from the God of the desert.

Toward a Description of the Desert

Just as the God of the desert does not show us his face, only his back, so too the desert itself defies easy definition. What I will offer here and throughout the book, then, is not definition but description. What *is clear* from this brief survey is that people of faith in every era have found wilderness to be a useful metaphor for the spiritual life.

---

[11]Belden C. Lane, *The Solace of Fierce Landscapes: Exploring Desert and Mountain Spirituality* (Oxford University Press, 1998).

Within the biblical text and beyond, I take wilderness to be an aggregate image for opposing experiences or feelings, such as the absence and the hyperpresence of God, silence and speech, darkness and luminosity, barrenness and fecundity, dislocation/exile and homecoming, betrothal and divorce, consolation and desolation, hunger and satiation, abuse and nurture, and divine abandonment and divine succor, to name a few. In short, wilderness involves disorientation, waiting, suffering, restlessness, confusion, spiritual malaise, darkness, stripping away of all the usual things on which we can rely, and, provocatively, encounter with God. Here again, the varied expressions of wilderness suggest what we know intuitively from our own lived experiences—there are many different types of wildernesses, and wilderness is not just a spiritual experience. We experience wilderness as an actual reality in many ways: Through the global fear caused by a major pandemic. Through illness closer to home such as a tragic, surprise personal diagnosis. Through the pain of infertility or some other family trauma. Through a vocational crisis at midlife, prolonged unemployment, or the financial exhaustion of sustained underemployment. Through geographical displacement. Through many other things I have not named here, all of which might prompt a faith crisis of some kind. No matter how it happens, we experience wilderness *in* bodies and *as* bodies.

This means that we may not be able to define wilderness, but we can feel it in our bones.

In certain extreme cases, wilderness is when everything in our life falls apart and we have to begin again. Though it may not feel like it at the time, sometimes that is a gift, a severe mercy. Much like the God of the desert, the wilderness is a paradox—it can be harsh and painful yet restorative at the same time. What I have found to be true, both in my scholarship and in my own life (which are one and the same), is that yes, the God of the desert makes tracks beside us. We need a God who is neither saccharine nor nihilistic, and that is precisely the God we find in the desert. The God of the desert is deeply embedded in our own embodied lives, seeking to convert our fragmented pieces into a unified whole. This is one of the gifts of the desert—a conversion of sorts in which we do what the desert fathers and desert mothers did—*ora et labora*, bring prayer and work together as one.

Letters from the Scholarly Desert

This is a conversion that does not happen by accident—but through our willingness to bring learning and holiness together, knowledge and vital piety no longer divided. Such is the gift of the desert—no longer to compartmentalize our lives but to join these disparate halves. This means that for scholars, pastors, and educated laypeople, prayer and scholarship conjoin. For many of us, this is a deep conversion—a movement from a life of fragments to a whole, full, embodied existence.

My own desert scholarship has taught me just how *deserted* our scholarship can sometimes be. Scholarship is spiritually impoverished when it fails to take an *affective turn*. In particular, a book about wilderness falls short if we do not deal with it as something more than an exercise in biblical cataloging and categorization. Just as the contemplative life (which, I might add, is depicted in wilderness texts of the Old Testament) was intended to lead to action, the road of our collective scholarly cleansing goes through the heart—and the heart of the desert. The wilderness is a school of humility, a vehicle of holiness, a place where we learn that God is the one before whom we are all laid bare. To make any meaning out of the wilderness, biblical and personal, we must deal with it *spiritually*.

This means that, while I am an Old Testament scholar, this project will combine biblical studies with spiritual formation, which M. Robert Mulholland defines as "the process of conforming to the image of Christ for the sake of others."[12] The interdisciplinarity of this particular work of scholarship is appropriate because our lives are not all just one thing.

---

[12]M. Robert Mulholland, *Invitation to a Journey: A Road Map for Spiritual Formation* (InterVarsity Press, 1993), 15.

Likewise, the wilderness is also not one straight line but a meandering path. This means that individual chapters may also meander from one opposing picture of wilderness to another, and that I will intersperse spiritual practices and discussion questions that can help sustain us as we take the roundabout way of the wilderness together.

In chapter one, I explore the biblical character of Hagar through the embodied experiences of African American women in history and in today's world, suggesting that those of us in power examine our complicity in keeping unjust systems of oppression in place. In chapter two, I examine the patriarch Jacob through the spiritual concept of the true and false self, relying on wise guides such as Parker Palmer, Henri Nouwen, Richard Rohr, and Thomas Merton. In chapter three, I read the Israelites' grumbling for the convenience of Egyptian food and rejection of manna as something akin to our own dry and deserted reading of biblical texts and our need to read spiritually. M. Robert Mulholland, Euguene Peterson, Hans Boersma, and others help us read spiritually and, I argue, eucharistically. In chapter four, I discuss darkness and disorientation as critical moments in our own unlearning, drawing on the apophatic tradition with Pseudo-Dionysius and Gregory of Nyssa, among others.

In chapter five, I argue that Moses functions as spiritual director, storyteller, and midwife of the word for the Israelites, who struggle to narrate their experience of wilderness. Moses' narrative of abundance in Deuteronomy 8 helps us confront our functional theologies honestly and to strain toward telling more hopeful narratives about our desert experiences. Chapter six examines Elijah's experience of solitude and silence, in which I layer the insights of Richard Foster and Macrina Wiederkehr over the rhythm of the Liturgy of the Hours. In chapter seven, I explore the prophet Hosea's rhetorical use of wilderness as a mechanism of both purging and betrothal, overlayed with the insights of Meister Eckhart and the mystical tradition. In chapter eight, I invite us to pray with the psalmist, whose kinship with God bears resemblance to modern psychological notions of secure attachment, arguing that in God, we find a safe haven and a secure base that sustains us in wilderness. In the conclusion, I pull these diverse strands together, demonstrating how the wilderness passages in the Old Testament can nurture our spiritual formation.

As we make this journey together, I pray the same for you that I pray for myself—that the God of the Desert continues to form me into both a saint and a scholar.

1

VISION AND CONFESSION

Casting Ourselves into the Wilderness and Setting Hagar Free

I went to see the preacher in charge of the African society . . . the Rev. Richard Allen . . . to tell him that I felt it my duty to preach the gospel. . . . He said our Discipline . . . did not call for women preachers. . . . On the second morning, I took a stage and rode seven miles to Woodstown. . . . I was desired to speak in the colored meeting house, but the minister could not reconcile his mind to a woman preacher—he could not even unite in fellowship with me even to shaking hands as Christians ought.

Jerena Lee, "Religious Experience and Journal"

This is the great work of a person: always to take blame for one's own sins before God and to expect temptation to one's last breath.

Desert Father Abba Antony to Abba Poemen

Jerena Lee, "Religious Experience and Journal," in *Spiritual Narratives*, ed. Henry Louis Gates Jr. (Oxford University Press, 1988), 3-4.
Benedicta Ward, trans., *The Sayings of the Desert Fathers: The Alphabetical Collection* (Cistercian Publications, 1975), 2.

I'll never forget the Wednesday night my pastor picked up his guitar, pans still clanging in the kitchen and chatter at a high volume over dinner in the fellowship hall, and led us all in "The Hokey Pokey." I had just graduated seminary in Birmingham, Alabama, and was about to move to snowy New Jersey. There I would begin doctoral work, trading my flip-flops for snow boots and, as one of the Hokey Pokey-ers jokingly advised, putting snow chains on my VW Bug.

That night, I laughed as I watched our senior adults put their right foot in, take their right foot out, put their right foot back in, and shake it all about. These are the same people who taught me to love liturgy, an unusual feature of worship for a church in my tradition. Over the years, I have prayed the Scriptures alongside them, stood in awe as we have dedicated babies, blessed backpacks, and ordained senior adult women to ministry when they discovered their calling in the second half of their life. At this same church, I have also taught many Sunday school lessons and Bible studies, attended spiritual retreats, and engaged in contemplative prayer in the small chapel where my husband and I were married. In the quiet of his office at church, my pastor helped me discern God's presence when my life felt unmoored. This same pastor and congregation blessed me when I moved to New Jersey and welcomed me back home after graduation. Before my husband and I moved off to Texas for me to take a teaching position at Baylor University, my pastor invited me to preach the sermon on the last Sunday before we left. (Happily, I am just one in a long line of women who have stewarded that pulpit over the years.) And when my husband and I moved back home from Texas, I took my place in the pews again, where I recited the Lord's Prayer alongside those who have affirmed and nurtured me in the nearly fifteen years I have been a member.

Our Father, who art in Heaven, hallowed be thy name . . .
You put your right foot in, you take your right foot out . . .
I now pronounce you husband and wife . . .

I carry these verses and half verses of prayers and songs and moments with me as I drive to church on Sundays. This church has formed me to see the world and God's vision for the world in particular ways.

On my drive each Sunday, I pass another church within the same basic denominational family as my own. Because I have been in Birmingham off and on for over twenty years, I don't experience the proverbial six degrees of separation between myself and everybody else. Instead, I am connected to just about the entire city by about half that amount, which means that I know and love many people who worship at this other church. These are sincere believers, and I have worshiped there from time to time myself over the years. Like me, these Christians are being formed to see the world and God's vision for the world in particular ways.

And while I love and respect them, I am fundamentally at odds with their vision of God and God's world. Even though we read the same Bible and are stamped denominationally with a similar embossing, our visions for God and for the world are quite different. In some cases, it appears that we are worshiping different Jesuses altogether.

For example, I'll be the first to admit that I'm not called to preach, not because I'm a woman but simply because that is not God's call on my life. I preach on occasion when asked, but it's a rare privilege, and I'm just fine with that. Nevertheless, I can't understand why much of my tradition edges out the voices of other women so clearly called to this vocation. Try as I might, I can't seem to find a single story in which Jesus discourages the devotion and vocation of women. Why should women either kowtow or knee their way to a place at the table when Jesus has already put a chair for them there? This is a significant interpretive difference between my church, filled with sincere believers who see God a certain way, and this other church I drive past each Sunday, also filled with sincere believers who see God a certain way.

We also understand the nature of God's love and justice differently. I will freely admit that I am a recipient of God's grace, which is, as the old hymn goes, "greater than all my sins." Yet when I look at the cross of Jesus in my church sanctuary, I see God's smile and I feel God's love. The cross, for me, is not a symbol of God's wrath or a scolding reminder of all the things I have done and left undone. For many sincere Christians at this other church, however, God seems to be primarily a God of wrath, and guilt and shame are the down payment on a grace that doesn't feel very gracious to me at all. We are all diligently reading the same Bible, yet I can't seem to find a picture of a God who loves Jesus but merely tolerates the rest of us.

These two examples demonstrate that while the same lectionary reading may be preached on any given Sunday at both churches, these theological convictions cast God in two very different lights. These differences are not the twenty-first-century version of how many angels dance on the head of a pin.[1] Instead, these are significant theological distinctions, resulting in two opposing ways of seeing the same God. Even so, I can say with complete confidence that these two congregations worship God, as best as we know how, in spirit and in truth.

Every Sunday, worship takes place in churches all over the world, well beyond my hometown. Many faithful Christians worship according to their convictions, sometimes differing in substantial ways. This has been the case since the foundation of the church, evident in the writings of the earliest Christians. Yet the particularity (*and perhaps peculiarity*) of this political moment seems to cast these differences in sharp relief, creating palpable (*and understandable*) anxiety on both sides.

I can envision that for some Christians, this political moment also feels like a battle for God: Who is God, and what does God stand for? Many Christians voted for Donald Trump, for example, out of a deep and laudable sense that his party would support life as they see it. Such Christians might look at the other theopolitical side, which supports life

[1]This famous statement was probably used by Christians in the seventeenth century to mock the scholastic movement of the Middle Ages, which saw intellectual Christians posing complex theological arguments. These later Christians saw the scholastic movement as wasting time and energy arguing about inconsequential theological points.

in a different way, and find much to fear in policies that erode traditional values as they see them. While I disagree, I can sympathize with Christians who feel this way. However, I look at *everything* Donald Trump stands for and see it as utterly antithetical to *anything* Christ stood for. Frederick Douglass's searing statement, "For, between the Christianity of this land, and the Christianity of Christ, I recognize the widest possible difference," feels just as relevant to the faith now as it did two centuries ago.[2] Between the (*supposed*) Christianity of Trump and the person of Jesus, I recognize the widest possible difference.

Despite my own convictions, I can absolutely understand, hermeneutically speaking, how both sides could accuse the other of calling evil good. It is all a matter of perspective, with one person's image of God differing from another's. My own feeling is that we are in an unprecedented moment in which some Christians have closed their hearts to the fact that people of color, children, immigrants, women, the LGBTQ+ community, non-Christians, and anyone not sharing a certain skin color, ideology, or gender identity are being targeted as outsiders who must be cast into the wilderness. The picture of God is on the line. The state of the church is on the line. People's very lives are on the line. And many so-called good religious people not only sanction these atrocities but actively participate in them because they have been formed to see God and to see the world in a particular way.

No matter where we find ourselves in this theopolitical moment, we are faced with two opposing visions of God and of God's world. It is safe to say that we all find ourselves in an ideological desert, wondering which way to turn.

Yet the stories of Hagar, Abraham, and Sarah remind us that the desert has always been a place of *divine encounter*. Abraham and Sarah are characterological depictions of the ripple effects of our actions. Abraham and Sarah demonstrate that our lives are intertwined and that

[2]Frederick Douglass, *Narrative of the Life of Frederick Douglass: An American Slave Written by Himself* (Belknap, 1960), 155.

we are, all of us, implicated in the lives of others. Hagar, by contrast, teaches us that even in wilderness, we can see and be seen by the God of the desert. While each character experiences wilderness differently, they all experience it. These desert stories lead us to examine our own vision of God: both our seeing (or our refusal to see) and our being seen. These stories also perhaps prompt *confession*, which is a key spiritual practice of the desert beyond the pages of the Old Testament. To these desert stories, this desert God, and this desert practice we now turn.

Seeing and Refusing to See

Abraham and Sarah's story begins in an *emotional wilderness* familiar to many couples—in the struggle to conceive a child. They are, as we may remember, past their prime, "old and advanced in years," as the Old Testament frequently likes to put it, the narrative offering continued and painful reminders that Sarah is barren (Gen 11:30; 15:2-3; 16:1-2). In the biblical text and in our actual lives, infertility is nothing unique. The struggle to conceive is so recognizable in the biblical text that scholars refer to it as the myth of the barren ancestress, with Sarah, Rebekah, and Rachel all facing infertility until the eleventh hour, when Yahweh opens their wombs. Key female characters beyond Genesis also face this struggle, notably Hannah, whose inability to conceive is depicted in an especially pathos-laden way by the biblical narrator (1 Sam 1).

Nevertheless, its ubiquity need not desensitize us to the depth and particularity of this pain—every couple experiences the struggle to conceive uniquely. In the case of Abraham and Sarah, the culture of the ancient Near East determined that a man's value was in his ability to raise sons in his name, and a woman's value was in her ability to conceive those sons. It was a gendered system that shackled men and women alike. While this cultural reality does not excuse Abraham and Sarah's treatment of Hagar, it does add a layer of emotional complexity that may lead us to empathize with more than one character in the story. As readers, *we see them* as they see (*or refuse to see*) Yahweh and one another.

Refusing to See Hagar

For a narrative culminating in two separate acts of seeing and being seen by God (Gen 16:13-14; 21:19), Abraham and Sarah's profound lack of vision for their own oppression of Hagar is startling. In the world of the narrative, Hagar, whose name can be translated "the stranger," "the immigrant," or "the resident alien," is *other* in every way. She is a *she*, already lower in the cultural mindset of the ancient Near East, she is Egyptian, and she is a *shiphkhah* ("slave-girl"), the property of Sarai, Abram's primary wife. In fact, this appellation—*slave-girl*—is the only way in which Abram and Sarai speak about Hagar. We know Hagar's name through the narrator's initial comment, "And she had a slave-girl from Egypt, and her name was *the immigrant*" (Gen 16:1), and through the question posed by the angel of the Lord: "And she said, 'Hagar, slave-girl of Sarai, where have you come from and where are you going?'" (Gen 16:8). While the narrator *names her* and the angel of the Lord *addresses her by name*, Abram and Sarai reify Hagar's positionality as *shiphkhah* repeatedly, never once addressing her in any other way. Indeed, the narrative intentionally reminds readers of Hagar's compromised social location, using various grammatical forms of *shiphkhah* no fewer than six times (Gen 16:1-3, 5-6, 8).

Likewise, the grammar itself paints a bleak and beleaguered picture of Hagar. Abram and Sarai are subjects, and Hagar is the passive grammatical object. In Genesis 16:2, Sarai tells Abram, "Go into my slave-girl," with the narrator revealing Abram's wordless passivity before his wife, "And Abram obeyed the voice of Sarai." The verbs that follow in Genesis 16:3 demonstrate the celerity and the emotionless of the action: She is *wattiqqakh* ("taken") and *wattiten* ("given") to Abram *lo l'ishah* ("as wife"). Genesis 16:4 details plainly what Sarai had intended in Genesis 16:2: "And he went into Hagar." In all this, Hagar is passive—passed from Sarai's hand to Abram's bed—and voiceless. Abram *wayyabo* ("entered") Hagar, and she conceives; but the conception of a child is not thought to bring her emotionally closer to her husband, as it might have with Sarai. Rather, now that Hagar's body has been used for its intended purpose, she is easily discardable. Abram and Sarai refuse to see Hagar as anything other than a slave-girl, one whose body belongs to them and whose body can be discarded when it is no longer useful. For as many times as eyesight, seeing, and vision are a part of the narrative, Abram and Sarai don't *see* Hagar at all.

When Abram tells Sarai that Hagar is "in your hands," a metaphor for power in the Hebrew Bible, and that Sarai should "do what is good in your eyes," Sarai's response is to "afflict her" to such a degree that Hagar runs from before the face of Sarai. John W. Waters notes that Hagar's status as the mother of Abram's child threatens Sarai's position in the family; thus Sarai's affliction of Hagar reestablishes Sarai's position in the household.[3] Later, when Sarah sees that Ishmael is a potential threat to Isaac and to their family unit once again, she demands that Abraham cast her out (Gen 21:8-10).

While Abram and Sarai are often remembered in church tradition as good people of faith, when I read these stories afresh with my students, they are often shocked by Abram and Sarai's actions. This is supposedly a narrative about people who follow the Lord, yet their treatment of Hagar takes a surprising narrative turn. Indeed, Hagar's encounters with the God of the desert cast into question the actions of Abram and Sarai, a couple who enslave her yet claim to follow God at the same time. In this way, their actions are disappointing and surprising. The ease with which they abuse another is a sobering invitation for us to look inwardly and to confess our own refusal to see, a reality I will explore later in this chapter. For a few narrative moments, however, Abram and Sarai recede into the background while Hagar's life and body are brought into the narrative foreground.

Hagar Sees Herself

Hagar's resilience is one of the first surprises in the narrative. Hagar resists the system of oppression in Genesis 16 in three ways: through an

[3]John W. Waters, "Who Was Hagar?," in *Stony the Road We Trod: African American Biblical Interpretation*, ed. Cain Hope Felder (Fortress, 1991), 197.

inner sense of autonomy and self-worth following the birth of her child, depicted by the narrator; through her flight from Sarai to the wilderness; and through naming the God she encounters. Hagar realizes she can do something Sarai cannot do—have a child. Indeed, Sarai realizes this much herself, and she echoes the cultural belief of the time—that it is the Lord who has prevented her from bearing a child: "Behold, *the Lord* has restrained me from giving birth" (Gen 16:2). Once Hagar gives birth to Ishmael, the narrator brings Hagar's eyes into focus: "And her mistress was lowered in her eyes" (Gen 16:4). From the root *qalal*, interpretive possibilities range for the term I translate "was lowered," from looking on Sarai with contempt, looking on her as someone who is now "slight" or "trivial," or even "cursing" her existence.

For Danna Nolan Fewell and David M. Gunn, Hagar's response demonstrates the self-worth she now feels: "Hagar, having caught a glimpse of self-autonomy, is not willing to return to her former status. She runs away into the wilderness. Just as she had threatened Sarai's importance in the family, Hagar now temporarily usurps her place in the narrative's spotlight."[4] As Waters puts it, after being elevated culturally as a mother, Hagar refuses to be lowered into the position of a house slave.[5] Indeed, after Genesis 16:6, the narrative focalizes Hagar entirely, detailing her second act of resistance—running away.

In her groundbreaking book *Sisters in the Wilderness: The Challenge of Womanist God-Talk*, Delores Williams notes that Hagar is the first woman in the Bible to liberate herself from oppressive power structures. Like African American women before her, Williams draws on the Hagar story as a picture of God's provision and liberation. Williams hints that, once she encounters the angel of the Lord, Hagar's act of naming God is itself an act of resistance: "In light of Hagar's Egyptian heritage, in light of her brutal treatment by Sarai and Abram's complicity in this brutality, a question can be raised. Is Hagar's naming action a strike against

[4]Danna Nolan Fewell and David M. Gunn, *Gender, Power, and Promise: The Subject of the Bible's First Story* (Abingdon, 1993), 46.

[5]Waters, "Who Was Hagar?," 197.

patriarchal power at its highest level, since the ultimate head of this ancient Hebrew family was its patriarchal God?"[6] Williams's suggestion is a fascinating one. Voicing our experiences, especially when they differ from the hegemonic power structures, *is* an act of resistance, a way of *seeing ourselves* and casting a vision for our own lives, even if that vision contradicts a more powerful person's vision of God.

Hagar is an undeniable figure of oppression in the early portions of the patriarchal narrative, yet she is also remarkable for her resistance to the power structures that enslave her, for the resilience she displays in the inner desert of her own life, and later as a survivor in the actual desert she inhabits. All these things ought to preclude our labeling her a victim only. Hagar refuses to recede into the narrative background as a victim, and neither does the God of the desert allow her to do so. Hagar has an identity all her own, rightly taking up space in the story as a character who refuses any longer to tolerate systems of abuse. Perhaps knowing that Abram and Sarai's house would be a more dangerous space than the desert itself, Hagar flees there and discovers a surprising hospitality.

Seeing Hagar

Both within the biblical text itself and in the postbiblical experiences of early Christians, the desert was a place of divine encounter. Robert Barry Leal lists several biblical characters who experience God in the desert, noting that Hagar is the first person in the Pentateuch to "highlight the importance of the wilderness as a place of divine encounter and call."[7] Indeed, Hagar is visited by God both times the narrative places her in the wilderness (Gen 16:7-16; 21:14-21), once to assure her that God sees her predicament and will vindicate her lineage, and later to provide physical support when she is expelled from the home of Abraham and

[6]Delores Williams, *Sisters in the Wilderness: The Challenge of Womanist God-Talk* (Orbis Books, 1993), 3, 24.

[7]Robert Barry Leal, *Wilderness in the Bible: Toward a Theology of Wilderness*, Studies in Biblical Literature 72 (Peter Lang, 2004), 100-101.

Sarah.[8] In both instances, the wilderness proves to be a hospitable space, one in which she is incorporated into salvation history.

Drawing on the power dynamics in the Abraham story, Hemchand Gossai interprets Hagar's sojourn in the wilderness as a "hospitable setting," a setting counter to Sarai's abusive household. "As much as the wilderness has come to be identified with hardship and all that is difficult," Gossai states, "it is also a place for encounter with the divine, and regardless of the inherent dangers that the physical wilderness poses, this is a time for newness."[9]

For Thomas B. Dozeman, the "newness" Hagar experiences puts her squarely within salvation history itself, particularly through innerbiblical allusions to Moses. Dozeman points to family conflict, ambiguity of identity, encounters at wells in the wilderness, naming of God, the assuming of new roles (Moses as a liberator, Hagar as a mother), increased conflict as a result of those roles, expulsion by either Sarai or the Pharaoh, and the secondary experiences in wilderness proving increasingly threatening as points of connection between Moses and Hagar. In both instances of expulsion, however, Dozeman notes that while inherently a dangerous space, the wilderness proves liberative, a release from slavery for Hagar, Moses, and the Israelites. Dozeman's further explication of the Ishmael story and its connection to salvation is beyond the scope of this chapter, yet it is worth noting his conclusion: The wilderness setting plays a central role in the Torah and is a location where God is encountered, where personal transformation takes place, and where community is forged.[10]

As the womanist scholarship of Williams shows, sometimes community is forged by foregrounding biblical characters long relegated to

---

[8]Different authorial traditions undoubtedly underlie these two stories, with the angel of the Lord used in Gen 16 and Elohim used in Gen 21. While we could parse the differences in understanding of these deities from a historical point of view, discussion of source criticism is beyond the scope of this chapter and indeed would prove distracting. What is important for the purposes of my work in this chapter is that it is some form of God whom Hagar encounters in both texts.

[9]Hemchand Gossai, *Power and Marginality in the Abraham Narrative*, 2nd ed. (Pickwick, 2010), 15.

[10]Thomas B. Dozeman, "The Wilderness and Salvation History in the Hagar Story," *Journal of Biblical Literature* 117, no. 1 (1998): 29-31, 43.

the sidelines by largely White, historical-critical scholarship, and centering her within the lived experience of real people. Williams explores the Hagar story within the female-centered tradition of African American biblical appropriation. Naming the Hagar story an "analog" for African American women's historical experience, Williams draws on the striking similarities between Hagar's story and the experiences of African American women's history in North America.[11]

Hagar's heritage was African, as was Black women's. Hagar was a slave, while Black women had emerged from slave heritage and survived despite it. Hagar was brutalized by Sarai, her slave owner, while Black women were frequently abused by the wives of male slaveholders. Hagar had no control over her body, Sarai offering it to Abram to procure a child, and when Sarah felt threatened by Hagar and Ishmael, both were cast into the wilderness. Time and again, Black women were raped by their slaveholders, forced to bear children whom slaveholders refused to claim, and then cast off into a similar emotional wilderness through the act of selling them to other slaveholders. Hagar resisted slavery by running away; many Black American women did the same. Hagar and Ishmael were expelled by Abraham and Sarah with no real resources to sustain them in the wilderness; after slavery, Black American women and their children were frequently cast out with nothing to help them make a life. Hagar, like many African American women in history, was a single parent forced to make a way where there seemed to be no way. Hagar had significant salvific encounters with God that demonstrated God's witness of her life and provision for her life. Likewise, African American women in churches testified to their own encounters with the God who provided for their needs when no one else would.[12] Williams's work is groundbreaking for its deep connection of the Hagar story to African American history, as well as for the language she has developed around speaking about such stories in light of Christian commitment.

---

[11]Williams, *Sisters in the Wilderness*, 3.

[12]Williams, *Sisters in the Wilderness*, 2-3.

A cornerstone of Williams's work is in the way she chooses to interpret God in the Hagar story. While some scholars have focalized the experiences of the women in the story rather than focus on the role of God, and others do not question or critique God's actions at all, Williams appears to take a middle way, arguing that God's response to Hagar's story is not liberation but the provision of resources that ensure survival.[13] She names the female-centered tradition of African American biblical appropriation the "survival/quality-of-life tradition of African American biblical appropriation." For Williams, this naming is consistent with the Black African community's view that God provided hope in slavery as well as through the social, sexual, and economic struggles of contemporary African American women.[14] For Williams, this survival/quality-of-life tradition is most evident in the correlation of Hagar's experience in wilderness and the encounters of Black African women, who saw the wilderness as a place of solitude and divine encounter.

According to Williams, "Although many themes in African-American women's history correspond with many themes in Hagar's story in the Bible, nothing links the two women together more securely than their religious experience in wilderness."[15] Williams demonstrates that among slaves, spiritual songs often referred to the wilderness as a place in which they encountered God, such as the following spiritual:

> How did you feel when you came out de wilderness, came out de wilderness, came out de wilderness? Tell me, brudder, how did you feel when

[13]Williams, *Sisters in the Wilderness*, 4. For solid examples of those who focalize the experiences of the women in the story, see the groundbreaking work of J. Cheryl Exum, *Fragmented Women: Feminist (Sub)versions of Biblical Narratives* (JSOT Press, 1993), and Ronald Hendel et al., "Gender and Sexuality," in *Reading Genesis: Ten Methods*, ed. Ronald Hendel (Cambridge University Press, 2010), among many others. For examples of those who do not question or critique God's actions at all, Elsa Tamez, "The Woman Who Complicated the History of Salvation," in *New Eyes for Reading: Biblical and Theological Reflections by Women from the Third World*, ed. John S. Potter and Barbel Von Wartenberg-Potter (Meyer Stone, 1987); Hemchand Gossai, *Power and Marginality in the Abraham Narrative*, 2nd ed. (Pickwick, 2010), among others.

[14]Williams, *Sisters in the Wilderness*, 5.

[15]Williams, *Sisters in the Wilderness*, 96.

> you came out de wilderness, came out de wilderness? Tell me sister, how did you feel when you came out de wilderness, came out de wilderness? How did you feel when you came out de wilderness, came out de wilderness? Did you love your brother when you came out de wilderness, came out de wilderness . . . ? Did you love your sister when you came out de wilderness, came out de wilderness . . . ? Did you love back sliddin' Christians when you came out de wilderness, came out de wilderness . . . ? Tell me, brudder and sister, did you meet Jesus in de wilderness?[16]

Such songs reveal that slaves saw the wilderness as a momentary reprieve from the tyranny of the slave master's household, as a place of solace, and as a place to encounter God.

The question that remains for me in light of all this is as follows: Is the God of the oppressor the same God of the oppressed? Abram and Sarai are two abusive individuals who also profess to follow God. Likewise, Hagar experiences God. As Danna Nolan Fewell, my own former teacher, puts it in her beautiful, midrashic, Levinasian retelling of the Hagar story, Hagar turns to the angel of the Lord and asks, "How could you possibly be the god of Abram and the god of the slave woman too?"[17] While Fewell's is an *imaginative* retelling, it is a fair question. Within the text and beyond it, how sure are we that the God we worship is not a false messiah? It is not difficult to draw parallels from the abuse of an immigrant named Hagar and our world today. Before turning to those parallels, I'll offer one, more explicit word about Hagar's experience with God.

Seeing God

In ancient Near Eastern culture, Hagar's naming of God (and the subsequent naming of the well) was atypical, an authority reserved for a patriarch, but in Genesis 16:13-14, "Hagar's authority substitutes for male

---

[16]William Frances Allen et al., *Slave Songs of the United States: The Classic 1867 Anthology* (Dover, 1995).

[17]Danna Nolan Fewell, *The Children of Israel: Reading the Bible for the Sake of Our Children* (Abingdon, 2003), 44.

authority."[18] Indeed, Phyllis Trible reminds us that Hagar is the only person in the Bible who names God.[19] Trible, Williams, and Helmer Ringgren each point to the uniqueness of the name Hagar chooses, with Ringgren noting:

> El is . . . familiar as the highest god of the Canaanites (as of most of the Semitic peoples). . . . These names [i.e., those compounds with "El"] are never associated with patriarchs, either as individuals or as tribes; instead, with the exception of El Shaddai, they are always linked to specific cultic sites. . . . El olam, "the Everlasting God," appears in Genesis 21:33 in connection with Beer-sheba. El ro'i, "God of seeing," appears in Genesis 16:13 at another sanctuary in southern Palestine. Beyond this we have no information about these two divinities.[20]

Discussion of Israelite religion and its evolution is beyond the scope of this chapter, but Ringgren's research highlights an astute observation by Williams: It is interesting that Hagar's deity is not associated with Hagar's oppressors, Abram and Sarai. As Williams puts it, "Though she obeyed God's mandate for her life, Hagar dared to give a name to the God she met in the wilderness. In a sense, this God is her God and possibly not the God of her slave holders Abram and Sarai."[21]

While the drama between the patriarchal family and their oppressed slave, Hagar, is worlds away from us historically and culturally, the idea that people of faith seem to worship vastly different versions of the same God is a present reality, one I hope my opening story about driving to church demonstrated well enough.

Recently, Beth Moore, a figure cast out into the wilderness by the Southern Baptist Convention, critiqued church culture: "When our story is told a century from now—and it will be—how much of the American church ran after idols and delusions, false christs and

---

[18]Williams, *Sisters in the Wilderness*, 21.
[19]Phyllis Trible, *Texts of Terror: Literary-Feminist Readings of Biblical Narratives*, Overtures to Biblical Theology (Fortress, 2009), 18.
[20]Helmer Ringgren, *Israelite Religion*, trans. David E. Green (Fortress, 1966), 21-22.
[21]Williams, *Sisters in the Wilderness*, 22, 97.

conspiracies, history will not only fault the pastors for not confronting us with the truth but the congregations who forbade them to."[22] Moore's comments confront our present moment. Ours is the era of George Floyd, #metoo, #churchtoo, the invasion of schools and churches by Immigration and Customs Enforcement (ICE), the suppression of news, the ambiguity of "facts," and the reality that sometimes it seems as though Christians *do* see two very different versions of the same God.

Seeing Ourselves

Even as I have joined Moore and offered my own critique of this current church moment, I confess that I am always in danger of failing to remove the theological plank from my own eyes while focusing on the theological speck in the eyes of my brothers and sisters. Because we all tend to cling to our own way of seeing things, it is wise to examine our ways of seeing God, God's world, and ourselves. Years of worshiping in the same place, watching the same news channels, or vilifying the same kinds of people in our minds often close our eyes to the possibility that our vision of God and of ourselves might be wrong. As my own pastor is fond of saying, "I repent of the things I used to believe." These are wise words that critique my own hardheartedness and quickness to judge others, inviting me to look within.

It is a basic hermeneutical fact that I am conditioned to see characters in the biblical text in much the same way that I see real people in the world—through the lens of my own vision of God, of my life experiences, my race and ethnicity, my gender and sexual orientation, my socioeconomic class, and any other identifying fact of my personhood. Because my students are human beings in the world, I assume much the same about them, which is why for many years now I have required my students to write "Letters to a Biblical Character," an assignment in which I ask them to choose a particular character within the scope of

[22]Beth Moore (@BethMooreLPM) wrote this prophetic critique on Twitter (now X) on November 15, 2020, https://x.com/BethMooreLPM/status/1327983702979321858?lang=en.

the biblical text we will read for the day. They compose an old-fashioned letter to that character, in which I ask them to personalize their reading experience and, hopefully, to develop empathy for people who lived long before them, whose customs and history differ markedly from their own, with an attempt to understand and express *caritas*, charity and love of humankind. I encourage them to select characters with whom they struggle or even disagree so that they can *practice* empathy. When we arrive at the wilderness stories in Genesis, many of them write letters to Abraham, Sarah, or Hagar. Beyond developing empathy for these characters, their letters provide a window into their own prejudices, into whose actions they are apt to view with suspicion and whose bad choices they are inclined to overlook.

In *Reading Other-Wise: Socially Engaged Biblical Scholars Reading with Their Local Communities*, Nicole M. Simopoulos's engagement with real women reading the Hagar story from various social locations accomplishes much the same, demonstrating how social location affects how we read and with whom we are willing to empathize. Simopoulos compiles reader responses of the stories in Genesis 16 from Latina Presbyterian immigrants and refugees from Mexico and Central America living in Northern California; Black South African Protestant women from both rural and urban South African townships enrolled in a yearlong theological training program in Kwa-Zulu-Natal, South Africa; and White, middle- to upper-class Catholic and Protestant women, mostly of divorce.

Perhaps unsurprisingly, the White women, many of whom had been divorced by adulterous husbands in favor of new sexual partners, identified with Sarah's jealous rage toward Hagar, seeing in Hagar a picture of the "other woman." Conversely, they also identified with Hagar's loneliness in the wilderness after being cast out by Abraham. The Latina women identified with Hagar as an exile from her native country and an outcast living in a foreign and hostile land. Black South African women identified with Hagar's exploitation as a slave who worked under oppression.[23] These are all readings done on the ground—that is, from a particular context. None of these women are scholars—they are people like many of us who sit in the pews on Sunday mornings at the churches we have come to love.

It is easy to remain in these same pews mentally, reminiscing about the times we have sung the words to "Father Abraham" as children. Too often, this nostalgia keeps us from seeing characters in the text such as Hagar that we sometimes miss. This nostalgia can also prevent us from *reading other-wise*, from seeing Abraham and Sarah as faithful servants only. The earliest Christians were no different, remembering the stories that portrayed Abraham and Sarah as faithful servants, with the book of Hebrews inserting them into its Hall of Faith (Heb 11:8-19) and the epistle of James baptizing Abraham as "the friend of God" (Jas 2:23; cf. 2 Chron 20:7; Is 41:8). These New Testament writers read the stories about Abraham and Sarah and interpreted them for their own expositional ends, in much the same way we do when we teach or preach these passages in our churches. There's nothing inherently wrong with that, and I am certainly no one to argue with the New Testament writers. These individuals faithfully read the Hebrew Scriptures and, through the inspiration of the Holy Spirit, have given us the Word of the Lord.

Thanks be to God.

But the original stories about Abraham and Sarah do not always depict them as faithful, and the Hebrew writers have rightly preserved those stories too.

Thanks be to God.

These stories and our involvement with them—how we read them and in which characters we see a picture of ourselves—are undoubtedly linked to the image of God we hold. Our reading of these stories is also connected to our spiritual formation, as God may be nudging us to a

---

[23]Nicole M. Simopoulos, "Who Was Hagar? Mistress, Divorcee, Exile, or Exploited Worker: An Analysis of Contemporary Grassroots Readings of Genesis 16 by Caucasian, Latina, and Black South African Women," in *Reading Other-Wise: Socially Engaged Biblical Scholars Reading with Their Local Communities*, ed. Gerald O. West (Society of Biblical Literature, 2007), 63-72.

new way of seeing. African American biblical interpretation helps raise important critiques about how we read and live in God's world, especially for White readers.

Confession as Spiritual Practice: Casting Ourselves into Wilderness

Rodney S. Sadler's exploration of the patriarchal narratives touches on many important questions for African American biblical interpretation. He offers insightful questions that are poignant and important:

> How can we sing "Father Abraham" without examining his exploitation of Hagar, or "We are Climbing Jacob's Ladder" without ever questioning his treatment of Bilhah, Zilpah, and Leah? How is that we have traditionally identified with the protagonists of these narratives who have perpetuated the patterns of oppression, the legacy of which we continue to suffer? . . . Whether our ability to read such texts with the protagonist is a manifestation of DuBoisian "double consciousness" or simply the result of a naively uncritical appropriation of a sacral tradition at odds with our life experiences, we owe it to ourselves to discern clearly what it is that these stories *really* say about the nature of God and family.[24]

As a White woman with a background more privileged than many, I cannot understand in a visceral, embodied way all that Sadler has expressed above. It would be naive and arrogant to assume otherwise. What I can offer is the following: that I will not discard his view into an ideological wilderness because it might threaten my readerly hegemony or my own personal life; that I will attempt to read and to lift up those scholars (*and my own students*) who attempt to read other-wise, perhaps not agreeing at every point but making an effort to shake hands with them; and that I will cast myself into an inner wilderness in which I examine my own racism, latent misogyny, and other prejudices. No

---

[24]Rodney S. Sadler, "Genesis," in *The Africana Bible: Reading Israel's Scriptures from Africa and the African Diaspora*, ed. Hugh R. Page Jr. (Fortress, 2010), 76. The phrase "DuBoisian double consciousness" refers to two different ways in which African Americans navigated their identity in the world—through their own eyes and also through the eyes of the dominant culture.

matter who we are, we all need the perspectives of others to help us see the world less myopically. The desert tradition encourages me, after all, not to say I see when I do not but rather to cast myself into the wilderness and to make my confession.

While the God of the desert is one of grace, much of the wilderness tradition reminds me that I have to work in tandem with God, who opens my eyes, who provides manna that I must stoop down to gather, and who calls me not to succumb to the demons who assail at this, the noon of my life. God knows, the Hagars of the world have been in the desert long enough. It might be time for those of us who see ourselves more in the position of Abraham and Sarah to cast ourselves into the wilderness.

Beyond the pages of the Bible but before the slave spirituals of the American South, the desert fathers and desert mothers of the fourth century saw the wilderness as personally transformative. For those Christians who would come to be known as the desert fathers and desert mothers, the new power granted by the emperor Constantine to their religion proved more spiritually destructive than martyrdom. As a result of this new power, baptisms rose and religious standards slipped. The church began to compromise between the things of God and the things of Caesar (see Lk 20:25). People including Antony of Egypt, the father of desert monasticism, fled to the deserts of Egypt, Syria, and Arabia, where they could reengage the narrow way of Jesus (Mt 7:13-14). For these men and women, "the voice of the desert's heart replaced the voice of the martyr's blood." As John Chryssagis puts it, these desert fathers and mothers "became witnesses of another way, another age, another kingdom."[25] Voluntarily stripping themselves of the power granted them through Constantine's sudden conversion, they chose the desert for its solitude, its stark and barren quality, and its silence.

The Greek *erēmos*, which we translate as "desert," means "abandonment," and from *erēmos* we derive the term *hermit*. For these

[25]John Chryssavgis, *In the Heart of the Desert: The Spirituality of the Desert Fathers and Mothers*, rev. ed. (World Wisdom, 2008), 17.

Christians who had deserted a Christianity that was growing in cultural influence and power for the austerity of Jesus' narrow way, the desert was an invitation to transfiguration. For those of us who think about the desert way as something akin to a church retreat, Chryssavgis offers a helpful corrective: "The desert is a place of spiritual revolution, not of personal retreat. It is a place of inner protest, not outward peace. It is a place of deep encounter, not of superficial escape. It is a place of repentance, not recuperation."[26]

The key word for me in Chryssavgis's statement above is *repentance*, the actions we take after we look at ourselves and confess to God whatever complacency or cruelty contributes to individual and institutionalized oppression in our world. The father of the monastic movement, Abba Antony, offered a definition of *confession* to Abba Poemen: "This is the great work of a person: always to take blame for one's own sins before God and to expect temptation to one's last breath."[27] Not only do we confess what Richard Foster calls our "concrete sins," but more deeply, we put ourselves under the gaze of God. For Foster, *confession* is both a grace and a discipline. He clarifies: "Unless God gives the grace, no genuine confession can be made. But it is also a Discipline because there are many things we must do. It is a consciously chosen course of action that brings us under the shadow of the Almighty." Confession is both a private and corporate discipline, one in which we acknowledge that we are "sinners together." "In acts of mutual confession," Foster writes, "we release the power that heals. Our humanity is no longer denied, but transformed."[28]

Indeed, the spiritual discipline of confession is apt for our time, a time in which we call good evil and evil good. We would do well to cast ourselves into an inner wilderness through the spiritual discipline of confession. Doing so is one way in which we cooperate with the same

---

[26]Chryssavgis, *In the Heart of the Desert*, 33-35.

[27]Ward, *Sayings of the Desert Fathers*, 2.

[28]Richard J. Foster, *Celebration of Discipline: The Path to Spiritual Growth*, 25th anniversary ed. (HarperSanFrancisco, 1998), 152, 145-46.

God who sees the Hagars of the world and asks us to do better by them. We have been complicit in the emptying of empathy. We are "good people" who are willing to cast into the wilderness those who are already powerless, the poor, the immigrant, the child of the immigrant, the person of color, the woman, the LGBTQ+ person, or the person of different faith or of no faith at all. We are Abram and Sarai, the "good people of faith" who are trying to follow the Lord while we cast out Hagar and Ishmael, the slave girl and her son, into the desert in which only God can take care of them. We have misplaced our empathy in a religious desert, naming as sin anything that interferes with our religious agenda. When we call empathy a sin, we're a long way from the gospel.[29] Douglas Steere writes that an examination of conscience is "where a soul comes under the gaze of God and where in His silent and loving presence this soul is pierced to the quick and becomes conscious of the things that must be forgiven and put right before it can continue to love One whose care has been so constant."[30] Part of the things that must be put right, as Steere writes, is surely the confession of our temptation to become dispirited in this age, to lose heart.

The Noonday Demon

"Expect temptation to one's last breath," Abba Antony said. This is the reality of the noonday demon about which Evagrius Ponticus wrote. Evagrius referred to this noonday demon as acedia, which is often translated as "sloth," "apathy," or "despair."[31] While the meaning of *acedia* shifted from Evagrius, who saw it as lack of care about one's spiritual life,

[29]Ben Garrett encouraged his followers, "Do not commit the sin of empathy." Garrett (@tompawnbadil), "Do not commit the sin of empathy. This snake is God's enemy and yours too. She hates God and His people. You need to properly hate in response. She is not merely deceived but is a deceiver. Your eye shall not pity," X, January 22, 2025, https://x.com/tompawnbadil/status/1882115502061068777?lang=en. In recent days, some in Christian circles have used this line to push against liberalism and its supposed support of political polices they feel are not in line with the gospel. Naturally, many Christians in other circles view Garrett's statements as a contradiction to Jesus, who attended to the poor and marginalized in his own society.

[30]Douglas Steere, *On Beginning from Within* (Harper & Brothers, 1943), 80.

[31]Hans Boersma, *Pierced by Love: Divine Reading with the Christian Tradition* (Lexham, 2023), 52.

to a kind of laziness under Thomas Acquinas, which included sadness about the good and disgust with activity, the term's etymology is linked to an absence of care or concern.[32] It is not only a weariness in doing good (*though it certainly is that*)—it is also a hopelessness that our confession will be heard and our sins will be forgiven.

Hans Boersma explains it this way: "When we cave into the temptation of acedia, we give up on life. Looking at our past, we cannot face the future. Our memories render us incapable of hope. Acedia arises, therefore, from an inability to forgive ourselves. Or, put more sharply, acedia stems from doubting *God's* ability or willingness to forgive us."[33] This inability to believe in God's forgiveness can lead to a spiritual disintegration in which we experience loss of meaning. A kind of nihilism sets in, leading, if left unchecked, to one of acedia's daughters, despair.[34] Confession pushes against the demon of unbelief, because in confession we trust that God forgives us. Thus, when we enter an inner wilderness and make our confession about the ways in which we have been complicit as an Abraham or a Sarah, we are to trust that God restores us.

When faced with the noonday demon, Athanasius had this story to tell about Abba Antony:

> When the holy Abba Anthony lived in the desert he was beset by *accide*, and attacked by many sinful thoughts. He said to God, "Lord, I want to be saved but these thoughts do not leave me alone; what shall I do in my affliction? How can I be saved?" A short while afterwards, when he got up to go out, Anthony saw a man like himself sitting at his work, getting up from his work to pray, then sitting down and plaiting a rope, then getting up again to pray. It was an angel of the Lord sent to correct and reassure him. He heard the angel saying to him, "Do this and you will be saved." At these words, Anthony was filled with joy and courage. He did this, and he was saved.[35]

---

[32]Jean-Charles Nault, OSB, *The Noonday Devil: Acedia, the Unnamed Evil of Our Times* (Ignatius, 2015), 28, 58; Boersma, *Pierced by Love*, 52-53.

[33]Boersma, *Pierced by Love*, 53.

[34]Nault, *Noonday Devil*, 108-11.

[35]Ward, *Sayings of the Desert Fathers*, 1-2.

I take this to mean that when we feel dispirited and when the demon of despondency assails us, we do what we already know to do—*ora et labora*, we pray and we work. We keep on keeping on. Indeed, of the five remedies for acedia that appear in the writings of Evagrius, perseverance is the essential remedy.[36] We persevere in our work, in our prayer, and in the vocation to which we are called. Each of these things risks empathy—and empathy *is a risk*; we pay a hefty price for it. The risks of empathy include vulnerability, confession and repentance, lamentation, and sometimes the willful ceding of our own power to someone else. We pay an even weightier price for refusing to risk it.

There are very few wilderness hills I would stake my life on, but the desire of God that all should receive and proclaim the gospel is one of them. The story of Hagar shows that my failure to see her is not God's failure and that God uses her as a mouthpiece too. Without Hagar's proclamation, a cipher for all those whose voices we tend to squelch, the gospel proclamation is stunted. I would go so far, perhaps, as to say that the very Spirit of God is quenched. When there is not a seat for everyone at the table or a lectern offered to all who are called to proclaim the gospel, we are already in a wilderness. If the Hagars of the world are not given a voice, oppression is not far behind—indeed, the squelching of voice *is* oppression. The gospel is the ultimate egalitarian message, transcending race, gender, social status, and every identifying reality of our social location (Gal 3:28). Now is the time to write, to speak, to preach, to act, and to recognize that, as Jesus said, if they are not against us, they are for us (Mk 9:38-41).

The character of Hagar, *the immigrant*, stands before us in Scripture and asks us to confess what kind of believer we will be. Will we close our eyes and refuse to see immigrants in our own day and time being carted off to the wilderness of prison in El Salvador? If Hagar confesses

[36]Nault, *Noonday Devil*, 37-43. Evagrius also includes tears, the acknowledgment that one needs to be saved; prayer and work; the antirrhêtic method, or contradiction, in which we use Scripture to talk back to the demon who is assailing us; and meditation on our death, which rightly orders our earthly sufferings and reminds us of our union with God in the life to come.

anything in the story, it is this—her dependence on the God who has seen her. In this way, Hagar's is a confession we all ought to heed, because we all stand powerless and in need before the God who loves us and the whole world too.

If we believe in a trinitarian God, then the same Lord of Abram and Sarai is the Jesus we encounter in the Gospels, the same Jesus who ties one's position before God to the sobering realities of social justice—seeing and caring for those who are naked, hungry, sick, and in prison, and putting not our mouths where our money is but our bodies where our theologies are (Mt 25:31-46). It is a fearful thing to fall into the hands of a seeing God and to recognize that *we* are the ones who have not seen God rightly at all. When empathy ceases to be a category for us, we have utterly failed as a country, as a church, as individuals. I am an otherwise "good White woman" who is sometimes guilty of doing nothing, of not wanting to rock the boat, or of allowing my own uncertainty of what to do or how to do it prevent me from, as Mary Oliver puts it, "taking my place in the family of things."[37] It is vital, now more than ever, that we take our place in the family, however fractured that family may be, and seek to make it better.

As the next chapter will show, this sometimes requires radical reorientation, one that only our sojourn in the wilderness can accomplish.

Questions for Reflection and Discussion

1. With whom do you most identify in the story—Abraham, Sarah, or Hagar? What about that character's experience in wilderness reminds you of your own?
2. With whom do you most struggle to empathize? Is there a person in your own life who reminds you of that character? What is the invitation of God to you in light of that realization?
3. Do you recognize acedia creeping into your own life? How does the desert tradition offer wisdom for fighting it?

---

[37]Mary Oliver, *Devotions: The Selected Poems of Mary Oliver* (Penguin Books, 2017), 347.

2

DREAMS AND LADDERS

Jacob at Bethel

Jacob left the town of Beersheba and started out for Haran. At sunset he stopped for the night and went to sleep, resting his head on a large rock. In a dream he saw a ladder that reached from earth to heaven, and God's angels were going up and down on it. The Lord was standing beside the ladder.

Genesis 28:10-13 CEV

"To my colleagues in the religion department at Baylor, it is with gratitude for my time in our department and at Baylor that I submit my letter of resignation."

I pushed back my chair from the dining room table where I had been writing and stared at my computer screen in disbelief.

This was not the letter I sat down to write.

I had been teaching at Baylor for six years, and it was time to write the formal letter to the faculty requesting promotion from lecturer to senior lecturer. I took a seat at the dining room table in my good friends' house, where I had been dog-sitting for the weekend, fully intending to write that letter.

Without thinking about it, I wrote a letter of resignation instead. I swear that letter wrote itself.

In the quiet of the house that morning, I breathed deeply and stared at the computer screen again.

I'm the kind of person who's never sure about anything, but I was more sure about that decision than any other decision I've made in my life. I was also sure that in writing that letter of resignation, I was giving up the dream I had for my life. Yet in resigning from my dream job, I felt a peace wash over me that I had never felt before and haven't felt since.

Jesus said the truth will set you free.

The truth was that the dream I had for my life, at least as I was living it at that time and place, wasn't life-giving. While my colleagues were wonderful and the institution top-notch, I found myself overworked, burned out, and wanting to move back home.

And so instead of writing a letter requesting that I climb up the ladder, I decided to fall down the ladder instead.

I wrote a letter of resignation to my own dreams.

Our trusted (*if not wordy*) friend Merriam-Webster defines *resignation* as an "act or instance of resigning something: *surrender*." It also offers a secondary definition: resignation is "the quality or state of *being* resigned: *submissiveness*."[1] I like the passive voice of that second definition—*being resigned*—because it suggests resignation is something we submit ourselves to—it happens *to* us and maybe *in* us. Originally from the Latin *resignare*, meaning "to unseal" or "to cancel," *resignation* these days is mainly associated with formally resigning from a position.

In my case, resignation meant all those things. It also meant that I had resigned myself to the fact that this thing I thought I wanted so badly was not all it was cracked up to be.

It was a couple of months before I had the guts to submit that letter. My husband and I went back and forth about it. He was anxious about my relinquishing the security of a full-time job, especially one I had

---

[1] "Resignation," Merriam-Webster, www.merriam-webster.com/dictionary/resignation.

worked so hard for. I had given my whole adult life to this dream, nine years of graduate school, two major moves across the country, a mountain of student-loan debt, and many other sacrifices at once too personal and too prosaic to name here. His anxiety was understandable. I felt it too.

The other thing I felt was failure—I had failed to make my dream work. For a chronic (over)achiever, failure is a hard thing to admit, yet there it was, staring me in the face. But one thing I learned is that failure is a gift—and like grace, it's a paradox. It's both a pearl of great price, costing everything that we have, and yet totally free.

I failed—*praise God*. I really mean that. I failed—*praise God*.

Ultimately, I submitted my letter of resignation exactly as I had written it from my friends' dining room table that day. No extra explanations, because I didn't have them. No commas or ellipses, because I didn't know what the future held and there was nothing more I could say.

Everything inside me that for years had felt depressed, frenetic, unsure, and anxious turned strangely calm.

I resigned from my teaching position at Baylor, yet there was a much deeper kind of resignation at work in my life. Resignation, as Merriam-Webster defines it and as our own lived experience certainly demonstrates, is often multilayered. Some of our most treasured spiritual teachers have left us a record of their own resignations. Their resignations are guides for us if we are willing to submit ourselves to their wisdom.

In his memoir, *The Road to Daybreak: A Spiritual Journey*, Henri Nouwen recounts his discernment process in leaving a career on the faculty at Harvard University for the quieter vocation of pastor to handicapped persons at L'Arche Daybreak. Nouwen describes his confusion as he sorted through his feelings, unsure whether he would be following or betraying his vocation by leaving. On the other side of his decision, he was able to say the following:

> The fruits of the Spirit are not sadness, loneliness, and separation, but joy, solitude, and community. After I decided to leave Harvard, I was surprised

> that it had taken me so long to come to that decision. As soon as I left, I felt so much inner freedom, so much joy and new energy, that I could look back on my former life as a prison in which I had locked myself.[2]

I had spent six years at Baylor thinking that if I just willed myself to feel differently, I would feel the way I was *supposed* to feel—happy to have achieved my dreams. But vocation, as another great spiritual teacher later put it, does not come from grim determination or willfulness but from listening. Parker Palmer phrases it like this: "I must listen to my life and try to understand what it is truly about—quite apart from what I would like it to be about—or my life will never represent anything real in the world, no matter how earnest my intentions."[3] Palmer and Nouwen both offer deep wisdom for listening to our own souls, and this—exercising a grim determination to pursue a lofty vision that is not the vision God has for us—amounts to little more than a white-knuckled life in which we wedge ourselves into places that do not fit us.

Jesus said the truth will set you free.

The truth of the matter is sometimes we are miserable because we are bruising ourselves on ladders that are not ours to climb. If we do not belong on a particular ladder, no amount of trying harder will change that fundamental reality.

I climbed off the ladder, set my dreams aside, deeply disillusioned with institutional academic life.

And yet somehow, strangely free.

I have known many wonderful teachers in my life, *angels*, all of them. Faith, hope, and love are a few. Others have been strange guides, and here are a few of their names: disillusionment, frailty, consequence, silence, stopping, and failure.

Disillusionment is a teacher.

Stopping is a teacher.

And oh boy, failure sure is a teacher.

---

[2]Henri J. M. Nouwen, *The Road to Daybreak: A Spiritual Journey* (Image Books, 1988), 22.
[3]Parker J. Palmer, *Let Your Life Speak: Listening for the Voice of Vocation* (Jossey-Bass, 2000), 4.

Yet we must entertain these strangers, because the New Testament tells us they may be angels in disguise, angels in the biblical sense of that word—messengers sent by God.

So these three remain: disillusionment, stopping, and failure. And the greatest of these is failure.

Without pursuing our own dreams and finding them wanting, perhaps we would never discover God's dream for us. Yet to pursue God's dream for us, we often have to learn a different way to climb.

The familiar story of Jacob at Bethel is also a story about dreams and ladders, and so this is where our story of wilderness begins.

Dreams

Jacob's dream begins with exile, *wayyetse*, "and he left" (Gen 28:10). The narrator provides Jacob's travel coordinates—he leaves Beersheba and sets out for Haran. Both places are significant in the spiritual biography of the Israelites—these are places where the patriarchs encountered God. These places are also part of Jacob's spiritual geography and therefore essential to his life with God. In particular, Beersheba is a place with strong family associations—a place where Jacob's father and grandfather often stayed (Gen 22:19; 26:23, 33). Beersheba was also associated with security (Gen 21:31; 26:25-33), divine assurance (Gen 26:24), and patriarchal worship and the presence of God (Gen 21:33; 26:25; 46:1). Kevin Walton notes that Beersheba is a place as near to anywhere that Jacob might have called home: "Thus the reminder that Jacob is leaving this place, emphasizing the sense of absence he is to feel—from place, from family, and from God."[4] The biblical writer offers two reasons for Jacob's leaving—the need to find an acceptable wife (Gen 27:46–28:2) and the fear of Esau's anger (Gen 27:42-45).

In his midrash, Rashi states that the leaving of a righteous person from a place *makes an imprint*.[5] Given the relationship between *yaaqov* ("Jacob") and *aqev* ("heel" or "footprint"), it is likely that Jacob left his

[4]Kevin Walton, *Thou Traveller Unknown: The Presence and Absence of God in the Jacob Narrative* (Paternoster, 2003), 42-43.

[5]Avivah Zornberg, *The Beginning of Desire: Reflections on Genesis* (Schocken Books, 2011), 181.

imprint—his footprints—throughout Beersheba.[6] Similarly, the memory of the footprints of *yaaqov* has been imprinted on the mind of the Israelite audience throughout the long stretch of patriarchal narrative. Yet Avivah Zornberg notes that the void in Beersheba may have been felt within Jacob also after his absence, a kind of "necessary detachment."[7] Zornberg frames this separation from his origins through the passage of time:

> In leaving home, Jacob goes out into exile. This is an exile not only from his geographical home but, in some radical sense, from himself. His going out makes an imprint on himself: how is he to know himself in that strange country, that darkness of exile? As he begins his journey, the sun sets (Gen. 28:11); when he returns, twenty years later, the narrative describes a sunrise (Gen. 32:32). Both these markers of time, the Midrash suggests, are functions of Jacob's personal sense of time. Between these two points, there is darkness, the Dark Night of the Soul.[8]

For Jacob, the darkness of exile is the wilderness on the way to Haran, and it is this sojourn in wilderness that is the very thing on which his personal transformation hinges. Indeed, the name *Haran* itself, which means "crossroads" in Hebrew, suggests transformation. Thus, the spatial and temporal setting of Jacob's dream—both the darkness of night and the wilderness (which both the narrator and Jacob describe only as "a certain place," Gen 28:11, 16-17, 19, *as though in his sleepy and startled state this is all Jacob knows*)—and the place Jacob is journeying to (Haran, "crossroads") point to a spiritual space rife with possibilities for divine intervention in Jacob's life. His GPS coordinates have changed, and his life will too.

Jacob finds himself at a crossroads, a place of spiritual significance. And as is often the case when we're going through something significant, Jacob's dream life is rich and vibrant.

At significant junctures in my own life, my nightly dreamscape has been particularly vivid, even God-shaped.

---

[6] F. Brown et al., *A Hebrew and English Lexicon of the Old Testament* (Oxford University Press, 1962), 211.

[7] Zornberg, *Beginning of Desire*, 181.

[8] Zornberg, *Beginning of Desire*, 185.

Two years before I decided to leave Baylor, I took a trip home to Alabama and climbed the dark, familiar stairs to the loft in my friend's house, where I often stayed on trips back home. Over twenty years of friendship, I have climbed those stairs and slept in that loft more times than even I remember. On that particular night, like I had so many times before, I turned off the lights, climbed into bed, and fell asleep. I don't know what time it was when I woke up, but I remember that the room was quiet and heavy with darkness. I felt a presence in the room that was as close and as real as my own breath. In that stillness, I heard a voice as clear as glass: "What do you want me to do for you?"

And in that moment, in the stillness of that room bathed in a presence I can only describe as numinous, heavy, and knowing, I confessed to God a dream I did not even know I had.

I'll never forget that night, because everything about my life changed after that, in ways that continue to unfold as I write this.

Our wildernesses—our places of unknowing and transition—can often feel like groping for the railing as we climb stairs in the dark. Yet it is frequently in these places where we struggle to name and struggle to see our way through that God shows up. With my own dreamscape vivid and rich that night, all I can say is, like Jacob at *Bethel*—God's house!—God was in this place, and I did not know it.

God's House

Jacob has a dream in the wilderness of Bethel, which means "house of God" in Hebrew. The Hebrew writer juxtaposes the isolation Jacob experiences in running away from home with Yahweh's dream for Jacob's life. Where previously Jacob's world closed in around him, leaving him in a fearful and constricting darkness, at Bethel, God's house, Jacob begins to see the possibilities of a larger world, a bigger life, one in which his own tiny earth connects to heaven.

Yair Zakovitch traces Jacob's expanding vision through the three usages of *wehinneh*—"and behold" (twice in Gen 28:12 and once in Gen 28:13). In the first stage, Jacob witnesses the stairway that is set on the ground and reaching to the sky. In the second stage, Jacob sees that angels of God are ascending and descending on it. In the third and final stage, Jacob looks at the top of the staircase and sees God standing on it.[9] At each stage, Jacob's world opens, becoming larger. Zakovitch puts it this way:

> Whereas a moment previously Jacob's world had suddenly been compressed by an all-encompassing darkness closing around his weary body, a vast world was now opened before him. Three axes become apparent: the vertical connection between earth and heaven; the horizontal dissemination of Jacob's descendants in all four directions; and a temporal line embracing both past and future, reaching from Abraham and Isaac to Jacob and the generations that will issue from him.[10]

Until now, Jacob's desires have been small, involving only himself. In a strange irony, it will take isolation for Jacob to realize that God's dreams for him involve more than just him. Jacob will have to be alone to realize that God's dreams for Jacob are not for Jacob alone. Like Abraham, Jacob will come to realize that the dreams of God involve blessing for the many and the whole, not only the one (Gen 12:1-3). As Madeleine L'Engle describes the scene, God invites Jacob (and by extension all of us) to move from independence to interdependence: "We need to remember that the house of God is not limited to a building that we visit for only a few hours on Sunday. The house of God is not a safe place. It is a cross where time and eternity meet, and we are—or should be—challenged to live more vulnerably, more interdependently."[11]

Our spiritual formation cannot and does not begin and end with us. If our formation is to be something more than a hollow self-actualization, less therapeutic and more Christocentric, then it must involve *the all*. We are implicated in the good and the flourishing of *the all*, just as we take our place in God's big world. We do not have to be good—Jacob, that wily heel-grabber, was not good. I'm not particularly good either. However

---

[9]Yair Zakovitch, *Jacob: Unexpected Patriarch* (Yale University Press, 2012), 47-49.

[10]Zakovitch, *Jacob*, 49.

[11]Madeleine L'Engle, *A Stone for a Pillow: Journeys with Jacob*, The Genesis Trilogy (Convergent Books, 2017), 10-11.

constricted, small, or self-involved our life might be, we need only look outward—*excurvatus ex se*, the self looking beyond the self—to see that we are part of the greater whole. It is that greater whole that invites us not to a rugged independence or fearful self-subsistence but to an interdependency in which we all have a place. The Christ of the poets and the Christ of the theologians and the Christ of the alcoholics and the Christ of the single mothers and the Christ of the fearful and antagonistic and the Christ of the babies rolling around on their tummies and the Christ of our political enemies is the same Christ that spins the planets round and round. That same Christ is Jacob's Christ and my Christ and the Christ of us all. That same Christ invites us to move from the edges of our lives to the very center of his house, where in that risk we find our belonging.

It's what Jesus said, isn't it? When we loosen our chubby-fingered grasp on our tiny little life and how we think that life ought to look, we find ourselves living a bigger and richer life than we could have imagined (Mt 16:25).

The house of God invites us into the possibility that we have not quite pinned God down, even at the eve of our life.

At the dawn of our life, we are so very sure of things. But somewhere at the noon of our life (I am forty-two as I write this, surely the noon of my life, when desert tradition soberly warns me that the proverbial noonday demon threatens to overtake me), we become less and less sure. Too much has happened to us and in us and for us and because of us and in spite of us for all the old ways to hang together quite as tightly as they once did. As we move from the dawning of our life, with its dark energy and vibrant force; to the noontime of our life, with its tired, disillusioned, and emerging, hard-earned wisdom, gray creeping into our temples; and surely to the dusk of our lives, we find that God also exceeds our grasp. L'Engle puts it with such forceful honesty:

> The human being's attempt to understand the Creator can never be final, but dynamic, in motion, almost as though we were climbing that ladder of angels joining heaven and earth. Do we get dizzy on the ladder? Refuse to climb? Turn over and tell the vision to go away? . . . Our God becomes too small when we

> make God in our own image, instead of heeding the image of God in us. In us, not outside us, but in us, waiting to be recognized. Our call, no matter what our vocation, is to witness to the God within, the God who is One.[12]

The Gospel writers envision this in a way Jacob never could. The Jesus of John's Gospel says it this way:

> Do not let your hearts be troubled. You believe in God; believe also in me. My Father's house has many rooms; if that were not so, would I have told you that I am going there to prepare a place for you? And if I go and prepare a place for you, I will come back and take you to be with me that you may also be where I am. You know the way to the place where I am going. . . .
>
> And I will ask the Father, and he will give you another advocate to help you and be with you forever—the Spirit of truth. . . . I will not leave you as orphans; I will come to you. . . .
>
> Anyone who loves me will obey my teaching. My Father will love them, and we will come to them and make our home with them. (Jn 14:1-4, 16-18, 23 NIV)

In Jesus, Bethel is no longer a place—it is a person—every person, in fact, who loves Jesus and obeys his teachings.

We are Bethel, the house of God. God has made it so. And so it is that in every moment and in every circumstance, we live and move and have our being in God's house—this great big world in which we are all interconnected and in which God's presence is ascending and descending invisible ladders all around us. As poet Gerard Manley Hopkins puts it, our world is "shot through with the grandeur of God."[13] We only *think* we live in a secular age; the truth is, we live in a world much closer to that envisioned by the poets and the storytellers, with their enchanted wildernesses, mystical landscapes, and vibrant dreamscapes, than we dare imagine. From the first breathy *wayehi* ("And it was") brooding over the dark waters at creation, to Jesus' ascension and descension of the ladder

---

[12]L'Engle, *Stone for a Pillow*, 140-41.

[13]John F. Thornton and Susan B. Varenne, eds., *Mortal Beauty, God's Grace: Major Poems and Spiritual Writings of Gerard Manley Hopkins* (Vintage Books, 2003), 21.

of the cross, to the pouring out of God's breath at Pentecost, God has enchanted our world. It is shot through with God's own grandeur. It is God's good pleasure that the world be so. At Bethel, God shows Jacob a much bigger world than the one he imagined, one that, as Barbara Brown Taylor writes, is "so thick with divine possibility that it is a wonder we can walk anywhere without cracking our shins on altars."[14]

Because God's dream for Jacob and God's dream for the world is much bigger than Jacob envisioned, he will have to learn a new way to climb. To get in on what God is doing, I suspect we will too.

Climbing Ladders

About two months after I made my decision to step away from Baylor but before the school year had ended, I found myself at a weeklong retreat in Alabama. It was a welcome relief during an exhausting and confusing season in which the initial euphoria of that decision gave way to the more practical aspects of how my husband and I would support ourselves. We had begun to wonder where our lives were going in the midst of what many people (*us too, at times*) surely considered an unwise decision. The retreat came as a relief—I knew I needed both quiet and community, a place to pray and a place to listen to the prayers of others. Yet when I arrived, I was too tired to pray and too tired to journal. The week I was there, the only personal praying I did included a single line in my journal, which I wrote immediately upon my arrival: "I feel too tired to talk to You right now, but I long for a word from You." I wrote that line in my journal, went about the perfunctory mealtime and small group time with others at the retreat, went back to my room, closed my eyes, and went to sleep.

The next morning, I was jolted awake when it was still dark outside, with a single sentence, clear as a voice spoken aloud, ringing in my mind: "It's time to climb off the ladder."

A few hours later, I sat in our first session for the day, in which our speaker opened his lecture with the following: "Today I want to talk to

---

[14]Barbara Brown Taylor, *An Altar in the World: A Geography of Faith* (HarperOne, 2009), 15.

you about climbing off ladders and climbing trees with God instead." What followed was a forty-five-minute lecture that gave shape to all I had been feeling and affirmed that our decision, however unorthodox, was the right one.

Most of us spend our lives climbing the ladder of success. This is especially true for the first half of our lives, in which we chase after things. We might pursue our education, find a romantic partner, and seek to build a home with a community around us. Richard Rohr refers to this first-half-of-life activity as building a "container" for our lives. We ask necessary questions such as, "What makes me significant?" or, "How will I support myself?" and, "Who will go with me?" According to Rohr, what our lives are *actually* about—who we *actually* are—remains largely undiscovered until the second half of life, when we begin to examine the contents of our container.[15]

It's sort of like reading prose all our lives and one day discovering poetry. Prose is important—it provides shape and narrative structure to our lives. Prose is a literary device that helps us recount our life story, relaying our successes and allowing us to follow along logically from one life plot point to another. Prose makes sense unless we're talking about William Faulker or Virginia Woolf's stream-of-consciousness prose, which is a very different kind of reading experience altogether. For that, we need a whole lot of coffee, prayer, and some sort of literary decoder ring. But for the most part, prose makes sense. It's orderly, linear, structured, and logical—our life plot points follow sequentially one after the other. We need prose because it helps us track and make sense of our lives. It's a first-order sort of narrative wisdom.

Poetry is not like that. The form of poetry itself is meandering and searching and certainly not always logical. As Old Testament scholar John Webster says about the relationship between God and the Bible, the form is fitting, even as the subject exceeds the form.[16] Likewise, the

---

[15]Richard Rohr, *Falling Upward: A Spirituality for the Two Halves of Life*, rev. and updated ed. (Jossey-Bass, 2024), 1.

[16]John Webster, *The Domain of the Word: Scripture and Theological Reason* (T&T Clark, 2012), 129.

form of poetry is fitting to grapple with our deep questions as we strain perhaps not toward full discovery but toward acceptance. Poetry allows us to rest inside its own spaciousness, inviting us to look inward to the mystical and untouched places within our deepest self, where God has made God's house. Like the old Shaker song, poetry invites us to turn, turn till we "come 'round right." It's there, in the turning of our lives 'round right, that we lay claim to the gift to be simple, the gift to be free, the gift to come down where we ought to be.

We need not be very old to feel the rhythm of the poetry of our lives—there are people I know who are very young who have discovered it and people I know who are quite old who have not. The point is that one day, we feel its rhythm, hear its call, knocking at our door. In engaging with the poetry of our lives, we are set free from the exacting demands we make that suggest our lives look a certain way. The voice that makes those demands is not the voice of the Poet, capital *P*, *God*, but emerges from a voice outside. Even if the voice comes from inside our own minds, that voice still exists at a distance from us—from a place outside our deepest self. That voice is therefore not of God.

Prose keeps us at the surface, protecting a narrative of our lives that is *prosaic*, commonplace, unromantic, and lacking in adventure and fearful beauty. Yet prose gives us the illusion of order and control. In other words, the narratives we strain to hold together keep us safe but largely dissatisfied. About poetry, Emily Dickinson once wrote, "I dwell in Possibility— / A fairer House than Prose."[17] It is precisely inside this house of possibility where we find God and our deepest selves too. The narratives we write about our lives are not only exacting—they're loud. They shout at us about how hard we've worked, about what other people will think, about what success must look like and how our lives must, *simply must*, turn out the way we've planned or we will be nothing more than failures who've been fooled by life and by the whole system.

---

[17]Emily Dickinson, *Hope Is the Thing With Feathers: The Complete Poems of Emily Dickinson* (Gibbs Smith, 2019).

But there will come a time when everything must fall apart, and there we will find God.

We will find God in the poetry of possibility. And inside that poetry we will find perhaps not every answer (*because by now, the answers have unraveled*) but a place to begin again, a place to rediscover the souls we've lost on our way up the ladder as we've chased our own dreams. Anne Lamott, in her typically poetic way, says: "No wonder some of our parents forgot to mention soul, as it is apt to distract one from serious goals and aspirations. It is as playful and illogical as a kitten, as watchful as God or a baby. It rubs its back lazily against trees. It stops and gasps at beauty and is bathed in it. And sometimes it begins to weep."[18] In rediscovering soul, like Jacob, we take a journey toward something approaching wholeness. As we do so, we find perhaps that the imagery of the ladder depicts not success but ascent toward God, often not by traveling up but by traveling down.

The old saint John Climacus understood the imagery of the ladder quite differently from our own picture of upward mobility and outward success. Drawing on the story of Jacob's ladder, Climacus depicts the ladder as an image of the spiritual life: "The holy virtues are like the ladder of Jacob and the unholy vices are like the chains that fell off the chief apostle Peter. The virtues lead from one to another and carry heavenward the man who chooses them. Vices on the other hand beget and stifle one another."[19] Drawing on many different stories from the Hebrew and Christian Scriptures, Climacus understood each rung on the ladder as a step toward virtue and therefore toward God. Beginning with step one, the renunciation of life, through step thirty, the cultivation of faith, hope, and love, Climacus claimed that saints travel the ladder upward toward God, rung by rung.

Climacus's third step, what he calls "On Exile," seems particularly apparent in Jacob's dream at Bethel. Climacus describes exile as "a separation from everything, in order that one may hold on totally to God. It is a chosen route of great grief. An exile is a fugitive, running from all

---

[18]Anne Lamott, *Dusk Night Dawn: On Revival and Courage* (Riverhead Books, 2021), 31.

[19]John Climacus, *The Ladder of Divine Ascent*, The Classics of Western Spirituality (Paulist Press, 1988), 152.

relationships with his own relatives and strangers." Climacus's step of exile is an "irrevocable renunciation of everything in one's familiar surroundings that hinders one from attaining the ideal of holiness." While Jacob does not choose this exile, this detachment, as Climacus writes, "Detachment is good and its mother is exile."[20] For Jacob, everything depends on a detachment not only from his origins but also from his own shadow. As Zakovitch puts it, "Alone in the backcountry, as the dark night cast its all-encompassing shadow, without his flock or sheepdogs to ease the loneliness, Jacob must suddenly have become singularly aware of his solitary predicament."[21] On this note of exile—*wayyetse*—"and he left"—Jacob's story moves into what other scholars will call "boxing the shadows."

Boxing the Shadows: Submission as Spiritual Practice

Esther Spitzer, like many scholars before and after her, myself included, describes Jacob's story as a progression toward wholeness. She describes the two flights into the wilderness and Jacob's dream as an "initiation" experience or a "rite of passage" in which Jacob becomes aware of his mission and destiny.[22] It is the second flight into the wilderness, about which I have written previously, in which he deals with his shadow side.[23] At the Jabbok River, Jacob wrestles with a mysterious figure shrouded in darkness, and there Jacob faces the darkness or the shadow within himself. Throughout his story, Jacob grasped for birthright (Gen 25:19-34), deceived his father for a blessing (Gen 27:1-29), ran away from his brother (Gen 27:41-45), and sent his family ahead of him toward possible death by the hand of Esau while he remained at the Jabbok River at night (Gen 32:1-21). Jacob, whose name means "the heel-grabber,"

---

[20]Climacus, *Ladder of Divine Ascent*, 85-86.
[21]Zakovitch, *Jacob*, 47.
[22]Esther Spitzer, "A Jungian Midrash on Jacob's Dream," *Reconstructionist* (October 1976): 22-23.
[23]Noel Forlini Burt, *Encounters in the Dark: Identity Formation in the Jacob Story*, Semeia Studies (SBL Press, 2020).

lived a selfish and small life, one in need of transformation, of breaking open.

Following the Jungian mode of individuation, Spitzer argues that transformation can take place only through suffering and an active struggle with the shadow, the dark side of the self.[24] Likewise, Rohr names three parts of the self—the shadow self, which he describes as "what you refuse to see about yourself and what you do not what others to see"; the persona or mask, which we construct during the first half of life; and the "best and deepest self," which is typically referred to as the true self. Movement to what Rohr calls second-half-of-life wisdom requires "shadowboxing," the movement from denial of the shadow self to the acceptance of its work in one's life and the process of recovering the true self.[25] This true self is the saint who dwells inside us, *the who we are before the world began*. As Thomas Merton wrote so beautifully long ago: "Make ready for the Christ, whose smile, like lightning, sets free the song of everlasting glory that now sleeps in your paper flesh like dynamite."[26] It is the Christ hidden in us that is the "hope of glory," as Paul puts it (Col 1:27). The reality about us is this: We are saints; and much of our lives is about uncovering—or rediscovering—that fundamental reality. To do so we must shadowbox those parts of ourselves that are merely masks, illusions, not the really real.

As Rohr says,

> The saint is precisely the one who has no "I" to protect our project. Their "I" is in conscious union with the "I AM" of God, and that is more than enough. Divine union overrides any need for self-hatred or self-rejection. Such people do not need to be perfectly right, and they know they cannot be anyway, so they just try to be in *right relationship*. In other words, they try above all else to be loving. Love holds them tightly and safely and always. Such people have met the enemy and know that the major enemy is "me." But you do not hate "me," either. You just see through and beyond

---

[24]Spitzer, "Jungian Midrash," 23.

[25]Rohr, *Falling Upward*, 81-83.

[26]Thomas Merton, "The Victory," in *Collected Poems* (New Directions, 1946), 115.

> "me." Shadow work literally *saves you from yourself* (your false self), which is the foundational meaning of salvation to begin with.[27]

There is a freedom, a *wayehi*, a creative "let it be," a genuine exhale from needing always to protect the self. Second-half-of-life wisdom, as Rohr describes it, is understanding that one's true self is hidden with Christ in God. It is this self that is both who we were as children in the mind and heart of God and who we uncover as wise adults or wise elders. It is this childlike self whom God protects who can truly enter the kingdom as a child, which is the only way we can ever enter the kingdom at all. This word of Jesus was so important that two Gospel writers decided to include it (Mt 18:3; Mk 10:15). This child, in their simplicity, has a childlike wisdom that is the real hallmark of the elder, the one who has undergone a second naivete.

The tension between living in a childlike way while becoming maturing disciples is captured in the spiritual discipline of submission. The spirit of submission is best described in the prayer of Thomas à Kempis: "As thou wilt; what thou wilt; when thou wilt."[28] In the spiritual discipline of submission, we offer our wills to God, seeking to do things God's way.

Richard Foster has identified seven practical areas of submission, which play out both vertically in our relationship to God and horizontally in our relationships with other people. We first submit ourselves to the triune God, into whose hands we put our day. Our second act of submission is to Scripture (I will discuss elements of this in chapter three, "Feasting on the Word"). Yielding ourselves to hear the Word, to receive the Word, and to obey the Word, we submit ourselves to the Spirit who will help us interpret and apply the Word to our lives. Third, we submit ourselves to our family, living graciously with one another. The fourth act of submission is to our neighbors and other people in our lives. Here we perform small acts of kindness, seeking ways to serve them in the daily things of life. Fifth, we submit ourselves to the body of Christ, in which we worship locally and seek to serve as the Spirit and our skills move us

---

[27]Rohr, *Falling Upward*, 84.

[28]Thomas à Kempis, *The Imitation of Christ*, in *The Consolation of Philosophy* (Random House, 1943), 139.

to do so. Sixth, we submit ourselves to the broken and despised, acknowledging that it is care for the "widows and orphans in their distress" that constitutes true fidelity to God. Finally, we submit ourselves to the world, living responsibly in an increasingly irresponsible world.[29] Like all the spiritual disciplines, submission is not an end unto itself but a means of grace that positions us to continue to mature in the faith.

These days, one of the only things I know for sure is this—the God of Jacob is the God of Paul and the God of us all, and God will not finish with us until we belong to him completely. It's what the biblical writer knew too as he reports God's words to Jacob: "For I will not let you go until I have done what I said to you" (Gen 28:15). It's also what Paul knew about Jesus—that the one who began a good work in us *will* see it to completion (Phil 1:6).

One of the ways in which God will bring the good work that is us to completion is through the Word itself. As we'll see in the next chapter, the Word who is God addresses us inside wildernesses of our own making, inviting us to integrate head and heart through a posture of eucharistic reading.

Questions for Reflection and Discussion

1. Is there a ladder you're currently climbing? Is it one God has invited you to climb, such as John Climacus's ladder toward virtue, or is it some other ladder?
2. Jacob is a complex character who nevertheless experiences profound moments with God. Is there a moment from his story that has caught your attention afresh?
3. Submission is one of the more challenging spiritual practices, both because it is simply difficult and because it can be easily abused. What is your knee-jerk reaction to submission, and what role does it play in your life?

---

[29]Richard J. Foster, *Celebration of Discipline: The Path to Spiritual Growth*, 25th anniversary ed. (HarperSanFrancisco, 1998), 122-23.

3

FEASTING ON THE WORD

Eucharistic Reading in Exodus and Numbers

The whole congregation of the Israelites set out from Elim and came to the wilderness of Sin. . . . The whole congregation of the Israelites complained against Moses and Aaron in the wilderness. The Israelites said to them, "If only we had died by the hand of the Lord in Egypt, when we sat by the pots of meat and ate our fill of bread, for you have brought us out into this wilderness to kill this whole assembly with hunger." Then the Lord said to Moses, "I am going to rain down bread from heaven for you."

Exodus 16:1-4; cf. Numbers 11; 14

As I refilled my coffee mug, sixty students began to sing "The First Noel"—their jovial way of alerting their absent-minded professor that it was time for class to start. I was in Illinois for a week as faculty for the Upper Room Academy for Spiritual Formation, speaking to pastors and spiritual directors on the theme of grace in the spiritual life. For someone who is accustomed to a semester of teaching, a week is a short amount of time, yet their silly, good-natured serenade is a picture of the connection we formed that week. I took my mug with me to the lectern and began the morning lecture.

I can't speak to exactly what endeared me to them, and I'm not ever likely to know. I can only say that I've lived long enough at this point to know that what we experienced together was not the grownup equivalent of a camp high. Something sacred took place in that classroom setting that enabled us to do tender work together that week. I shared vulnerably from the biblical text and from my own life, experiencing something that was full, not false or forced. I taught out of my truest self, and as a result I felt a sense of belonging. I was deeply at home, connected to those sixty people: They belonged to me, I belonged to them, and we all belonged to God. Likewise, the biblical text felt like a home I could move around in, not at a detached distance but intimately from within its pages. I belonged to the biblical text, and the biblical text belonged to me. As a result, that week was among the most intimate and life-giving experiences of my teaching life, one that reminded me of the sacredness of the teaching space and the sacredness of the Word itself.

The classroom is always a sacred space, yet I have often experienced it to be a lonely place. Every semester, I am intentional about creating a welcoming classroom space for my students, yet I do not always feel at home there myself. There may be any number of reasons for this—when the *realities* of teaching impinge on the *romanticism* of it, I'm reminded that even this noble profession has its frustrations: bored or uninterested students, a mountain of grading, and institutional pressures, to name a few.

While these things may be true sometimes or even often, I'm convinced that my own loneliness comes from a deeper place. My loneliness has less to do with these superficial things and more to do with *the self* who stands behind the lectern, the self who educates and explores the biblical text. I have been privileged to study the Bible at the highest level, to learn things most people never get to learn, and to convey a portion of those things in an academic setting. Yet somewhere along the way to becoming a "serious scholar," I began to treat the biblical text as a thing to be dissected, deconstructed, and held to the scholarly light of objectivity. On the way to objectivity (*as if there were such a thing*), I misplaced the self who found delight in its pages, relegating that particular self to the sacred (and solitary) place of the prayer closet. Over time, the place of prayer felt fertile, life-giving, bursting with energy, a place where my deepest self was at home. The other place, the classroom space where I spent most of my time, felt like an emotional desert, a place where my deepest self was buried under dry earth. Everything there felt detached and desiccated, and I did not feel like I belonged. It became clear to me that *I was composed of two selves in contradiction with each other.*

I have discovered that when the self who teaches and learns is a *divided self*, the mind and the heart disconnected from each other, both the classroom and the biblical text itself will be lonely places. Both will become emotional and epistemological deserts where no one feels at home. While this story is a personal one, I don't think I'm alone in feeling lonely.

Today, those of us who make our vocational homes in the academy and the church experience these as two separate, distinct places. Historically, however, these were not separate homes. Christians from the patristic era all the way through the monastic movement sought to engage the life of the mind and the life of prayer at the same time. Indeed, until the thirteenth century, theology was "foundationally a deeply experiential way of knowing."[1] As premodern Christianity gave way to Scholasticism and ultimately to the Enlightenment, theologians began to employ a dialectical or logic-based approach to the study of the biblical text, which foregrounded reason as the primary means of knowing. The aim of biblical studies shifted from prayerful engagement of the text and its intersection with one's own life to mastery over it. This approach differed greatly from the monastic context, which joined the life of the mind with the inner landscape of the heart.

---

[1]Todd W. Hall and M. Elizabeth Lewis Hall, *Relational Spirituality: A Psychological-Theological Paradigm for Transformation* (IVP Academic, 2021), 12.

Beginning with Scholasticism, then, biblical studies and spiritual formation were divided, each of them representing very different epistemological ends.[2] Citing something akin to irreconcilable differences, this amounted to the breakup of a disciplinary marriage in which the academy and the church existed in separate homes. Over time, the academy sought explicit knowledge, controllable facts that could be mastered. The church, on the other hand, approached knowledge from a supposedly more implicit, intuitive, and relational place.

This disciplinary divorce has vast implications for how we read the Bible. Hans Boersma has said as much, explaining the trickle-down effect of this breakup as a difference between patristic and modern biblical interpretation: "We often think of biblical exegesis as lying within the purview of the academy and of liturgy as the domain of the church; not so with the church fathers. For them, the way we read the Bible has everything to do with how it functions in the church."[3] For Boersma, what is at stake is who reads the Word and how. The academy reads the words of Scripture in a serious, exegetical way, while the church engages the affective dimension of those words through liturgy. Much of Boersma's excellent work in *Scripture as Real Presence: Sacramental Exegesis in the Early Church* is a call to retrieve or at least reconsider patristic exegesis as a worthwhile reading posture.

Boersma's assessment of the disciplinary divorce between biblical studies and spiritual formation is historically accurate, but he is overly optimistic in his view that the church reads the Bible in spiritually nourishing ways. While the two disciplinary houses may have experienced a formal separation, the terms of their estrangement are not as cut and dried as they may first appear. The epistemological inclinations of the academy impinge on the church in ways that go largely unnoticed, at least cognitively, by those of us who sit in the pews. Nevertheless, this epistemological impingement distorts us relationally, affectively, in ways

[2]Hall and Hall, *Relational Spirituality*, 12-13.

[3]Hans Boersma, *Scripture as Real Presence: Sacramental Exegesis in the Early Church* (Baker Academic, 2017), 66.

that militate against a personal, embodied engagement with the text. We are formed intellectually but not relationally. Would that liturgy impinge on, indeed, intrude into our seminary classrooms, but frequently it does not. Would that both our seminary classrooms and our churches were more affective and experiential, but often they are not. I am not saying (as I think Boersma is not) that in every case, liturgy is relegated to the church and biblical exegesis to the academy. What I *am* saying is that too often academic reigns supreme in the church too, and this comes at a high cost—we are lonely readers disengaged affectively from God and from our deepest selves.

This loneliness begins with the way our seminarians and religious academicians are trained. When we hierarchize biblical studies over spiritual formation in our seminary and university classroom curricula and separate them as two distinct disciplines, we separate head from heart. When we treat biblical studies (and other religious disciplines) as something akin to the hard sciences and relegate spiritual formation to a curricular afterthought, we send a message to seminarians who later become pastors of churches that it is mastery of a text rather than submission of our lives to God that matters most. We then perpetuate a system that says we control the texts we exegete, rather than allowing the Word to excavate our lives.

The consequence of this is far-reaching. We train seminarians who have separated head from heart and who then preach sermons and teach Bible studies that lead their congregations to do the same. The result is that we live in an epistemological desert of our own making, with words of life available to us yet unaware that we are starving to death. Wesleyan tradition has bemoaned this state of affairs, at least in its hymnody, with Charles Wesley penning the famous line, "United the two so long disjoined, knowledge and vital piety." Yet sadly, knowledge and vital piety are not joined, and the academy and the church, two houses that were once united, are both affective deserts. We can become other than the way we have been trained, but it will take hard work and, dare I say it, divine intervention.

How can we integrate the heart and the mind in such a way that the Word sustains us? Like manna in the wilderness, God has given us his Word as food. How can we stoop down to gather it? If we are in the desert, how can we find our way back home? These are the questions I seek to answer in this chapter. The story of Yahweh's gift of manna in the wilderness in Exodus 16 and its companion passages, Numbers 11 and Numbers 14, both provide a deeper diagnosis of our desert reading practices and invite us to *desert them* in favor of a eucharistic feasting on the Word. What is needed is academic rigor and vital piety joined beautifully together. Christians from the desert tradition through the monastic Middle Ages provided a picture of this, and our retrieval of both their philosophical positions and their reading practices may very well renew us and save us.

Stomach Growls

"What is home but the merging of our lost selves? What is home but our divided selves finally embracing?" Macrina Wiederkehr once wrote.[4] In Egypt, the Israelites are not home. They exist in a brutal system in which they are enslaved for 430 years. Their cry rises to Yahweh, who intervenes and demands that the Israelites journey into the wilderness for the purpose of *feasting*—"Thus says the LORD, the God of Israel, let my people go that they may *celebrate a feast* for me in the wilderness" (Ex 5:1). The jubilation proposed by Yahweh is captured by the root word *khagag*, which deals with making a pilgrimage feast, celebrated in part by the sacred procession and dancing, as the psalmist would later exclaim, "glad shouts and songs of thanksgiving, a multitude keeping festival" (Ps 42:4).[5] The celebratory nature of feasting in the wilderness was captured in the Covenant Code by a liturgical rhythm in which the Israelites offered thanksgiving for their freedom from slavery every four months (Ex 23:14-16). Yahweh's invitation to the wilderness was for the express purpose of liturgy, the worship of himself through a prayerful

---

[4]Macrina Wiederkehr, *A Tree Full of Angels: Seeing the Holy in the Ordinary* (HarperOne, 1988), 13.
[5]F. Brown et al., *A Hebrew and English Lexicon of the Old Testament* (Oxford University Press, 1962), 290.

and celebratory *feasting on words*. This celebration was to become a rhythm of life in which the Israelites remembered their freedom, the trading of one kind of life for another, a liturgical reminder that God really can spread a table in the wilderness (Ps 78:19).

Nevertheless, the words of joy initiated by this God of the desert gave way to a different kind of word in the wilderness. After about a month of living there, the Israelites began to *lun* ("murmur"). The word in the *qal* tense is used sparingly in the Old Testament, present only in the wilderness narratives of Exodus and Numbers. The narrator clarifies who is doing the murmuring in Exodus 16:1-2—it is all of Israel, *kol adath beney-yisrael* ("the whole congregation of the children of Israel"). In the initial verses of the companion passage in Numbers 11, the Hebrew writer uses slightly different terminology. There it is *haam* ("the people") who *kemithonenim* ("murmur"; Num 11:1), while *hasaphsuph* ("the rabble") among them feel a *hithawu* ("craving"; Num 11:4). Discussion of the authorship and redaction of these two passages is beyond the scope of this chapter, as is a thorough teasing apart of their differences.

Nevertheless, what is clear from both passages is that the collective hunger of the group led to their collective murmuring. In the assessment of the Israelites, Moses and Aaron have led them to the wilderness to die of starvation (Ex 16:3). The construction of the grammar is revealing—both the bringing out (*hotsethem*) and the killing (*lehamith*) foreground the agency of the subject.[6] The implication is that Moses and Aaron, working on behalf of the Lord, have *caused this*. Their assessment is not far off. As he looks back on the initial sojourn in the wilderness, the aging Moses offers a poignant reflection on their experience: "And he oppressed you and he let you starve" (Deut 8:3). There too, the starvation—*wayyariveka*—underscores agency. It is *caused* by the same Lord who brought them to the wilderness in the first place (*wayyassev*; Ex 13:17-18).[7] As Moses recounts the experience, however, he points to

[6]Both are in the *hiphil* verbal stem, which foregrounds the subject as the causative agent.
[7]These verbs are also in the *hiphil* verbal stem, indicating the subject as the agent of causation.

the *purposeful nature of their hunger pangs*—it was for the purpose of testing the hearts of the Israelites (Ex 16:4; Deut 8:3), ultimately resulting in their good (Deut 8:16). The Lord has caused it all—the leading into the wilderness, the hunger pangs, and later the giving of a mysterious kind of food wholly different from the kind they knew in Egypt.

All this causation has its attendant consequence—the people murmur, and they do so vociferously. In the first thirteen verses of Exodus 16, *lun* ("murmur") appears no fewer than eight times.[8] English dictionary definitions of *murmur* reveal the indistinct nature of its sound. A murmur is a soft, blurred, or low sound, seemingly spoken at a distance. It is also described as a half-suppressed or muttered complaint, like a grumble or a growl. Medically, a murmur is related to the heart, an abnormal sound caused by turbulent blood flow. Whether we define it medically or not, a murmur is an unintelligible sound with a very real source. These are words—unintelligible words perhaps, but words nonetheless—that signal to us something is wrong.

In the context of a chapter about the lack of food, the longing for food, and the provision of food, I would describe a murmur like a hunger pang. As a place both of deprivation and of silence, the wilderness is quiet enough to hear a murmur, a low growl signaling that something is wrong.

What becomes immediately apparent is that Wiederkehr's description of the divided self, parts of the whole lost from one another, characterizes the Israelites' behavior in the desert. The Israelites clamor for "all the food we wanted" (Ex 16:3), and the rabble experience a "gluttonous craving" (Num 11:4-6; cf. Num 14:1-4), yet the food they long for is not given for their good. Instead, Pharaoh feeds them table scraps, a begrudging effort to ensure the system of enslavement continues. This is nourishment given at a distance, scraps flung from a table of relational scarcity. Nothing about it is intimate, life-giving, or transformative but

[8]The triradical root is used in various forms throughout those thirteen verses, as a *niphal* preterite plus *waw* consecutive (Ex 16:2); in noun form as the direct object (Ex 16:7-9, 12), as a *hiphil* imperfect (Ex 16:7), and as a *hiphil* participle (Ex 16:8).

is instead intended to keep things as they are. This food is the opposite of abundance, and the Israelites are unknowing participants in this relationally broken structure when they clamor for it.

Likewise, we are unknowing participants in a self-perpetuating readerly system in which self is simultaneously at the center of the process and also nowhere to be found. We put ourselves at the center when we seek to control the reading process, communicating to God that we do not want what God can offer, which is relational engagement with its very Author. An Enlightenment-era mode of reading puts God at a relational distance, where the food of God's Word fails to nourish and transform us. Settling for intellectual readerly scraps instead, we are famished for genuine nourishment even as we demand we know what is best for us. In that way, we put ourselves at the center of the reading experience yet hide our deepest selves also.

Lest this all sound too indicting, Robert Mulholland notes that our reading habits have been ingrained in us through our earliest educational experiences: "You are the 'victim' of a lifelong, educationally enhanced learning mode that establishes *you* as the controlling power (reader) who seeks to master a body of information (text) that can be used by you (technique, method, model) to advance your own purposes."[9] This mastery begins by approaching the text from a place of information gathering, what Mulholland and others call informational reading.

Mulholland describes informational reading as involving several goals. First, informational reading seeks to cover as much textual terrain as quickly as possible. Second, informational reading is linear, moving sequentially through the parts of the text. Third, informational reading seeks to master the text, to grasp it, to get our minds around it, thus bringing it under our control. Fourth, informational reading views the text as an object out there for us to control or manipulate according to our own purposes, intentions, or desires. Fifth, informational reading

---

[9]M. Robert Mulholland, *Shaped by the Word: The Power of Scripture in Spiritual Formation*, rev. ed. (Upper Room, 2001), 19.

is analytical, critical, and judgmental. Finally, informational reading is about problem-solving, discovering whether something will "work for us."[10] This mode of knowing is a form of *incurvatus in se*, a bending toward the self, that forces its way onto the thing known through an act of epistemological pillaging. In the wilderness, the Israelites' *demand* for food and their treatment of Yahweh as a *thing* to be bartered with rather than a Subject to engage demonstrates that they misunderstand the spiritual purpose of the desert—to engage God in a life-giving, transformative way.

Engagement of God in a life-giving, transformative way is also the purpose of reading the biblical text. Thus we are fundamentally at odds with the biblical text itself when our *only* approach is dryly exegetical. Mulholland is clear to say (as am I) that this type of reading is not wrong in itself, and it *does* have its place. Recovering authorial intention, historical circumstance, redaction history, and other elements of exegesis bolsters our explicit knowledge, *lessening* (though not eliminating) our chances of doing real interpretive danger with the Scriptures. We need look no further than nineteenth-century interpretations of the curse of Canaan (Gen 9:25-27) as textual justification for slavery in the American South to affirm the need for sound biblical exegesis. At a time when facts are disturbingly up for debate, we need the work of scholars. My own book is a scholarly engagement with the biblical text, so I am not advocating we desert these important methods.

What I am suggesting is that we are fundamentally at odds with the biblical text itself when our *only* approach is to recover authorial intention rather than to hear the address of the Author in our own lives. The biblical text itself does not invite us to exegete but to hear an address. That address is deeply personal because we are dealing with persons: the Person, capital *P*, who addresses, and the person, lowercase *p*, who receives that address. That address must be personal because God is not a concept—God is a Person. If we habitualize reading only for information,

[10]Mulholland, *Shaped by the Word*, 51-53.

drowning out God's personal address to us, the text itself will become a dry desert, one that fails to nourish us.

This mode of reading is malnourishing partly because it fails to grasp us with the Bible's essential wonder. Like Hall in my discussion above, Cheryl Bridges Johns traces this lack of astonishment to the Enlightenment. She follows the reception history of the biblical text into the modern era's battles over biblical inerrancy and to our current postmodern, ex-evangelical moment. Her conclusion is clear—when the Bible is stripped of the miraculous world in which it is situated, we are left reading a "modern Bible" within a disenchanted world. As a result, the Bible is a text that is "neither alive nor mysterious." It is a "disenchanted text."[11] Her aim is not to choose a side between evangelicals or their more left-leaning counterparts, as though one side were more to blame for our readerly desert than the other. Her aim, in fact, is not blame at all but something more akin to lamentation:

> When the grand narrative of the Bible is reduced to a set of biblical principles that are propositionally distilled from the text, the human subject reigns supreme over the text, deducing its principles or laws and conceiving of ways to apply the truths of Scripture. This is not the same as abiding in the mysterious realm of sacred Word. It is not the same as having the Word of God alive in one's life so that the Bible becomes a habitation of the heart. It is not the same as "knowing" in the sense of the Hebrew term *yada*, which conveys an encounter with God resulting in a loving relationship.[12]

Johns laments what is obvious in Exodus 16:1-12 and its companion passages, Numbers 11 and Numbers 14—a preference for the tangible over the mysterious, a craving for the mundane rather than the miraculous, and a desire to manipulate rather than to relate. As the manna was incomprehensible to the Israelites, so too relational ways of engaging the Word of God are a miracle our modern mind struggles to comprehend.

---

[11]Cheryl Bridges Johns, *Re-Enchanting the Text: Discovering the Bible as Sacred, Dangerous, and Mysterious* (Baker Academic, 2023), 3.

[12]Johns, *Re-Enchanting the Text*, 32.

Instead, we settle for the crumbs of control, which means that the self who reads is a *false self*, one incapable of forming a generative relationship with the Bible and its Author. This kind of relationship will not allow the biblical text to, as George MacDonald says, break the "crust of the false self."[13] Reading in ways that reify the false self cannot conform us to Christ because there is not an authentic self to receive the Christ who exchanges our readerly crumbs with genuine manna. As Parker Palmer puts it, "Since self and a world that do not allow themselves to be known by love have a distorted self-image, the outcome of that struggle is always unfreedom and untruth. Such an education either turns out people who force their own inner distortions on the world, or it produces people who have succumbed to the world's distortion of themselves."[14]

We are, as Wiederkehr said, "divided selves," a Hebrew verb not fully parsed, common singulars and common plurals in search of a first person. In the modern era, the academic study of the Bible has taught us to take ourselves out of the reading process (reader-response criticism and autobiographical criticism notwithstanding), which we know to be impossible. We project our interests and prejudices onto everything we read, including the biblical text. The great irony is this—we have lost ourselves in the reading experience and overemphasized the self at the same time. In short, our reading is not personal enough. We have buried something in the desert of our readerly experience, and that something is the self. Like the Israelites in the wilderness, we must first recognize our lostness, our hunger within, before we can open ourselves to receiving true bread. For the Israelites and for us, this starvation is not a punishment but one intended for our good (Deut 8:16).

The mystical tradition also affirms this reality—hunger pangs are given to us by the God who loves us. Writing in sixteenth-century Spain, John of the Cross used the imagery of the night and the desert to

[13]George MacDonald, *Diary of an Old Soul* (Augsburg, 1975), 104.

[14]Parker J. Palmer, *To Know as We Are Known: Education as Spiritual Journey* (HarperSanFrancisco, 1983, 12.

describe dryness in the spiritual life. John drew on many biblical texts to describe and allegorize this reality, one of which is the giving of the manna in Exodus:

> For, as long as the soul rejects not all things, it has no capacity to receive the Spirit of God in pure transformation. Of this we have a figure in Exodus, where we read that God gave not the children of Israel the food from Heaven, which was manna, until the flour which they had brought from Egypt failed them. By this is signified that first of all it is meet to renounce all things, for this angels' food is not fitting for the palate that would find delight in the food of men.[15]

The failure of the food from Egypt, for my context in this chapter at least, is in reading the Scriptures in ways that are counter to, as John of the Cross puts it, "pure transformation." Trusting Yahweh, who waited until the flour of Egyptian ways of living in the world had failed before showing them a new way to live in the wilderness, so we must arrive at a place where our old readerly ways fail to satisfy us. *It is through this failure that God generates desire, one of the great gifts of the desert.* This desire positions us to receive the God of the desert and the gift of the Word itself.

In my own life, God used loneliness within an institutional system that separated academic engagement from spiritual formation. That deep distancing of two things that ought to be joined together created within me two *lowercase selves* in contradiction with each other. My divided self was the desert God used to create a desire in me to read more deeply. How each of us arrives at this place of desire for readerly manna is as mysterious, I suspect, as the manna itself. My own experience is a mystery to me, one I still strain to articulate. I will trust that this God makes desert tracks beside each of us as we are ready to recognize their faint outline. All I know is this: The God of the desert is not bound to any particular method other than love itself. It is the heart of desert love itself that God guides us to read relationally, uncovering the very self who reads.

---

[15]John of the Cross, *The Essential St. John of the Cross* (Wilder, 2008), 80-81.

Bread from Heaven

The biblical text reveals several things about the manna, the "bread from heaven," that highlight its sacred character. Most importantly, it is given by the Lord—it is not something the Israelites procure for themselves. Like Simon Peter's insight into Jesus' identity as the Messiah, revealed not by "flesh and blood" but by the Father in heaven (Mt 16:17), here also the manna falls from heaven like an epiphany, a fresh insight given from above. It is sheer grace, a benediction analogous to Jesus' "blessed are you," the giving of what is needed at just the right time.

Intertwined with this *givenness of things* is a clear indication of the presence of the Giver. For a community stubbornly uncertain about the Lord's presence (Ex 17:7), the manna points to that fundamental reality. The intertwining of the gift with the Giver is especially important in this desert setting in which everything feels unmoored. How often does the provision of God in wilderness point us to the greater reality that God really does indeed care about us! In my own wilderness experiences, the giving of the thing I need has transformed mere (and at times morbid) relief into the higher virtue of joy, because I realized that I was not out there in the hinterland alone. The God of the desert is present there too. The gift I receive diminishes in importance when I discover that *God* is the gift. The gift is just the symbol of that reality and a reminder that I am cared for by God.

This care does not always come in the way we might want or expect, but it always comes in the way that we need. The bread from heaven given to the Israelites makes this important point. The name *manna* means "What is it?" and underscores the mystery of the gift. Like the wilderness itself, which is a circuitous and unexpected path (Ex 13:17-18), so also are the things that happen to us on the wilderness road. The element of surprise is fundamental to the life of faith, and many of the deepest blessings of my own life have been surprises. I have a vivid memory of waking up, looking out a window in a place I never expected to be, and feeling the surreal nature of that moment. The manna is that—surreal and surprising.

The Israelites pick at it like a child trying a new food for the first time: "What is this? What is the flavor like? I'm not sure I like the texture. This isn't what I'm used to." And yet manna is the table spread in the wilderness, the very thing the Israelites need. We learn again, to our surprise, that God knows us better than we know ourselves. "God is not a tyrant, and God knows what we need," I have said to my own students as I have sat with them in their own wildernesses. That God knows us is a mystery far more wonderful than the manna itself.

And so it is that we must bring ourselves to God—that is our one act. All else is grace. This is also true when we bring the self who reads to the God who loves us.

Readerly Bread from Heaven

If one of the results of reading the Bible for information is a loss or division of the self, then reading *with* the God of the desert moves us toward a retrieval of that self. Desert father Abba Poemen had this to say about the relationship of the Word of God and the self: "The nature of water is soft, that of stone is hard; but if a bottle is hung above the stone, allowing the water to fall drop by drop, it wears away the stone. So it is with the word of God; it is soft and our heart is hard, but the [person] who hears the word of God often opens his [or her] heart to the fear of God."[16]

Poemen's word out of the desert is the advice to *put ourselves under the Word habitually*, acknowledging that there is a hardness in us that must be softened. That softness involves finding our self, our identity, in the words God speaks over us. As Roberta Bondi suggests, we must ask persistently, "What does this passage tell me about my identity in God?" Bondi goes on to say that the Bible forms our identity in several key ways: through salubrious words about us from the creation account, which emphasizes our being made in the image of a God who longs to

[16]Benedicta Ward, trans., *The Sayings of the Desert Fathers: The Alphabetical Collection*, rev. ed. (Mowbray, 1981), 192-93.

befriend us; through an examination of Jesus' selfhood and his refusal to form that selfhood based on other people's expectations of him; and through looking to Jesus, whose interactions with others suggest that their value does not come from what they do right and that their value does not diminish when they are imperfect. Even as Bondi points to these comforting aspects of identity formation in God, she also provides a discomfiting reminder fully in keeping with Scripture—namely that the call to find our identity in God is also an abandonment of every other egoic scaffolding, what surely feels like a death.[17]

As Poemen puts it, the hard is worn away by the soft. This process must be, by necessity, both habitual and humbling, requiring a radical trust in the God who has taken us to the readerly desert in the first place. This also means that none of Bondi's suggestions are possible without a foundational reorientation of our readerly position. We must recognize ourselves as a "word" from God, as Robert Mulholland has said. Drawing on Paul's statement in Ephesians 1:4 that God has "chosen us in Christ before the foundation of the world," Mulholland notes that the Greek *eklektos* ("chose") derives from the preposition *ek*, "out of," and the verb *legō*, which means "to speak." Thus we are a "word spoken forth." Just as the Word became flesh in Jesus (Jn 1:14), so too our own word is incarnated: "Now our 'word,' this word with a small *w* that God is breathing forth, is to be incarnate in us. Our physical life, our psychological, mental, emotional life—our whole created being is a vehicle for the expression of that 'word' God speaks forth to be in the lives of others." Soberingly, Mulholland adds that the whole of our word is being shaped either positively, by the Word who is God, or negatively by the world (and, I would add, even the readerly world). When it is shaped by the world, that word becomes "distorted" and "garbled" by the "false and incomplete expressions of our being." These realities are largely the places of frustration about which Paul writes in Romans 7.[18]

[17]Roberta C. Bondi, *To Pray and to Love: Conversations on Prayer with the Early Church* (Fortress, 1991), 86-89.

[18]Mulholland, *Shaped by the Word*, 34-36.

This means that if the whole of our "word" is distorted, there is a relational distance between us and the Word of God that only the Word who is Jesus can bridge. To bring Mulholland into conversation with Poemen, this means that we must continue to put own distorted word under the Word of God and allow it to do its converting work, the soft wearing away at the hard. We must move from graspers of the text to gatherers of it, from putting our own agenda over it to placing ourselves under it, allowing it to wear away our hearts of stone, as the desert prophet Ezekiel might say (Ezek 36:26). We trust that the God of the biblical desert is the God of our own readerly deserts too, and that this God can and does use the Word to retrieve the selves we have lost.

This retrieval happens through what Mulholland calls "focal perceptual shifts," one of which is the movement from lofty academic postures of readerly distance to the intimate posture of placing ourselves under the Word. Mulholland calls this spiritual or formational reading, and he outlines six characteristics of formational reading that serve to balance informational reading approaches. First, formational reading involves slowing down. Here, we are not concerned with covering a certain amount of textual terrain. Rather, the point is meeting God in the text.[19] Eugene Peterson draws on the language of the Old Testament itself to highlight the slow nature of spiritual reading. He draws on the Hebrew word *hagah*, which can refer to moaning, growling, uttering, speaking, or musing.[20] While the word is frequently translated as "meditate," Peterson views this as too tame an option, taking preference for the grittier word, "growl." Whatever translation choice we opt for, *hagah* was used by our Hebrew ancestors to refer to the kind of reading that deals with our souls.[21]

This spiritual reading is slow, pushing against a reading posture that values reading quickly for information. It involves waiting before the

[19]Mulholland, *Shaped by the Word*, 36.

[20]Brown et al., *Hebrew and English Lexicon*, 211.

[21]Eugene H. Peterson, *Eat This Book: A Conversation in the Art of Spiritual Reading* (Eerdmans, 2009), 2.

text as the Israelites waited before the manna (Ex 16:26-30), what Wiederkehr calls "keeping vigil with the word of God."[22] Just as there was a Sabbath from striving to gather manna, so there is a Sabbath from striving to gather crumbs of information from a Word that is given to us freely for the formation of our souls. We do not control the process but wait for the word God gives us, chewing on what is given at each sitting, trusting that God will make for us a feast that will nourish and sustain. As Peterson says, "Words spoken or written under the metaphor of eating, words to be freely taken in, tasted, chewed, savored, swallowed, and digested, have a very different effect on us from those that come at us from the outside, whether in the form of propaganda or information."[23] Like the Israelites who are called to a Sabbath, so we are called to rest before a text. Is there a word or a phrase that catches our attention? God invites us to rest before it, looking inward for how it might nourish us (or convict us) rather than moving too quickly past it.

Second, formational reading calls us to the deep places inside ourselves, where "you seek to allow the text to begin to become that intrusion of the Word of God into your life, to address you, to encounter you at deeper levels of your being." This means that the word we receive may come in the form of either consolation or censure. We must pause long enough to hear its address, for God may use this word to "disturb the foundations" of the false self.[24] What, for example, motivated the Israelites to crave something other than what God could provide (Ex 16:1-13; Num 11; 14)? What internal longing did that craving point to? What insecurities or fears did it highlight? Likewise, we might ask ourselves what it is in us that prefers scholarly distance to intimate relationship with this Word.

Third, formational reading allows the text to master *us*. Here we come to the text with an openness to hear, receive, respond, and become a

---

[22]Macrina Wiederkehr, *Abide: Keeping Vigil with the Word of God* (Liturgical Press, 2011).
[23]Peterson, *Eat This Book*, 10.
[24]Peterson, *Eat This Book*, 56.

servant of the Word rather than its master.[25] The Israelites learned they could not manipulate the Word who was the God of the desert. They had to humble themselves before what was given, both manna and law, and stoop down to gather and obey.

Fourth, formational reading requires a radical inversion of subject/object position. The Word is the subject who addresses us, and we are the object who receives its address. We stand before the Word and wait for its address, ready for the Word to "exercise control over the 'word' we are."[26] When we recognize that we are a small *word*, the object before the subject of the incarnate, preexistent *Word*, we can partner with God in becoming God's message of love, justice, and fellowship in the world. Just as the Israelites were shaped in the wilderness to become a "kingdom of priests" (Ex 19:6) and a "light to the nations" (Is 49:6), believers are to be the "light of the world" (Mt 5:14-16). We cannot shine a light that is dimmed through our own self-deception. The Word intrudes and invites a level of self-knowing that is necessary if our spiritual formation is to be "for the sake of others," as Mulholland says elsewhere.[27]

Fifth, in contrast to the analytical, critical, judgmental approach of informational reading, formational reading requires a humble, detached, receptive, loving approach. Rather than making simple adjustments to our informational mode that continue a pattern of our false self in control over the Word, we yield ourselves to the "penetrating address of God that confronts our distorted word."[28] This calls us not to façade-like adjustments but to what Dallas Willard calls a "renovation of the heart."[29] Such a radical adjustment is in keeping with the prophetic call that the Israelites keep the law not on tablets of stone but on the tablet of their heart (Ezek 36:26; cf. Rom 2).

---

[25]Peterson, *Eat This Book*, 57.

[26]Peterson, *Eat This Book*, 57.

[27]M. Robert Mulholland, *Invitation to a Journey: A Road Map for Spiritual Formation* (InterVarsity Press, 1993), 15.

[28]Mulholland, *Shaped by the Word*, 59.

[29]Dallas Willard, *Renovation of the Heart: Putting on the Character of Christ*, 20th anniversary ed. (NavPress, 2021).

Sixth, formational reading is not focused on problem-solving but in an openness to mystery.[30]

Like the Israelites, when we lean into astonishment, we rediscover the element of surprise at what God provides. The narrator tells us that, when the people of Israel saw the bread from heaven, they were astonished: "And each man said to his brother, 'What it is it?' For they did not know what it was" (Ex 16:15). Moses had to explain that it was *hallekhem*, the food given by the Lord for their nourishment, because it differed markedly from what they were accustomed to. Likewise, for those of us who are biblical scholars, ministers, or people overly familiar with the biblical text, spiritual reading helps us recover the mystery of the Word's essential *whatness*. When we lean into this essential whatness, we experience the second naivete necessary to unearth the self buried under the desert of academic readerly expectations.

Recovery of this self occurs through returning to the desert tradition, such as that reflected in the advice of Abba Poemen. We are also wise to take a page out of the church fathers, who were not bound by scholarly convention in the same way we are. Instead, they found freedom in what I will call *eucharistic readings* of the Old Testament text, in which encounter with Christ himself becomes our aim.

Eucharistic Reading

Because Christ is the Word, Christ himself is the feast. As Jesus tells us in John's Gospel, he is the bread of life (Jn 6:32-40). It is Christ himself whom we feast on when we read the Word of God spiritually. But I would push us further—the inevitable conclusion of spiritual reading is what I will call *eucharistic reading*, feasting on Christ even in the Old Testament. Such an invitation pushes against my natural inclinations as an Old Testament scholar and, indeed, much of my training. Patristic-era interpreters were not bound by these scholarly conventions, which

---

[30]Mulholland, *Shaped by the Word*, 59.

are rooted in the Enlightenment. Such interpreters often relied on allegorical reading to situate both Christ and reader in the Old Testament. The term *allegory* derives from two Greek words, *allos* (other) and *agoreuein* (to speak); thus *allegory* means "to speak other"—that is, to speak other than what the words themselves appear to say.[31] While the New Testament Christianizes Exodus 16 through the words of Jesus in John's Gospel, is Christ to be found in Exodus 16? Are we?

The allegorical interpretations of patristic-era interpreters would respond in the affirmative to both these questions. Drawing on the allegorical readings of Exodus 12 by both Melito of Sardis and Origen, Boersma argues that an "unabashedly christological reading of the text" stands out in their interpretations. Boersma goes on to say, "In fact, Christology is so central to both writers that they were convinced that Christ (and, by implication, the church) is already present within the history described in Exodus 12. That is to say, Christ and the church constitute the New Testament mystery that is sacramentally already present within the Old Testament text."[32]

Such an interpretive impulse was not atypical but was in fact the normative posture for patristic exegesis. While we might balk at the exegetical license taken in separating the Old Testament from its historical context, patristic writers did not fear what we might call its "arbitrary character."[33] Patristic writers did not mind freewheeling interpretations of the biblical text because they believed the Bible belonged to the church.

A key takeaway of Boersma's patristic analysis of Exodus 12 involves the sacramental and embodied nature of the text itself: "At bottom, this exegesis is grounded in one underlying conviction: as God's people we are implicated directly in the exodus that takes place in Christ. We ourselves are taking the exodus journey." Drawing on Paul's discussion of table grace in 1 Corinthians 10, a "broad-ranging allegorical network

---

[31]Boersma, *Scripture as Real Presence*, 81.
[32]Boersma, *Scripture as Real Presence*, 82.
[33]Boersma, *Scripture as Real Presence*, 82.

emerged": Egypt became the world of human passions; the waters of the Red Sea were salvific in nature; Pharaoh and his soldiers were interpreted as the devil; the pillar of light was Christ and the pillar of cloud the Holy Spirit; the blood of the lamb was the blood of Christ; the three-day journey into the wilderness was turned into Good Friday, Holy Saturday, and Resurrection Sunday; the manna was the Eucharist; and the water from the rock was understood either as the cup of salvation or as baptism.[34]

Such a framework situated the exodus event liturgically within the sacraments of baptism and Eucharist, becoming a way Christians could embody the text through ritual. For patristic Christians and for Christian readers today, this method allows us to enter the wilderness experientially, finding Christ present with us. When we do so, we find that Christ himself is the manna in the wilderness. And because Christ himself is the feast, we are invited to read eucharistically.

Eucharistic Reading as Spiritual Practice

Because eucharistic reading practices are imaginative, they are fundamentally autobiographical. When our readings take an *autobiographical turn*, they also take an *affective turn*—it is our loves, our appetites, our deep disappointments, our joys, our great hopes that rise to the textual surface. In short, eucharistic readings focalize our *feelings* more than anything else. We may find that by placing ourselves in the text in this way, we become very tender, vulnerable, and emotional. We trust that Christ is meeting us in these feelings, even as Christ is stirring our imagination.

Through his study of the New Testament, Alexander Whyte describes the process this way: "With your imagination you are anointed by holy oil, you again open your New Testament. At one time, you are the publican: at another time, you are the prodigal. . . . At another time, you are Mary Magdalene: at another time, Peter in the porch . . . till your whole

[34]Boersma, *Scripture as Real Presence*, 89, 91.

New Testament is all over autobiographic of you."[35] In this way, the God of the desert is Christ himself. It is this very Christ who sits with us when the feelings evoked by our eucharistic reading practice turn tender.

One way to connect ourselves to the biblical text imaginatively is through an exercise L. Roger Owens calls "watching the play."[36] While Owens uses the story of Jesus asleep in the boat in Mark's Gospel to explain the exercise, I will use our focus text for this chapter, Exodus 16, as a minor adaptation of his exercise. In watching the play, we imagine ourselves in the third row of a theater, where we watch the play of Exodus 16 unfold. We follow the two major acts of the play, Exodus 16:1-13 and Exodus 16:14-36, picturing what takes place and asking ourselves the following questions: "What do you hear?" "What do you taste?" "What do you feel?" "What do you see?" In the next stage of the exercise, Owens advises us to break the fourth wall, stepping out of our seats and imaginatively stepping onto the stage. Here we move closer to the action—we are in the desert with the Israelites. We ask those same questions again about what we hear, taste, feel, and see, and we ask ourselves where we are in the scene. Do we feel angry and hungry, along with the Israelites, wondering where our next meal might come from? Do we feel anxious to defend the God of the desert, whom we have come to know, urging the Israelites to patient trust in God's disciplinary methods? We allow ourselves to feel our feelings, to be right there in the wilderness.

In the third stage of the exercise, what Owens calls "going off script," we allow ourselves to have a conversation with this God of the desert in which we talk about what is going on with us. Here, we improvise, we go off script, sitting down with God to say whatever is on our mind and heart—"I am frustrated that what was supposed to feel like freedom

[35]Alexander Whyte, *Lord, Teach Us to Pray* (Harper & Brothers, n.d.), 251.

[36]I am indebted to L. Roger Owens's five-session talk, "Attentiveness to the Word," which he delivered in fall 2018 for the Upper Room Academy for Spiritual Formation in Gallant, Alabama. Owens's practice of "watching the play" is inspired by Ignatius of Loyola, whose imaginative methods of reading Scripture have shaped affective approaches to the Word for centuries.

feels frightening instead," for example, or we name whatever comes to mind. We're then invited to listen to what the God of the desert says back to us. Finally, Owens advises, "When it's over, pay attention." Were there moments of prayer in which we found ourselves particularly moved or drawn to something? Where was our *affect* most clearly stirred? Here, we simply sit, "savoring and paying attention" to what happened.

One of the oldest and most well-known practices in formational reading is lectio divina ("sacred reading"), which comes to us from twelfth-century monk Guigo. Referring to sacred reading as a ladder on which we might climb or be lifted up from earth to heaven, Guigo describes the four stages of lectio divina thus: "*Reading* seeks for the sweetness of a blessed life, *meditation* perceives it, *prayer* asks for it, *contemplation* tastes it. Reading, as it were, puts food whole into the mouth, meditation chews it and breaks it up, prayer extracts its flavor, contemplation is the sweetness itself which gladdens and refreshes."[37]

Here again, I use the focus text for this chapter, Exodus 16 to demonstrate this practice, but any biblical text can be used. In the first stage, *lectio*, we simply read the passage, aiming for a short amount of text. We might, then, take just five or six verses from Exodus 16. We read slowly, with the heart. We imagine we have entered the world of God's wilderness story, simply reading the passage and sitting with it in silence for several minutes. In the next stage, *meditatio* (meditation), we read the passage a second time, looking for a particular word that arrests our attention. Here we meditate on that word, with the idea of a cow chewing the cud, masticating, slowly turning it over and over again in its mouth. When that idea feels too antiquated for me, I picture my basset hound chewing on his bone, enraptured and totally focused. We sit with that word or phrase in this way, not allowing anything to distract us.

In the third stage, *oratio* (prayer), we read the passage a third time, again with no other agenda except to listen to God. Here it might be

[37]Guigo II, *The Ladder of Monks* 3, in *A Letter on the Contemplative Life and Twelve Meditations*, trans. Edmund College and James Walsh (Cistercian Publications, 1981).

helpful to consider Mulholland's advice: "If there is a particular word or phrase that has stirred in you, ask yourself: 'How do I feel about what is being said?' 'How do I react?' 'Why do I feel this way, or why am I responding in this way?' 'How is the Spirit of God touching my spirit?'"[38] We might also ask ourselves how we have been consoled, challenged, or moved in some way by the passage. Do we identify, for example, with Moses or the Israelites or even God in Exodus 16? Here we talk with God about that in prayer. In the final stage, *contemplatio* (contemplation), we read the passage one final time. Here we trust that whatever wilderness we find ourselves in, Christ is eucharistically present with us. Christ is in the wilderness, and Christ himself is the feast. His presence is the manna, given in just the right amount at just the right time to sustain us.

The exercises above are simply two of many formational (or eucharistic) practices that can help us make the autobiographical, affective turn. This affective turn is necessary to merge our lost or divided selves. Indeed, reengaging the affective dimension of the spiritual life is necessary if we are to face the disorienting darkness of the wilderness, which is the focus of the next chapter.

Questions for Reflection and Discussion

1. What is your relationship to spiritual reading? Do you find that, when you read the biblical text, you do so informationally or formationally?
2. What are the benefits and challenges to both types of reading?
3. Imagine you are in the wilderness with the Israelites: What do you see, taste, hear, smell, and touch? How might God use the text about manna in the wilderness to speak to your own story right now?

---

[38] Mulholland, *Shaped by the Word*, 22.

4

THE DARKNESS OF DISORIENTATION

Moses, Sinai, and Liminality in the Spiritual Life

Holy places are dark places.

C. S. Lewis, *Till We Have Faces*

Then the people stood at a distance, while Moses drew near to the thick darkness where God was.

Exodus 20:21 NRSVUE

Smoke wrapped around the mountain like a snake coiled through a tree as we made our way in the dark. My breathing was quick and shallow, my heart pounding as though I had swallowed several pots of coffee. I had no idea where I would go even if I *could* get out—I just knew that everything in me wanted to escape. Dizzy and disoriented, I felt like I could sprint for miles toward I knew not where. That rush of adrenaline was what I now know to be a panic attack, information my eight-year-old self didn't have at the time. I begged them to stop the car, but there were no guardrails on the side of the mountain in those days. There had been other ways to get there, but this roundabout way was still the better road, my father insisted. Now that we had chosen it, we couldn't turn back. We had no choice but to keep following the road as it curved upward into the unknown.

I would have been less afraid if we had been making this journey during the day. The terrain would have been the same, of course—the mountain still steep, the road still winding, the guardrails still nonexistent—but the familiarity of light brings with it the illusion of control. But it was not day, and the mountain continued to loom before us like a large wall, not exactly an impasse but not a straight road either. Even though we traveled together, I felt all alone, a tiny passenger in the back seat, trapped in an uncertain pause on a longer journey as my family made our way through the Great Smoky Mountains in the dark.

In some ways, the darkness and uncertainty of that mountain was a picture of God in my life then. It was a frightening thing not to know whether there was a *Great Someone* keeping watch over us in the Great Smoky Mountains that night, and *if* there was, *what* that Great Someone was like. I didn't know anything about prayer in those early days, so I wouldn't have known how to address that Great Someone even if I wanted to. That night, I was as uncertain about God as I was about the journey itself. *Fear* was my only orientation to God, to that dark mountain, and to the road we were on.

"Everything makes me afraid," I said many years later as I reflected on that night and many others in my life.

Those were among the most honest words I've ever spoken.

By eight years old, fear was a constant companion, seated next to me in the car that night and anywhere else I was, edging out desire for newness or adventure or life with a God who loved me. Maintaining control at all times was the only perceived way to keep fear at a distance. Consequently, I kept God, other people, and actual life at a distance too. I placed a wall in front of me as big as the mountain that night, a spiritual impasse that had the illusion of keeping me in control. Over time, I oriented myself to living on the edge of a life rather than in its dark and uncertain center. While this orientation was a decidedly toxic one, I didn't have to risk the disorientation that newness required.

The great writers of the spiritual life teach me that I'm not alone in this fear. The spiritual mountain or wall is a common phase in our lives with God. It is also the most critical experience in our faith formation. Along the spiritual journey, movement toward the wall is characterized by certainty fading into uncertainty like smoke on a mountain. Many of our answers become questions, and God seems to be released from whatever box we've placed God in.[1] Many different things may spur our movement toward the wall—a deep loss of some kind, sickness, the questions that naturally arise at midlife, some unforeseen crisis—but what is common to the wall experience is our will meeting God's will face-to-face. We decide anew whether we will surrender to God's will in our lives. At this stage, we recognize that we have spent our energy and are ready to learn about freedom, "the liberty of living without grasping."[2]

Despite this realization, the confrontation between the will of God and our own will is frightening and disorienting. Symbolically, the wall is a nighttime encounter in which we experience a deep unraveling of all we know. This unraveling is necessary if we are to risk newness, yet frequently we resist it. Strategies for resistance differ for each person. For some, the ego reasserts its will, believing we are in charge of our spiritual lives. Others whose early experiences of God or faith are tainted by painful memories engage in a kind of dance, in which we substitute other forms of spirituality that seem more comfortable, such as the shallowness of the health-and-wealth gospel. Other people rely on a familiar self-hatred to push this new and uncomfortable awareness of God's love away. For intellectuals, going through the wall requires intellectual

[1]Janet O. Hagberg and Robert A. Guelich, *The Critical Journey: Stages in the Life of Faith*, 2nd ed. (Sheffield, 2005), 98.

[2]Hagberg and Guelich, *Critical Journey*, 114-15.

humility and acceptance of ambiguity, which we try to resist through rational argument. High achievers will attempt to go through the wall by their own efforts, working harder than is required to get through the impasse. Some people appeal to doctrine, unable to withstand the uncertainty that such an unraveling produces. Those of us who teach or pastor others through their own unsettling experiences can deal with spiritual pride when we realize we must also face the wall.[3]

Our resistance can last for a long time, perhaps years. Invariably, we will experience grief at the wall, because we are often asked to give up something central to our identity.[4] While God's grace is the only means by which we may move through the wall, we must decide whether we will keep going or remain stuck there.

While such a confrontation with God is frightening, the wall represents fear *and* desire in equal measure. What emerges on the other side of the wall is a "melting down and reshaping" of our identity, in which our orientation toward God, others, and ourselves fundamentally changes. We gain a deeper sense of God's unconditional love for us, and we are able to extend that love to others. Such reorientation often involves moving forward into our true calling, discovering our life's purpose, and relinquishing our expectations of what is good for us. Fundamentally, there is a mystery to the wall, a darkness to it, a curving upward toward an unknown mountain.[5]

In the story of the Israelites, Mount Sinai is such a place. Indeed, Mount Sinai looms large in biblical memory as *the* critical experience in Israel's faith formation. Geographically and spiritually, Sinai is depicted as a "fierce landscape," one shadowed by wilderness on all sides (Ex 19:1-2).[6] At Sinai, the Israelites encounter Yahweh at the intersection of desert and mountain, two separate vistas that symbolize two separate ways of

---

[3]Hagberg and Guelich, *Critical Journey*, 115-18.
[4]Hagberg and Guelich, *Critical Journey*, 120.
[5]Hagberg and Guelich, *Critical Journey*, 123, 128.
[6]I have borrowed the phrase "fierce landscape" from Belden C. Lane, *The Solace of Fierce Landscapes: Exploring Desert and Mountain Spirituality* (Oxford University Press, 1998).

knowing in the spiritual life. Richard Rohr explains the spiritual implications of the two landscapes in this way:

> [Desert and mountaintop] are two different metaphors for the great mystery of what cannot be directly addressed in rational language. The tradition of the mountain is about presence; the tradition of the desert is about absence. The tradition of the mountain is about speaking; the tradition of the desert is about silence. The mountain is about knowing; the desert is about not knowing.[7]

Rohr accurately describes the spirituality of desert and mountain landscapes in Judeo-Christian tradition. Nevertheless, Sinai is simultaneously desert and mountain, the two stark spaces darkening into each other geographically, narratively, and spiritually. Therefore, Sinai merges presence and absence, speech and silence, and knowing and unknowing. The geography is both mountain and desert—the spirituality is both kataphatic and apophatic. Narratively and spiritually, Sinai is a reminder of the untrammeled *tohu wabohu*, the welter and the waste, that sprawled over the face of the deep, a stifling and dark silence before creation sighed its first word and dawn awakened (Gen 1:2). Sinai is therefore a spiritual *limen*, a place of theological and spiritual crossing. There, Yahweh invites the Israelites into the disorienting darkness. This very disorientation is an inevitable part of spiritual formation for all people of faith.

Liminality in Narrative Tradition

Drawing on the work of Victor Turner, who coined the term *liminality*, Robert L. Cohn notes three distinct phases in social rites: the separation of the ritual subject from their role in the social structure; the margin or limen, the transition stage; and the reincorporation of the subject into their new role in society. In the liminal phase, the ritual subject is "betwixt and between," having undergone a symbolic death to the old life and emerging into a new one.[8] Symbolically, wilderness and darkness serve

[7]Richard Rohr, *Things Hidden: Scripture as Spirituality* (Franciscan Media, 2008), 126-27.
[8]Robert L. Cohn, *The Shape of Sacred Space: Four Biblical Studies* (Scholars Press, 1981), 9-10.

as the primal expressions of liminality in the Sinai narrative. Liminal experiences can take place individually, and many famous stories in literature depict liminality as a necessary part of the hero's journey.

Liminal experiences can also take place communally, in which an entire group of people cross an epistemological, spiritual, or literal threshold. Turner uses the term *communitas* to describe communal liminality, in which liminars experience a type of bonding that does not depend on class, rank, wealth, or social status but that is an egalitarian, direct, nonrational, existential bonding of the "I-Thou." Liminars are said to experience a "common predicament"; thus the thinking (liminality) and the relating (*communitas*) of individuals during rites of passage are different from those in "fixed social positions."[9] At Sinai, Yahweh takes the "mixed multitude" (Ex 12:37-38) who were cast of Egypt and forms them into a people, the *beney-yisrael* ("the sons of Israel"). Thus the Israelites experience the strain of liminality communally. For all their grumbling (Ex 15:22-27; 16:1-13; 17:1-7; Num 11; 14), the Israelites know only *life together*. As a result, they also experience the liminal process together.

Much like the encounter at the wall, the liminal process occurs through a series of ideological or spiritual movements, which include orientation, disorientation, and reorientation/new orientation.[10] Orientation involves those things that provide stability and structure to our lives, even if those things are not altogether healthy. In Egypt, the Israelites experienced what I will call a *toxic orientation* under Pharaoh, who afforded them the certainty of provision, as their repeated complaints against Moses reveal (Ex 16:1-13; Num 11:1-6; 14:1-4). In the wilderness, the Israelites idealize the life they knew in Egypt, remembering it differently than it was. While orientation provides predictability, structure, equilibrium, and geographical or ideological groundedness to place, orientation can also be toxic, structured by faulty patterns of thinking

[9]Cohn, *Shape of Sacred Space*, 10.
[10]Walter Brueggemann, *Spirituality of the Psalms* (Fortress, 2001).

that keep us in systems of abuse. Slavery in Egypt provided just such a system, with the Israelites failing to recognize their lives as abusive until the work grew progressively harder. Indeed, it is their "cry on behalf of their taskmasters" (Ex 2:22-23; 3:7-9, 16-18) that catalyzes the narrative in the first place, prompts Yahweh's deliverance, and ultimately leads them into the disorientation they experience at the wilderness of Sinai.

In contrast to the toxic orientation in Egypt, for the Israelites, the wilderness is a place of disorientation. In disorientation, people experience life as upside down. Suffering, incoherence, and uncertainty mark the experience as one of deep discomfort. Walter Brueggemann describes disorientation as a fact of life: "Life is also savagely marked by incoherence, loss of balance, and unrelieved asymmetry."[11] Such is true for the Israelites. Earlier in the story, the Hebrew writer remarks that Yahweh led the Israelites through the "roundabout way" of the wilderness (Ex 13:18). While the author's note is surely a geographical one, the *spiritual geography* of the Israelites' wilderness experience involves disorientation.

The Israelites express fear around Yahweh's provision at many different points in the narrative (Ex 15:22-27; 16:1-3; 17:1-7; see also Num 11:1-6; 14:1-4). They also experience a different method of divine leadership through the pillar of cloud and fire (Ex 13:20-22; 14:19-24; 33:9-11; Num 9:15-23; 10:11-12, 34). They endure war (Ex 17:8-13), something the peculiar route through the wilderness was intended to avoid (Ex 13:17). Moreover, the numinous and thunderous way in which Yahweh speaks to the people provokes terror (Ex 19:16; 20:18-19). New rules of engagement for approaching God involving holiness and ritual must also be learned (Ex 19:10-15).

Desire, Danger, and Divine Choreography

While people of faith experience disorientation for many different reasons, the Israelites' arrival in the wilderness is no accident but a

[11]Brueggemann, *Spirituality of the Psalms*, 25.

divinely choregraphed movement in which, as the psalmist would say, "deep has spoken to deep" (Ps 42:7). The deep desire of the Israelites to be released from slavery has met the deep desire of Yahweh to take a particular people for himself. Disorientation therefore begins with desire, with the acknowledgment that things are not as they should be.

Desire is an act of courage in which we dare to name what we want in the face of an insurmountable obstacle. It is frequently the liminal places in our lives that nudge us toward voicing these unspoken desires. This liminality both compels us and companions us as we move from orientation (captivity) to disorientation (wilderness) and ultimately to reorientation (freedom). Desire is at once the *catalyst* for liminality, our *companion* in liminality, and the *gift* that emerges out of liminality. The author of the Exodus account depicts this liminality in part through Moses' ascent and descent of Mount Sinai. As readers, we are invited to ascend and descend Sinai, both mountain and wilderness, with Moses. As we do so, we discover that *Desire* and *Liminality* are other names for the God Moses encounters there, with desire functioning as the preamble for the Sinai encounter:

> "You have seen what I did to the Egyptians, how I bore you on eagles' wings and brought you to Me. Now then, if you will obey Me faithfully and keep My covenant, you shall be My treasured possession among all the peoples. Indeed, all the earth is Mine, but you shall be to Me a kingdom of priests and a holy nation." These are you the words that you shall speak to the children of Israel. (Ex 19:4-6 JPS)

In the preamble to the giving of the Ten Commandments, Yahweh expresses his own desire to take the people for himself. For the Israelites, this move toward a new orientation will involve danger and risk.

For Rudolf Otto, danger and risk are an inevitable part of any encounter with the *mysterium tremendum* ("aweful mystery"). For Otto, encounter with the *mysterium tremendum* begins with *tremor*. Otto describes *tremor* as something beyond the natural emotion of fear. Here the term is a specific emotional response, one tied to a "feeling of peculiar dread" when confronted with the holy and numinous.[12] Otto traces the evolution of dread of the numinous through its primitive stages of "daemonic dread," something akin to the shudder we experience in the telling and retelling of ghost stories, in which the hairs on our arms stand up, to the consummation of dread in the light of Christ, who prompts the hymnic response, "Holy, Holy, Holy." For Otto, the holiness of Yahweh (and of God canonically) is inescapably bound to the wrath of Yahweh:

> Anyone who is accustomed to think of deity only by its rational attributes must see in this "wrath" mere caprice and wilful passion. But such a view would have been emphatically rejected by the religious men of the Old Covenant, for to them the Wrath of God, so far from being a diminution of His Godhead, appears as a natural expression of it, an element of "holiness" itself, and a quite indispensable one.[13]

At Sinai, Yahweh's holiness is tied to repeated instructions not to "break through to the LORD to gaze, lest many of them perish" (Ex 19:21 JPS; also see Ex 19:24). Yahweh promises that death will result when the natural (the Israelites) cross the boundary of the numinous (both Yahweh himself and Sinai, which has been made numinous by Yahweh; Ex 19:12-13, 21-24). Death is such an assured reality that the Hebrew writer puts Yahweh's warning in the infinitive absolute: *mot yumat*—"you shall surely die" (Ex 19:12). The consequences of the natural mixing with the numinous are so dreadful that Yahweh supplements this warning: "And set boundaries for the people round about, saying, 'Keep yourselves from going up to the mountain or touching the border of it'" (Ex 19:12).

Beyond erecting physical boundaries, the Israelites express their terror by shrinking back at various points throughout the Sinai encounter, with the Hebrew writer describing the scene in this way: "And all the people saw the thundering and they saw the lightening and the sound of the shophar and the mountain smoking, and the people were

---

[12]Rudolf Otto, *The Idea of the Holy* (Oxford University Press, 1923), 13.
[13]Otto, *Idea of the Holy*, 18.

afraid and they shook violently and they stood at a distance" (Ex 20:18; see also Ex 20:21). The words on the Hebrew writer's pen are purposeful. He uses *qol* twice, once to describe the "sound" or the "voice" of the thunder and lightning, and the second time to describe the "sound" or "noise" evoked by the shofar. The experience is not something the Israelites *hear* but is instead something that they *see* (*roim*). For the rabbi Rashi, the *seeing* of Yahweh's voice is an enigma, one that is inconceivable and untranslatable in other terms. It is this enigmatic experience that causes the Israelites to "shudder" at the sound of each of the Ten Commandments, causing waves of fear all through the back of the camp.[14]

The fearfulness of the encounter continues through the thunder and lightning, which cause the mountain to "smoke" (*asen*). As the Israelites witness the imposing Sinai affected by this God they are just beginning to know, their response is not merely to *display* fear, though the Hebrew writer employs that term (*wayyar*). Rather, their response is visceral and embodied, more difficult to categorize than simple fear. The Hebrew writer uses a verbal form of the root word *nua*, the semantic range of which can express "shaking," "tottering," "trembling," or, in the passive, being "tossed about." The Israelites' terror is fully *embodied*, causing spasms in the body that force them to protect themselves and to stand at a distance. The standing at Sinai is frightful to the point of both spasm and paralysis. The mountain quakes, as do the Israelites who stand on it. Like the mountain on which they set their feet and the wilderness on which they tread, the Israelites are jarred and rattled. They tremble, expressing something akin to Otto's *tremor* at the "aweful mystery" that stands before them.

At a ritualistic level, the Israelites respond to the *mysterium tremendum* through a repeated emphasis on "washing," "purifying themselves, and abstaining from sexual relations" (Ex 19:10, 14-15, 22). Significantly, the Hebrew writer employs various forms of the triradical root *qdsh* ("holy, holiness, sanctify") throughout the narrative (Ex 19:6, 10, 14, 22-23; 20:8, 11).

---

[14]Avivah Zornberg, *The Particulars of Rapture: Reflections on Exodus* (Schocken Books, 2001), 263.

Holiness is clearly a lexical key to unlocking the theological and spiritual implications of encounter with Yahweh at Sinai. The holiness of Yahweh is also the reason for repeated commands for boundary keeping, the rituals of purity and holiness the Israelites must perform, and the trembling of the Israelites at the manifestation of Yahweh's "aweful mystery" at Sinai. Otto ties holiness and wrath together: "Something suprarational throbs and gleams, palpable and visible, in the 'wrath of God,' prompting a sense of 'terror' that no 'natural' anger can arouse."[15] Both in his person and in his proposed punishments, Yahweh is not only suprarational, to borrow Otto's term—Yahweh is also *supernatural*, existing beyond the natural world that the Israelites inhabit.

Yahweh's quiddity—his suprarational and supernatural essence—is an implicit reminder that Yahweh is fundamentally different from Pharaoh, whose power is natural and therefore limited to the realm of the natural world. Pharaoh has the power to kill the body, yet real fear and trembling rest with Yahweh, who could, as Jesus would say, destroy both body and soul in hell (Mt 10:28). At Sinai, Yahweh does something more awe-inspiring and more awe-full than Pharaoh could have envisioned. Altogether Yahweh is unique compared to any other deity the Israelites encounter, their terror and fear are (super)natural responses to the theological disorientation they experience at the wilderness of Sinai. Fear—prompted by the risk and the danger the Israelites face—is both the ending to the story of the Ten Commandments and the protection from sin: "that the fear of him may be upon your faces so that you may not sin" (Ex 20:20). The Hebrew writer's use of *peneykem* ("your faces") is a nod to the theological reminder later in the narrative that no one may look on the face of Yahweh and live (Ex 33:20).

While the human face of Pharaoh could be seen, the holy face of Yahweh could not. Yahweh's (super)natural nature is an apophatic darkness, a *not knowing*, in which darkness and holiness join together in an awe-full and tremulous way. Sinai is both desert and mountain, a

[15]Zornberg, *Particulars of Rapture*, 19.

liminal space in which the Israelites face Yahweh, the embodiment of desire, and risk being overpowered by that very Desire. It is this possibility of being overpowered that provokes humility, which is a necessary part of disorientation as well as a gift that emerges from it.

The Thick Darkness Where God Is

For Otto, an encounter with *overpoweringness* (*majestas*), what he terms *tremenda majestas*, "aweful majesty," provokes humility:

> It is especially overpoweringness that the creature-consciousness, of which we have already spoken, comes upon the scene, as a sort of shadow or subjective reflection of it. Thus, in contrast to "the overpowering" of which we are conscious as an object over against the self, there is the feeling of one's own submergence, of being but "dust and ashes" and nothingness. And this forms the numinous raw material for the feeling of religious humility.[16]

"Religious humility," a movement from knowing to unknowing, is a gift of disorientation that is necessary to move into a new orientation. Religious humility is also an expectation of Yahweh reflected in the first two commandments (Ex 20:1-6; Deut 5:1-10). Yahweh is unfettered, unbound, by any images the Israelites might make of him—the Israelites must receive Yahweh with the humility of those who cannot pin this deity down. Indeed, the inability to create an image representative of the God who cannot be fully known is a core feature of apophatic theology. Paradoxically, apophatic mysticism is not about the remoteness of God but is experienced by those who have already drawn close to the beautiful mystery that is Godself. Apophasis is the intensifying of desire in which we hunger for God *as Godself*, as God chooses to be apart from our projections about what we wish God were like. In this sense, we desert God; we leave God in a desert of unknowing. As Mark McIntosh puts it, "For what is so powerfully attractive about the true God is that one only journeys into deeper encounter with God by entering into the

[16]Otto, *Idea of the Holy*, 20.

desert of liberation. This is the fertile wilderness where one is freed from ideas and ways of life that are unmasked at last as traps and snares, subtle slaveries of spirit."[17]

The deeper encounter about which the mystics speak occurs through a dialectic of light and darkness, a duality apparent in Moses' encounter with Yahweh at Sinai: "Then the people stood at a distance, while Moses drew near to the thick darkness where God was" (Ex 20:21 NRSVUE). While most translations render the word *araphel* in the same ways as the NRSVUE, the semantic range can refer to "darkness" or "heavy gloom" as well as "cloud" or "heavy cloud."[18] Outside Exodus 20:21, *araphel* is used to describe the heavy, dark, and cloudlike presence of Yahweh dwelling inside Solomon's temple (1 Kings 8:12). By alluding to the cloud that dwelled within the tent of meeting during the wilderness wandering (Ex 40:34-35), Solomon's dedication of the temple reinforces that Yahweh's dwelling was within a heavy cloud. The otherworldly nature of Yahweh demanded distance between Yahweh and the people and required them to purify themselves.

The building of a "house for God" suggests Solomon's desire to contain or possess the God who guided the Israelites through the wilderness, even as that same God resisted theological domestication. Despite the implications of housing Yahweh and relegating him to just one place, in his dedication of the temple, Solomon acknowledges, "The LORD has chosen to abide in a thick cloud" (1 Kings 8:12a JPS). The imagery of the cloud provides a shadowy cover for a dark God who refuses to be pinned down theologically even by Moses, the friend of God (Ex 33:11). Yahweh's refusal to reveal himself fully reaches its climax in the definitive statement, "You cannot see My face, for man may not see Me and live" (Ex 33:20 JPS).

---

[17] Mark A. McIntosh, *Mystical Theology*, Challenges in Contemporary Theology (Blackwell, 1998), 123-24.

[18] For example, the ASV, CEB, ESV, KJV, and NIV, to name a few. By contrast, The Message pulls from the imagery of the cloud, translating the phrase "the thick cloud." The NLT renders the phrase "dark cloud," while the CSB translates it "the total darkness."

Rohr describes the scene between Moses and Yahweh in this way: "Here we can observe a brilliant and delicate balancing of knowing with 'don't you dare think you fully know'; of seeing with an immediate reminder that we have not fully seen. The integration of the two traditions is right in the text. The most that Moses can see is, humorously, Yahweh's backside (33:23)."[19] The moment we assume we have fully seen or fully known is the precise moment we have slipped into the idolatry Yahweh warns the Israelites against (Ex 20:4-6; Deut 5:8-10). As Liz Hoare says: "Our images of God have to be constantly shattered and rebuilt. Time after time we have to relearn what God is like, only to find later that this image also has become fossilized into an idol and has to go."[20]

Still, this rhythm of fossilization and relinquishment induces the religious humility required of disorientation. Our destruction of theological images is a description of mystical apophasis, which is intended to produce "the intensifying of desire to such a point that one is left hungering only for the living God."[21] Desire is the gift that emerges out of liminality—and Desire is another name for God. It is Desire who compels Moses to enter into the dark cloud, where Moses discovers that Yahweh exists *beyond* words, *beyond* images, *and beyond* knowing.

These insights are rooted in the imagery of the Hebrew Scriptures, Hellenized by Neoplatonic tradition and baptized by Christians as early as Gregory of Nyssa in the fourth century. His mystical work *The Life of Moses* was among the first texts to explore darkness as a metaphor for unknowing in Exodus:

> What does it mean that Moses entered the darkness and then saw God in it? . . . Scripture teaches . . . [that] as the mind progresses and, through an even greater and more perfect diligence, comes to apprehend reality, as it approaches more nearly to contemplation, it sees more clearly what of the divine nature is uncontemplated. . . . This is the true knowledge of what is sought; this is the seeing which consists in not seeing, because

---

19Rohr, *Things Hidden*, 127.

20Liz Hoare, *Using the Bible in Spiritual Direction* (Morehouse, 2016), 49.

21McIntosh, *Mystical Theology*, 123-24.

> that which is sought transcends all knowledge, being separated on all sides by incomprehensibility as by a kind of darkness. . . . When, therefore, Moses grew in knowledge, he declared that he had seen God in the darkness, that is, when he had come to know what is divine beyond all knowledge and comprehension, for the text says, *Moses approached the dark cloud where God was* (Exod. 20, 21).[22]

For Gregory of Nyssa, it is not absence but abundance, the excess of luminous darkness, that characterizes Moses' contemplative encounter with Yahweh.[23] Moses doesn't see everything—such a feat is impossible—but he sees just enough of Yahweh to be changed by the encounter. Indeed, Moses takes on a fearful quality not unlike the God he encountered in the thick darkness: "So Moses came down from Mount Sinai. And as Moses came down from the mountain bearing the two tablets of the Pact, Moses was not aware that the skin of his face was radiating, since he had spoken with him. Aaron and all the Israelites saw that the skin of Moses' face was radiant; and they shrank from coming near him" (Ex 34:29-30 JPS).

While the Hebrew Scriptures vacillate on the level of intimacy Moses experiences with Yahweh, claiming that Moses cannot see Yahweh's face and live (Ex 33:20), at other times suggesting that Yahweh spoke with Moses "face to face" (Ex 33:11; Deut 34:10), Moses was clearly changed by their encounter (Ex 34:29-35), gaining a greater confidence in his own leadership as the narrative of the Pentateuch unfolds. Indeed, what Moses knows of Yahweh (or, rather, *unknows*) also grows by degree as his own story intertwines within the larger story of the exodus. Moses is able to see *some things* about Yahweh and Yahweh's nature. These moments are important markers in Moses' spiritual life, just as key moments of encounter with God are important for the spiritual formation of all believers at every time and place. Yet Yahweh's *mysterium tremendum*

[22]Gregory of Nyssa, *The Life of Moses*, trans. A. J. Malherbe and E. Ferguson, The Classics of Western Spirituality: A Library of the Great Spiritual Masters (Paulist Press, 1978), 94-95.

[23]Denys Turner, *The Darkness of God: Negativity in Christian Mysticism* (Cambridge University Press, 1995), 17-18.

and *tremenda majestas*, displayed most robustly at Sinai, is a reminder that all we think we know of God is but seeing through a mirror darkly (1 Cor 13:12). This darkness is a necessary disorientation—a reminder of our own finitude and fragility before an infinite, all-powerful God. We are, as the hymn writer tells us, "frail children of dust." The darkness of disorientation also protects from doing ideological violence to our neighbor by demanding that their experiences of God align with our own. Ultimately, like the "roundabout way of the wilderness" (Ex 13:18), disorientation paves the way for greater spiritual freedom for ourselves and others.

Reorientation as Relationality

Indeed, the work of disorientation in the life of faith moves us toward a greater knowing—what Rohr calls reorientation or new orientation. Within Rohr's model of liminality, like the Israelites, people of faith move from captivity, through wilderness, and ultimately toward freedom. Freedom occurs when we integrate the uncertainty and chaos of the wilderness experience, relinquishing our images of God, self, and other and acknowledging their instability and impermanence. Choosing to do so is an act of radical hospitality in which we create space for God to do a new thing inside us. God's work reorients us so that we can awaken to wonder, surprise, celebration, deliverance, healing, and the new birth that is at the heart of the gospel. Such a bursting of categories is necessary for our movement toward a new orientation. While we do not deny the pain involved in disorientation, at the same time we choose to see the disorientation of wilderness as a severe mercy, as a gift from the God who loves us.

While Cohn has framed the Israelites' journey of liminality through three distinct phases that include the whole of the Hexateuch, elements of reorientation appear within the Sinai narrative itself.[24] For the

[24]Cohn labels phase one as the separation, the exodus from Egypt, in which the crossing of the Red Sea marks the "final break" (Ex 14:31; *Shape of Sacred Space*, 13). Phase two is the limen or

Israelites, reorientation is utterly relational. Earlier in the narrative, Yahweh frames his reason for the Israelites' departure from Egypt (orientation) and journey to the wilderness (disorientation) as the need for them to worship (Ex 3:18; 4:22-23; 5:1-3; 7:16; 8:1, 20, 27; 9:1; 10:3). This act of pulling the Israelites out of their toxic orientation to Egypt, causing them to take the roundabout way of the wilderness and experience disorientation, is rooted in Yahweh's desire to reorient them to their true identity as treasured and as priests formed into a holy nation (Ex 19:4-6). Reorientation can happen only in relationship to Desire, to Yahweh himself. At an identity level, the Israelites are not only called to trade their political allegiance from the Pharaoh to Yahweh (which is what is meant historically by Yahweh's command to "love the LORD your God" in Deut 6:4-5)—they are called to understand their fundamental orientation to the world around them as *belonging* to Yahweh, the *mysterium tremendum* whose proximity to them has transformed them into something wholly other than they were before. From a Christian perspective, the New Testament understands the transfer of allegiance from the world around us to God in different ways—as being buried and raised again (Rom 6:4) and as becoming a "new self" (Col 3:9-10).

An essential newness is at the heart of reorientation. As the dusk of disorientation fades with the glow of the dawn, *we become something other* than we were the night before. From the Old Testament to the New, God is about doing a new thing. That is God's essential work—from God's satisfied sigh of Sabbath rest after creation (Gen 1:31–2:3), to the voice of the prophet proclaiming freedom from Babylonian tyranny ("I am about to do a *new thing*; now it springs forth; do you not perceive it? I will make *a way in the wilderness* and rivers in the desert," Is 43:19 NRSVUE), to the final words of the Johannine Jesus on the cross ("It is finished," Jn 19:30), to the new heavens and the new earth promised at the eschaton (Rev 21:1-6). From the Old Testament to the

transitional period, the forty years of wilderness wandering; and phase three is the reincorporation, the crossing of the Jordan River, the conquest of Canaan, and settlement into the land.

New, God invites people to believe his words and to join his work in the present moment.

Rather than encouraging the Israelites to look behind their collective theological shoulder and fantasize about their life in Egypt, as they were prone to do, Yahweh meets the Israelites in their present wilderness. Yahweh is not chained to their Egyptian past, nor is Yahweh floating into the Promised Land ahead of them. Rather, Yahweh deals with them in the objective reality of the Sinai wilderness. Yahweh deals with them in the present, in the now, unfolding a new way of living right there where they are, in wilderness.

This is part of what we learn in the wilderness—*the present moment is who God is.*

ehyeh asher ehyeh

I am who I am.

Whatever else darkens into apophatic mystery, God *is*—and God is *now*.

Like the Israelites, we choose whether we will remain toxically oriented to the theological systems of the pseudo-religious or whether we will respond to the voice crying, "Let my people go" and follow that voice into a disorienting wilderness where we will encounter the *I am*. The pseudo-religious cannot hear the new thing the *I am* is doing because their ears remain glued to the past: "Afterward Moses and Aaron went to Pharaoh and said, 'Thus says *the I am*, the God of Israel: Let my people go, so that they may celebrate a festival to me in the wilderness.' But Pharaoh said, 'Who is *the I am*, that I should listen to him and let Israel go? I do not know *the I am*, and I will not let Israel go'" (Ex 5:1-2). Such an encounter requires a discerning ear—we must rightly divide new and salubrious words from the same old words we have always heard.

The cost of remaining toxically oriented to hegemonic systems of (pseudo-)religious authority is that we continue to misconstrue the nature of God. We hear the words of religious authorities whose messages are, like Pharaoh's, not centered on truth but on keeping power in their own hands. Yahweh spoke, but Pharaoh denied it, proclaiming Yahweh's invitation to worship in the wilderness *bedivrey-shaqer* ("words of deception," Ex 5:9). The narrative about Pharaoh is a textual mirror for those of us in positions of religious authority. His denial of the role of Yahweh in the Israelites' lives is a reminder that we too commit a great sin when we deny God's call in the lives of people of faith, relegating them, like Pharaoh, to nonliberative and soul-crushing theological systems intended to keep everyone—those with power and those without it—in their place.

We fool ourselves into thinking we are speaking for God when in fact we are furthering our own agenda, putting people who look like us and think like us into theological trophy cases and polishing them for display. In Christian organizations, this might look like a reticence or refusal to listen to the ideas of those with whom we disagree, heresy-policing minor differences in theological opinion, or, more darkly, ousting or refusing to hire individuals who don't fit perfectly into the theological groupthink culture created by the institution. When we behave in these ways, it is inevitable that we will act as mouthpieces for the malformed God created by our own prejudices. To put it more pointedly, this often edges out women and persons of color who are forced by the system to claw their way to a seat at the table. The language of rejection is frequently paternalistic and given a warped spiritual spin—"The Lord is leading us in a different direction," for example, a convenient and cowardly excuse that may be difficult to argue with but that nevertheless accomplishes what is intended—to couch the will of humans in religious terms, effectively delaying or denying a seat at the table to those genuinely called by God.

Like Pharaoh, when we continue to backtrack, offering the dangling carrot of freedom only to retract it again, we keep people toxically oriented to theological systems that paternalistically promise freedom *but not yet*, or freedom but *partial freedom*. In order for freedom truly to be freedom, it must be entire, it must be whole. God's people must be all the way free: "Let my people go," demands *the I am*, "so that they may celebrate a festival to me in the wilderness" (Ex 5:1 NRSVUE). When people hear a call intended to recalibrate the way we structure our institutions and those of us in power reify the same old systems, we function like Pharaoh. We gaslight people by telling them they have not heard a word from God. When we tell them that these new words they hear are "words of deception" (Ex 5:9), like Pharaoh, we stand in the way of the new thing God is doing.

In the wilderness, a place of disorientation, the Israelites bend their ears tentatively toward new words—the Ten Words, to be precise, which will curve their theological path toward a new orientation. The Ten Words—and the Law as a whole—are the *gift* of Liminality. These words put spacious boundaries around their freedom so that they can worship *the I am* in a new (reoriented) theological and geographical space as a new (reoriented) people who belong to Yahweh. In much the same way, Christians reorient themselves with the life-affirming words of Paul: "For freedom Christ has set us free. Stand firm, therefore, and do not submit again to a yoke of slavery" (Gal 5:1 NRSVUE).

Living in the freedom of the *I am* requires a certain willingness to travel the liminal road more than once. We take the roundabout way of the wilderness at various stages of our lives, moving from orientation, disorientation, and reorientation again and again. As Rohr says, "We must never presume that we see. We must always be ready to see anew." The road through liminality to reorientation, therefore, requires what has been called "beginner's mind." In Christian tradition, we call it having the heart and mind of a child. As Rohr puts it, "We need to be converted again and again. We aren't born again. We are born again and again and again."[25] This conversion—the reorientation of our thoughts about who God is and about who we are—requires courage to enter the disorienting darkness rather than shrinking back from it. This

[25]Richard Rohr, *Everything Belongs: The Gift of Contemplative Prayer* (Crossroad, 2003), 33, 52.

conversion also requires humility to relinquish religious suppositions rather than clinging to them. This is the letting go that, as Gregory of Nyssa writes, leads us from light to luminous darkness:

> What does it mean that Moses entered the darkness and then saw God in it? What is now recounted seems somehow to be contradictory to the first theophany, for when the Divine was beheld in light but now he is seen in darkness. Let us not think that this is at variance with the sequence of things we have contemplated spiritually. Scripture teaches by this that religious knowledge comes at first to those who receive it as light. Therefore what is perceived to be contrary to religion is darkness, and the escape from darkness comes about when one participates in light. But as the mind progresses and, through an ever greater and more perfect diligence, comes to apprehend reality, as it approaches more nearly to contemplation, it sees more clearly what of the divine nature is uncontemplated.[26]

When we choose to enter the disorienting darkness, we see all we do *not* know of God. At the wilderness of Sinai, the Israelites experience presence and absence, speech and silence, and knowing and unknowing, all markers of a liminal journey that traverses both mountain and desert.

Contemplation as Spiritual Practice

The insight needed to determine our areas of toxic orientation cannot come through sustained attention to work or ministry. As the previous discussion of the wall has shown, we often resist the grace of God because it disrupts what is comfortable. Just as the God of the desert proclaimed freedom for the Israelites under Egyptian domination, so also God is seeking to release us from our own areas of unfreedom. The spiritual practice of contemplation invites us, as Adele Calhoun says, to see with faith, hope, and love: "It asks us to seek God and the 'meanings' threaded through our days and years, so that our experience of being embedded in the triune life of God deepens and grows."[27] Moses'

---

[26]Gregory of Nyssa, *Life of Moses*, 94-95.

[27]Adele Ahlberg Calhoun, *Spiritual Disciplines Handbook: Practices That Transform Us*, rev. and expanded ed. (InterVarsity Press, 2015), 55.

experience at Sinai is a form of contemplation, one that produces a visible change in him afterward (Ex 34:29-35). When we slow down and contemplate the beauty and the goodness of God in the ordinary events of our days, we also begin to see those things that pale in comparison God's beauty. We begin to see what we have given ourselves over to that is counter to the cruciform-shaped life.

Contemplating our own desert experiences is one practical means God may use to move us from toxic orientation through disorientation and to reorientation. One way we can engage this practice is in prayerful silence to contemplate where we find ourselves right now: Does our life feel stable, predictable, grounded, structured, with a certain consistency and equilibrium? If so, we are probably in a state of orientation. Does life feel incoherent and uncertain? Are we experiencing a loss of balance or life upside down, with chaos at the center? These are markers of disorientation. Or does life feel like something is being born inside us? Are we filled with amazement, wonder, celebration, and surprise? Do we experience deliverance and healing? These are signs we are in a new orientation of some kind.[28]

As we discern whether we are in a state of orientation, disorientation, or reorientation, we pay attention to the feelings that rise within us. We may feel heat in our bodies or notice impatience or embarrassment, a need to hide or defend. When we leave the experience, we spend some time reflecting on what we noticed, asking ourselves where we responded out of past wounds. Where we felt resistance. Where we felt consolation. What did this particular experience of orientation, disorientation, or reorientation symbolize for us? What, if anything, gave it meaning?[29] These questions will draw us closer to movement of the God of the desert in our ordinary lives, for that is where God has pitched God's tent.

---

[28] I am indebted to Jerry Webber (Upper Room Academy for Spiritual Formation Four-Day Retreat, 2023) for his presentation on liminality in the spiritual life, which introduced me to these specific key words to describe the feelings of orientation, disorientation, and reorientation.

[29] I have adapted the questions of Calhoun, *Spiritual Disciplines Handbook*, 56, for this exercise.

In Exodus on Sinai, Yahweh has pitched his tent. The silence that begins the narrative is followed by words wending their way back up to the mountaintop. Silence and speech, divine and human, silent *shewas* closing syllables that will open to long vowels and long speeches in which Yahweh offers words of life. For the next wilderness generation in the book of Deuteronomy, a decision must be made about how to remember the experience of darkness and disorientation. To remember it with narrative grace, the people will require a spiritual director of sorts, a midwife of the word, in the figure of Moses.

Questions for Reflection and Discussion

1. What is dark about your life right now? Do you have a sense that there is something holy about that darkness?
2. Have you ever known yourself to be at a wall, a spiritual impasse? Have you been able to move through that wall? Or are you still stuck there?
3. What about Moses and the Israelites' experience at Sinai do you find most applicable to your own life right now?

5

NARRATING OUR LIVES WITH GOD

Storytelling as the Practice of Spiritual Direction in Deuteronomy 8

Remember the long way that the Lord your God has led you these forty years in the wilderness, in order to humble you, testing you to know what was in your heart, whether or not you would keep his commandments. He humbled you by letting you hunger, then by feeding you with manna, with which neither you nor your ancestors were acquainted, in order to make you understand that one does not live by bread alone but by every word that comes from the mouth of the Lord. The clothes on your back did not wear out, and your feet did not swell these forty years. Know, then, in your heart that, as a parent disciplines a child, so the Lord your God disciplines you.

Deuteronomy 8:2-5 NRSVUE

"It's difficult to swallow the fact that I've heard God wrong for the past twenty years," I told my spiritual director as I slumped back on the couch in my office.

I looked over my shoulder as I said it, double-checking that I had locked the door ahead of time to ensure my students wouldn't hear this or any other decidedly shocking revelation I shared.

"What if you didn't hear God wrong at all?" she asked. "What if you *are* called, you *did* hear correctly, and you *did* follow in obedience and faith? What if what you're experiencing is not a crisis of calling but a crisis of theology?"

In that moment, her words set me free.

More broadly, the takeaway for me from that conversation was that life in this world—and calling itself—was more complicated than I had allowed. The vocational path for women especially is often not linear, as it frequently is for men, moving from point A to point B—but circuitous, roundabout, much like the wilderness itself. Sometimes we step off a ladder to recalibrate. Sometimes the path for women is more like a garden than a ladder, in which we tend to different things in different seasons.

I had narrated my life in a spiritually constricting way, but my spiritual director opened up a larger storied space that affirmed my calling and gifting.

I don't think I would have arrived at that insight—or offered myself that level of grace—without someone else to listen to my story.

This is the work of spiritual directors: to listen to the stories we tell about God, about ourselves, and about the world around us, and to help us narrate them with greater clarity and grace.

As a spiritual director myself, I know that there is value in receiving spiritual direction in all seasons of life, yet it is frequently seasons of wilderness that draw people to this ancient practice. Spiritual direction is a storytelling practice, one undergirded by the fundamental assumption that God's story and our stories are intertwined. G. K. Chesterton, himself one of the great storytellers, puts it like this: "I had always felt life first as story: and if there is a story, there is a Storyteller."[1] Chesterton understood *God* to be this great Storyteller, and of course

[1] G. K. Chesterton, *Orthodoxy: With Annotations and Guided Reading* (B&H, 2022), 82.

Scripture bears this out. From the individual parables told by Jesus, to the short yet powerful tales of Jonah and Ruth, to the gospel story, which Frederick Buechner describes as tragedy, comedy, and fairy tale, to the sweeping metanarrative of Scripture itself—God has told us he loves us through the medium of the written word and through the mechanism of narrative, of story.[2] This means that God is a story-shaped God, and we are story-shaped creatures.

Thus it is a fundamental assumption that the ministry of spiritual direction will largely involve stories: telling them, listening to them, honoring them. Spiritual directors understand that the story of God and the story of the person they direct are interwoven, interlocking, intertwined, embedded deeply in each other. Indeed, there is an *intertextuality* between God's story and our story—a whispering of voices back and forth. Buechner all but says as much in his book *Beyond Words*: "It is absolutely crucial, therefore, to keep in constant touch with what is going on in your own life's story and to pay close attention to what is going on in the stories of others' lives. If God is present anywhere, it is in those stories that God is present. If God is not present in those stories, then they are scarcely worth telling."[3]

The role of a spiritual director is to listen to the story of another person's life with God. The spiritual director cups an ear to the holy ground that is the whispering back and forth between the spirit of the directee and the Holy Spirit. It is the always the Holy Spirit who is the true Spiritual Director in the Horebs or the Sinais, the Mount Moriahs, the Golgathas, in the story of each of our lives. Through a process of "one-anothering," or spiritual companionship, a spiritual director *listens* and *names*.[4] A spiritual director *listens* for the curvatures of the story the directee is telling and *names* the places and the chapters in that story

[2]Frederick Buechner, *Telling the Truth: The Gospel as Tragedy, Comedy and Fairy Tale* (Harper & Row, 1977).
[3]Frederick Buechner, *Beyond Words: Daily Readings in the ABC's of Faith* (HarperOne, 2004), 379.
[4]Angela H. Reed et al., *Spiritual Companioning: A Guide to Protestant Theology and Practice* (Baker Academic, 2015), 48-49.

where God is present. A spiritual director also names the places in the directee's story where God is decidedly *not* present. After all, not all the stories we tell about God, about ourselves, and about the world around us are aligned with the gospel and with the God who loves us. As my own spiritual director has said to me, "Noel, God is not *in* everything in your life." And indeed, Ignatian spirituality bears this out—there are voices of consolation, coming from the voice of the God who loves us, and there are voices of desolation, coming from some other place.

Part of the role of spiritual director is to disentangle the tangled Christmas lights of the stories we tell. Or, in the words of the hymn writer, to disentangle peace from pain. It is often these places of pain—or places of unfreedom—that lead a person to spiritual direction in the first place. Many of these places of unfreedom reveal themselves when we are in the wilderness. It was ironically in the wilderness, a place of freedom from Egyptian slavery, in which the Israelites' pain, brokenness, and sin revealed themselves. Moses' function in the book of Deuteronomy is to one-another the Israelites, to engage in holy listening, and to help them reframe the narrative about their wilderness experience.

The Heart of the Wilderness

In Hebrew tradition, Deuteronomy is named for its first two words, *elleh haddevarim* ("these are the words"). Aptly named, Deuteronomy is a book of words delivered by Moses at the eve of his life in which the first third of the book (Deut 1–11) narrates the Israelites' experience in the wilderness. Both the biblical text and Christian history reveal the wilderness to be a place where people learn to cast aside spiritual masks and to name their deepest desires. There are instances within the biblical text itself where a form of spiritual direction takes place, yet it is Christians in the early church (and later in the Middle Ages) who are most associated with spiritual direction.[5] Appropriately, many Christians

[5]In his correspondence with the churches at Corinth and at Galatia, Paul uses the language of "father" and "child," demonstrating his deep love and spiritual care for these particular groups of people. It is clear that both in his travels to these churches (particularly Corinth) and in his

received spiritual direction in the desert, where they traveled to meet with an older man who had made his home there, beseeching him, "Abba, give me a word." As L. Roger Owens beautifully describes his own experience of spiritual direction, "My life was the word we would look at together."[6] The wilderness setting is an appropriate setting to receive a word about our lives because it is in wilderness where we often need a word the most. In spiritual direction, the word we receive often helps us get in touch with the deeper desires underneath the superficial things we sometimes bring with us into direction. Such is the case in Deuteronomy 8, where Moses addresses the role of desire in the context of obedience through an emphasis on the heart.

Deuteronomy 8:1-2 describes the harsh realities of the desert experience while calling the Israelites to sustained obedience. Moses begins his speech by outlining what it will take to live (*khayah*), to multiply (*ravah*), and to possess (*yarash*) the land (Deut 8:1). He ends his speech with a warning that what has happened to the other nations—destruction (*avad*; Deut 8:20)—may also happen to the Israelites. Like much of Deuteronomy, which counsels obedience to Yahweh so that blessing can be received (Deut 6–7; 9; 28; 30), the entire speech juxtaposes remembrance and forgetfulness through the use of the Hebrew verbs *zakar* ("remember"; Deut 8:2, 18) and *shakakh* ("forget") (Deut 8:11, 14, 19). Here remembrance is tied to the whole of the wilderness experience, its hardship and the provision of God in the midst of that hardship. Remembrance serves as a bulwark against forgetfulness, which leads to haughtiness of spirit and ultimately *avad* ("destruction," "loss of way," "extermination"; Deut 8:20).[7] Avoidance of that destruction

---

epistolary ministry, he was asking questions and nurturing burgeoning faith in the way that a spiritual director does. 1 Cor 4:15 and Gal 4:19 are particular texts that point to the pain involved in coming alongside these communities and the deep affection and discerning ministry he exercised with them. In the Old Testament, Moses points to the relationship between younger men in the faith and older men, again demonstrating the spiritual nurture offered in the context of the faith (Deut 32:7).

[6] L. Roger Owens, *Abba, Give Me a Word: The Path of Spiritual Direction* (Paraclete, 2012), 45.

[7] This portion of the chapter was previously published in Noel Forlini Burt, "To Do You Good in the End: The Wilderness Experience in Israel's Communal Memory (Deut. 8)," in *Biblical and*

is tied to the keeping of the commandments, as Moses notes in the beginning of Deuteronomy 8:1. The use of the verb *shamar* points to a watchfulness, a keeping of the commandments as one would watch or keep one's own life. Used prolifically throughout the Old Testament, *shamar* and its various noun cognates, including *shemurah* ("eyelid"), *shimmur* ("watching, vigil," such as the vigil of nights kept in Ex 12:42), and *shemaryah* ("kept, preserved"), to name a few, deal with the vigilance of keeping or preserving the most important things in relation to one's life with God.[8]

In Deuteronomy 8:1-2, the ability of the Israelites to keep the commandments in the wilderness is tied to the heart. Hebrew tradition uses *heart* to characterize the inner person, which includes their mind, affections, and will, the seat of the emotions or passions.[9] Moses proclaimed that keeping the commandments would require the whole self. Thus, Moses implied that these words were inextricably bound up with the whole of life, both the inner and the outer, the deep things of the heart and the circumstances affecting the heart. For Moses, *heart* is a keyword, one he uses three other times in Deuteronomy 8: in Deuteronomy 8:5 to assure the Israelites that Yahweh's discipline in the desert was purposeful, and in Deuteronomy 8:14, 17 to warn the Israelites not to forget Yahweh in prosperity or harbor an inward thought that they had achieved blessing on their own.

As a spiritual director who is helping the Israelites narrate their lives with Yahweh, Moses invites the Israelites to an obedience not unlike that practiced by Benedictine Christians in the sixth century. About Benedictine obedience, Elizabeth Canham says:

> The kind of listening Benedict calls for is a deep hearing that moves beyond understanding with the mind to a willingness for the heart to be

---

Theological Visions of Resilience: Pastoral and Clinical Insights, ed. Christopher C. H. Cook and Nathan H. White, Routledge New Critical Thinking in Religion, Theology, and Biblical Studies (Routledge, 2019).

[8]F. Brown et al., *A Hebrew and English Lexicon of the Old Testament* (Oxford University Press, 1962), 1036-38.

[9]Brown et al., *Hebrew and English Lexicon*, 523-25.

> moved. Because ear and heart are inextricably connected, obedience to God's call follows. . . . The rote mouthing of prayers or doing duty does not constitute obedience; rather, open-hearted listening to God with a willingness to change equals obedience.[10]

It is this open-hearted kind of listening to which Moses directs the Israelites in Deuteronomy 8, one that keeps the word of the commandments as one would keep the word of one's own life.

Like a spiritual director, Moses listened to the complaints of the Israelites in the initial wilderness experience, privately processing his own grievances with Yahweh (Ex 5:22–6:13; 17:4; Num 11:10-17). In Deuteronomy 8, Moses invites the Israelites to do a deep listening of their own. This mutuality of listening is at the heart of spiritual direction—the director listens to the story of the directee, and the directee responds in obedience to the word of the director. As Owens notes, there is a close connection between obedience and listening. The Latin words for "to listen" and "to obey" are linked in origin and meaning. "Obedience," Owens says, is more than the act of "doing it now because I said so." Rather, obedience involves listening to the words of the director, "not unlike the careful, attentive listening the director offers you." Obedience is more about listening with the heart than following blind directions.[11] This is precisely what Moses does throughout his speeches in Deuteronomy 1–11, particularly in Deuteronomy 8:5, where he counters the Israelites' narrative of Yahweh's absence (Ex 17:7) or malignant intent (Ex 16:1-3; Num 14:1-3) and urges them to know deep in their hearts that their wilderness sojourn has been purposeful. In this way, Moses performs the most important role of a spiritual director—to challenge and reframe the Israelites' faulty narratives about God (and themselves) so that they can move toward freedom.

Set a generation after the initial wilderness experience in Exodus, Leviticus, and Numbers, the book of Deuteronomy is Moses' second

---

[10]Elizabeth Canham, *Heart Whispers: Benedictine Wisdom for Today* (Upper Room, 1999), 141.
[11]Owens, *Abba, Give Me a Word*, 63.

telling, which is reflected in its naming from the Septuagint, "The Second Giving of the Law." Accurately reporting what is true of an experience sometimes requires narrative distance, which is why Moses can reflect on the initial wilderness experience and reframe it as a story in which God was present and the wilderness was purposeful. In the Pentateuch, Moses fulfills many roles—prophet, priest, and lawgiver. In Deuteronomy, Moses also functions as a spiritual director, one-anothering the Israelites and helping them reframe their story from a narrative of scarcity to a narrative of abundance and hope. In particular, Deuteronomy 8 highlights Moses' storytelling capacity and role as spiritual director in the Israelites' wilderness experience.

Narratives of Scarcity

It is undeniably true that the biblical story, not only in its wilderness chapters, is in part a story about suffering. As David Carr notes, "The themes of suffering and resilience are woven throughout the Bible":

> The Bible's distinctive themes and emphases can be traced back to century after century of crisis. It certainly contains texts about other aspects of human experience—joy, gratitude, love, wonder, and the like. Nevertheless, it was during periods of crisis that the overall structure and emphases of the scriptures were shaped the most. Thus suffering, and the survival of it, was written into the Bible.[12]

Such is the case with Deuteronomy, which surely has two audiences in mind for whom suffering was a way of life: the audience within the world of the story itself, for whom wilderness was their only reality, both geographically and spiritually; and the exilic community, those Israelites taken from their land by the Babylonian Empire in the sixth century BC, who received the story and saw wilderness as a metaphor for their displacement. Deuteronomy strains to reconcile the harsh reality of the wilderness experience with a functional theology that proclaims the goodness of Yahweh (Deut 1–4; 8–10; 29; 32).

---

[12]David Carr, *Holy Resilience: The Bible's Traumatic Origins* (Yale University Press, 2014), 4.

This is true not only for the pages of Deuteronomy. It is true also for the pages in the narrative of our own lives. In church contexts, small groups, or even in spiritual direction, we may affirm the things about God *we think we should say*—such as God is near to us in our suffering or is good in spite of that suffering. Such conversations are often cognitive only, the affirmation of theological or doctrinal commitments that have been drilled into us by our faith communities or culture. In other words, the things we *think* are not necessarily the same things we *feel.* As W. Paul Jones reminds us:

> Each of us has a God, maybe several, that determines the dynamic of our lives. Ironically, it is often not the one affirmed credally on Sunday morning. One's functional God provides the *why* that flavors the *how, where,* and *who* of one's Monday mornings. Who we are depends on whose we are. A key issue of spiritual direction, then, is to discern from among the plethora of today's options for our loyalty which one actually functions as our God. Much of life's tragedy results not only from not knowing this identity, but from the deception of trying to hide that foundational orientation, even from ourselves.[13]

One of the blessings of the wilderness is that its upending quality can unknowingly reveal cracks in our own narrative. When our stories take, as they must, an embodied, visceral turn, and we discover that we are not, as James K. A. Smith says, "thinking things," a spiritual companion can help us make an affective turn. We can discover (or remember) that we are liturgical animals whose telos is oriented toward love.[14] As Moses emphasized it, we are to love and to obey with the *heart*, with the whole self. When we proclaim God's love with our theologies but don't feel that love in our bodies, the narratives we tell begin, if only in secret, to unravel, and we find the parts of ourselves divided.

---

[13]W. Paul Jones, *The Art of Spiritual Direction: Giving and Receiving Spiritual Guidance* (Upper Room Books, 2002), 45.

[14]James K. A. Smith, *Desiring the Kingdom: Worship, Worldview, and Cultural Formation*, Cultural Liturgies (Baker Academic, 2009), 37-74.

We may find ourselves hurt with God but too ashamed to say it. Worse still, we may feel hurt with God yet unable to access that hurt cognitively, let alone viscerally. Thus there is a wedge in the relationship that cannot be repaired because we haven't acknowledged it's there. As Angela Reed, Richard R. Osmer, and Marcus G. Smucker rightly say, "We become consummate actors, able to share casual pleasantries while hiding away our isolation, confusion, and curiosities about the spiritual life."[15] And so we begin to craft an internal narrative that questions whether God will truly be with us when everything falls apart, yet we are reluctant to share that narrative with anyone else, including ourselves and God.

These places of pain and unfreedom often emerge *because* we are in wilderness or reveal themselves *in* wilderness. It is in wilderness that the stories we tell about God and about ourselves reveal our functional theology, what we truly believe about God, as opposed to what we *say* we believe about God. This is true of the Israelites, whose grumbling against the Lord (Ex 15:22-24; 17:1-7; Num 11:1-3; 14:1-4), craving of different nourishment (Ex 16:1-12), and betrayal of covenant (Ex 32) peel back a narrative curtain on a functional theology, largely, of scarcity. The tangible and spiritual provisions of God—manna, clothing, and endurance—are central to remembering the wilderness experience (Deut 8:2-5). Nevertheless, it is that very provision that ironically highlights the basic physical deprivations of the wilderness.

Tucked just beneath the consoling language of provision lies the traumatic core of the wilderness experience. This traumatic core appears in Deuteronomy 8:2. When Moses tells the Israelites to remember *eth-kol-hadderekh* ("the whole way," "the entire way") that the Lord has brought the Israelites during the forty-year trek in the wilderness, what at first sounds comforting strikes a jarring note. Three verbs following the purpose clause *lemaan* bring this into sharp relief. The Israelites are to remember that the Lord brought them through the wilderness for the purpose of *annotekha* ("afflicting you," "humbling you," "making you feel your

[15]Reed et al., *Spiritual Companioning*, 15.

dependence"), *lenassotekha* ("to put you to the test," "to try you"), and *ladaath* ("to know") what was in in the Israelites' hearts, whether they would keep the commandments (Deut 8:2).[16] While Moses' speech is a jarring summation of their experience, the book of Numbers, the very book whose Hebrew title means "In the Wilderness," highlights the visceral experience itself. The majority of the wilderness generation dies, and even Moses is told he will die there (Num 11; 14; 15:32-36; 16; 32:6-15; cf. Deut 34). As such, Moses can refer to wilderness as "great and terrible . . . , an arid wasteland with poisonous snakes and scorpions" (Deut 8:15 NRSVUE).

Elsewhere, Moses refers to it as "a howling wilderness waste" (Deut 32:10 NRSVUE). Embedded into the language Moses uses here is the root word *tohu* ("formlessness," "confusion," "unreality," "emptiness," "wasteland"). Used sparingly in the Hebrew Bible (e.g., Deut 32:10; 1 Sam 12:21; Is 24:10; 45:19), the word is used most notably in Genesis 1:2 in conjunction with the word *bohu* ("emptiness"). Together, the two words convey that the primordial emptiness was akin to an uninhabited wilderness space. When brought into conversation with other places where *tohu* is used, including Genesis 1:2, the use of *tohu* in Deuteronomy 32:10 highlights the chaotic nature of the wilderness experience. Robert Barry Leal puts it this way: "Wilderness is Israel's historical entry into the arena of chaos which, like the darkness before creation, is 'formless and void,' and without hovering wind (Gen. 1:2). Wilderness is the historical form of chaos and is Israel's memory of how it was before it was a created people. . . . Wilderness is formless and therefore lifeless."[17] This lifelessness is all the more striking because it is *life being taken away*. What is implied here is a kind of uncreation.[18]

Moses' speech in Deuteronomy 8 is, therefore, an honest reporting. He does not gaslight the Israelites, nor does he offer glib pastoral pablum in response to their experience. Why would he? The Israelites'

---

[16]This portion of the chapter was previously published in Burt, "To Do You Good."

[17]Robert Barry Leal, *Wilderness in the Bible: Toward a Theology of Wilderness*, Studies in Biblical Literature 72 (Peter Lang, 2004), 71.

[18]This portion of the chapter was previously published in Burt, "To Do You Good."

experience is also Moses' experience. He spiritually companions them not from a narrative distance but in a close-up, intimate, embodied way. Like a good spiritual director, then, Moses does not deny their experience but sits *with them* in the painful truth of it. He doesn't deny their narrative, but he does reframe it by telling them that insufficiency is not the truth: Their clothing did not wear out and their feet did not swell, and they did receive the manna Yahweh provided (Deut 8:3-4).

The need to reframe our narratives from insufficiency to abundance is a challenge not only for the Israelites but for many of us. As Jennifer L. Holberg rightly notes,

> If we're honest, how rare is it to think that anything in our lives is, in fact, enough? . . . I suspect, that more frequently we worry about not having or being enough—not enough time, not enough talent, not enough resources. We have internalized stories about ourselves that highlight our failures or deficiencies. Insufficiency is the operational hermeneutic of our lives in so many ways.[19]

Holberg's trenchant analysis raises many questions. *Where* do our narratives of insufficiency come from? *How* do we reframe them? *What* is the new narrative God is unfolding before us? These questions can only be answered by choosing the kind of *summative trust* offered by Moses in Deuteronomy 8:16: "He fed you in the wilderness with manna that your ancestors did not know, to humble you and to test you *and in the end to do you good*" (NRSVUE). We take our cue from Moses, who does not deny the pain of the experience or offer glib pablum. Moses offers an honest assessment of the experience while doing two things—viewing wilderness under the God lens and inviting a third Voice into that difficult space.

Wilderness Under the God Lens

In spiritual direction, "We view life under the God lens. We look at life from the perspective of our desire for God, and with the presumption

[19]Jennifer L. Holberg, *Nourishing Narratives: The Power of Story to Shape Our Faith* (IVP Academic, 2023), 29.

that God's grace is always at work."[20] This is especially important in the wilderness, in which we must strain not only for God's goodness but even more so for God's presence. Like the Israelites, who are called to "know in [their] hearts" that Yahweh has not been a distracted bystander or an evil tyrant but an intimate participant in their experience (Deut 8:5), we must do the same. Like a spiritual director is one who allows a "third Voice into the room," Moses invites a third Voice into the wilderness. Moses acknowledges, to borrow a few words from Owens, that this third Voice speaks with "the authority of an author whose words have the power to shape the story and the character of our lives."[21] Throughout Scripture, God is a Voice crying out in the wilderness, heralding a joyful, abundant way. We must allow God to be the Voice coming alongside us to narrate our stories. Only then will we move from telling stories about our own (and God's own) insufficiencies. As Holberg puts it so beautifully,

> How, then, do we shift our mindset from "going back to Egypt" and being self-sufficient, and instead, find narrative models that are grounded in the conviction of God's plentitude? Not with a prosperity gospel based in our performance, but with a story rooted in our total belovedness and our complete inability to save ourselves. Put another way: What would happen if the stories we tell about God and about ourselves proceed from our absolute conviction of his loving generosity and our own "enoughness"?[22]

The wilderness shatters our unhealthy illusions of self-efficacy, a posture Moses warns the Israelites against in the final verses of Deuteronomy 8 (Deut 8:11-18). Such a posture invites a joyful self-forgetfulness, even as we understand ourselves to be truly loved and cared for by the God whose provision is plentiful. As Mary Oliver says, "Joy is not made to be a crumb," and the manna Yahweh provides for the Israelites in the wilderness is enough to sustain them for the moment.[23]

---

[20]Owens, *Abba, Give Me a Word*, 43.
[21]Owens, *Abba, Give Me a Word*, 65.
[22]Holberg, *Nourishing Narratives*, 31.
[23]Mary Oliver, *Devotions: The Selected Poems of Mary Oliver* (Penguin Books, 2017), 61.

Nourishing Narratives

Looking at the wilderness through the God lens, then, means at least three things: We tell our stories (and invite others to tell their stories) out of the depths of our own hearts, naming our deepest desires; we tell our stories looking through the eyes of a purposeful pedagogy that does not minimize the pain of the experience; and we read our stories eschatologically, which is to say, with the final chapters in mind. These three postures can reorient the narratives of scarcity we tell to more nourishing narratives, to borrow a phrase from Holberg.

It was during a period of wilderness in my own life that my spiritual director helped me wade through my scattered prayers to name the deeper desire hiding underneath. "What else (*other than this thing you so desperately think you want*) do you want from God?" she asked. I was shocked to discover that what I wanted was actually a desire given to me by God, one far deeper and more healing than the prayer at the surface. My prayer was one of scarcity, yet the desire underneath was far more abundant, nourishing, and risky than I would have uncovered on my own. She listened to me in a holy way, companioning me as I named what God had placed on my heart. This is the nature of spiritual direction, as Owens describes it: "In spiritual direction you learn to name your desires, noticing them and asking where they come from and what they are for. This naming and noticing is done in the conviction that our deepest desires are for God."[24] My own wilderness provided the spiritual space in which I could grapple with my misplaced desires and strain to tell my story with greater depth. My spiritual director helped me fold my wilderness and the desire I recovered there into the larger context of my life with God. As a result, I was able to reframe my narrative to one that was more hopeful.

Holberg describes (what I will call) the tension between wilderness and hope in this way:

> This push toward narrative hope is something that the Bible itself models for us. Isn't it interesting that Scripture doesn't erase all the bad things

[24]Oliver, *Devotions*, 55.

> that happened? One could imagine a religious text that might find it easier to simply give rules or assert spiritual abstractions. Wouldn't it have been easier to not give a report of all the times the Israelites were disobedient? Mightn't it have been more effective to have a New Testament full of clear rules, rather than assemble a collection of letters that chronicle all the dysfunctions of the early church? As a mental exercise, imagining a different construction of the Bible highlights the fact that the Bible doesn't shy away from the hard stuff—instead, it's almost exclusively the hard stuff. Except that the hard stuff doesn't get to win.[25]

It is true that Scripture doesn't erase all the bad stuff that happens—there are scorpions and snakes there, for example (Deut 8:15)—but Scripture does help us reframe those things, both in the here and now and eschatologically. In the here and now of the Israelites' wilderness story, Moses reminds them that their clothes didn't wear out and their feet didn't blister (Deut 8:4). In their immediate narrative future, Moses assures them that the Promised Land will be a place of abundance, with descriptions of gushing waters, flourishing vegetation, and mineral wealth (Deut 8:6-9). This is the language of food, of satiation, of abundance, of enoughness.

Eschatologically, the whole of the biblical story reminds us that we are swept up into something bigger in which nothing is wasted, not even the most vile and disturbing things (Rom 8:18-39; cf. Deut 8:5, 16). This is the comedy and the fairy tale of the gospel, and these comedic and fairy-tale chapters are the narrative thrust of the whole narrative, one that reorients our own positionality in this present world. As Holberg says, "An orientation towards hope changes our stories about ourselves."[26] As it did for Moses and the Israelites, it will take courage and trust to reframe our wilderness narratives, yet we must—we simply must—strain toward the final pages of our own narratives. As Brueggemann puts it so well: "What we know about our beginnings and our endings, then, creates a different kind of present tense for us. We can live

---

[25]Holberg, *Nourishing Narratives*, 174.

[26]Holberg, *Nourishing Narratives*, 180.

according to an ethic whereby we are not driven, controlled, anxious, frantic or greedy, precisely because we are sufficiently at home and at peace to care about others as we have been cared for."[27]

It is this care and provision in the midst of our anxiety and panic that is a hallmark of the God of the desert, something the prophet Elijah discovers in the next chapter.

Questions for Reflection and Discussion

1. What does one-anothering mean, and how have you experienced it in your own life?
2. What kind of narrative are you telling about your own life—one of scarcity or one of enoughness? How nourishing is the narrative you are telling about your own life?
3. Is there someone God is inviting you to one-another through their own wilderness experience?

[27]Walter Brueggemann, "The Liturgy of Abundance, The Myth of Scarcity," *The Christian Century*, March 24, 1999.

6

THE SACRED PAUSE

Practicing Solitude and Silence with Elijah

Guide us waking, God, and guard us sleeping; that awake we may watch with Christ, and asleep we may rest in peace.

Prayer at the Close of Day

Let us be silent—so that we may hear the whisper of the gods.

Ralph Waldo Emerson, "Friendship"

I climbed the stairs to his office, small and tucked away on the third floor of the divinity school. He is an average-sized man, yet he remains, all these years later, larger than life in my mind. I often tease him about the antique recliner in his office, medium blue and dainty: "This old thing is more suited to a tiny grandmother with knitting on her lap than a towering figure in the world of preaching," I told him.

Pink crept onto his brown cheeks as he smiled and looked down.

Gospel Canticle and Benediction, Prayer at the Close of Day (Compline), in *Lutheran Book of Worship* (Augsburg, 1978), 159-60.

When I tease him, this seventy-something-year-old man still blushes like a little boy, and that amuses me.

I love him for it.

"My dear, this is the chair I sat in to pray for you throughout your doctorate, and throughout your marriage, and your move to Texas, and all the other events of your life," he said.

I know that, of course.

I also know it's the chair he sits in when he naps.

I took my seat in the chair opposite him, as I had done so many times over the past twenty years, first as his student, then as his teaching assistant, and later as a professor still in need of a word of wisdom from this man I love.

I can't remember the fancy college word I used that night in his office, only his response: "You love words," he said, grinning.

It is true that I love words—I have made my home in them. Teaching and writing about the spiritual life requires words. But like pencil smudges on the page, words merely shadow the ineffable. Silence comes closer to the divine than words ever will. This means that my true vocation is not first to speak but to listen. Silence is the home out of which speech is born.

I arrived at this conviction during arguably the two busiest years of my teaching life. It was during this season that God invited me to incorporate intentional pauses into all the noise. Through a two-year apprenticeship to the monastic life, I devoted myself to the familiar rhythm of prayer expressed in the Psalter. I discovered solace in the cessation of words, a sacred pause in which I was baptized by silence and prayer.

Centuries ago, the psalmist understood the need for sacred pauses, exclaiming, "Seven times a day do I praise you" (Ps 119:164). This statement by the anonymous prayer poet reveals that a rhythm of prayer had been established in Judaism long before the birth of Jesus. At seven fixed hours of the day, Jews would offer prayer to Yahweh. The book of Acts demonstrates that the earliest Christians maintained this practice (Acts 2:42-47; 3:1).

Over time, monastic Christians institutionalized this rhythm of prayer, naming it the "Divine Office" or the "Liturgy of the Hours." For Saint Benedict and Christians both before and after him, fixed hour prayer was the *opus dei*, "the work of God," the most important office Christians were to assume.[1] Whatever other work Christians engaged in, whether within the monasteries or in secular occupations, prayer remained the central work for the whole church. Today, the Divine Office still connects Christians in different time zones to one another. As one brother or sister says, "Amen" and falls asleep, another rises with the dawn and continues the prayer. In this way, the Divine Office is a connective tissue for the global church that binds us together regardless of time and place.

Macrina Wiederkehr refers to these set times for prayer as "seven sacred pauses," which awaken us to God's grace at every hour. Wiederkehr states: "It is possible to develop a kindred spirit with these rich historical hours that does not require praying specific texts or going to a particular place for prayer. Each hour has its own unique mood and special grace. . . . No matter what you are doing, you can pause to touch the grace of the hour." For those who practice the Liturgy of the Hours, the final graced hour is Compline, or night prayer. The word *compline* comes from the same Latin root as the word *complete*, and it is an invitation to look within rather than without. Wiederkehr describes Compline through a series of themes: silence, rest, sleep, darkness, trust, protection, personal sorrow, completion, and intimacy. After the final prayer of the night, Christians enter into "the Great Silence," a period of darkness and silence until Vigils, the first hour of prayer. As Compline darkens into the Great Silence, we are moved to a place of *apophasis*, a place beyond images and beyond words: "We come now to the moment when there is nothing more to see or hear, nothing more to say. Silence is for the ears as darkness is for the eyes. We travel within to the deep places where we do not need words or images."[2]

---

[1]Phyllis Tickle, *The Divine Hours: Prayers for Autumn and Wintertime* (Doubleday, 2000), xii.
[2]Macrina Wiederkehr, *Seven Sacred Pauses: Living Mindfully Through the Hours of the Day* (Sorin Books, 2008), 2, 156, 154.

The Great Silence is a place of deep introspection in which we are invited to depart on a journey inward. Such a journey requires trust. It also requires us to let go of our plans and expectations as well as what we think we know about ourselves and the world. In doing so, we trust that treasures await us in the dark earth of silence. Such a journey also requires a certain degree of protection, as there are enemies without and within that we will face. Wiederkehr offers a wise reminder that in humility, we must beseech God for protection:

> The enemies of the soul are all around us. Who among us is not acquainted with these undesired guests that visit us on a daily basis: apathy, indifference, self-righteousness, greed, control, selfishness, lust, resentments, bitterness. . . . The obstacles to spiritual and human development are plentiful. Most of us are quite familiar with those things that detain us on our day's journey.[3]

As the confidence of the day shades into the uncertainty of the night, Compline and the Great Silence depict a variety of darknesses. The darkness of humility is the darkness of unknowing, in which God disentangles truth from mendacity. There, God invites us to a conscious examination of our motivations—revealing our self-delusions and the deceit that sometimes drive our actions. This darkness is the tomb, the womb, or the cave out of which newness, grace, genuine devotion, and rebirth occur. Comfort is a gift that emerges from this kind of darkness, in which we experience delight in drawing us into the "Holy Darkness of God."[4] By contrast, the darkness of suffering entails those things that happen to us over which we have no control. Nevertheless, this darkness can yield a similar growth. However we parse the particular darkness that faces us as Compline blackens and quiets into the Great Silence, this is a sacred pause that is necessary on the journey of our spiritual growth.

For the biblical character Elijah, the journey from the wilderness to the cave at Mount Horeb is such a sacred pause. Elijah's experience at

---

[3]Wiederkehr, *Seven Sacred Pauses*, 156.

[4]Wiederkehr, *Seven Sacred Pauses*, 161.

Mount Horeb reveals the importance of the spiritual disciplines of solitude and silence.

The Inward Departure

Micha Roi describes Elijah's experience in 1 Kings 19 as a "departure on a journey story," which entails two journeys across two pericopes: the flight into the desert (1 Kings 19:1-8a) and the journey to Horeb (1 Kings 19:8b-21).[5] As a literary genre, the departure-on-a-journey story contains the following elements: a description of the protagonist's setting forth, which includes uncertainty regarding its nature as enterprise, flight, or expulsion; fear or worry highlighted by the term *yrh* on the part of the protagonist; the reaching of a sacred spot; revelation and prayer, typically about protection from danger on the protagonist's journey; a divine response, in which God commits to accompany the hero on their journey; a divine reply to the protagonist's prayer that is practical in nature, a carrying out of what God promised in God's earlier response; and a description of the continuation of the protagonist's journey.[6] The first eight verses of 1 Kings 19 contain elements of the genre outlined by Roi, with a particular emphasis on fear and flight.

The pericope opens with a recollection of what has occurred in the previous chapter, Yahweh's triumphal victory at Mount Carmel and Elijah's subsequent slaughtering of the prophets of Baal. Jezebel's resulting anger prompts a sending of a *malakh* (surely no "angel" but a messenger in human form) to proclaim a curse on Elijah—that his own life will be taken from him like the lives of the prophets he slew on Mount Carmel. The repetition of the triradical root *nephesh* indicates Jezebel's intention to eradicate the whole of Elijah's life, his life force, his inner being, his entire self. Jerome T. Walsh notes that the seven times in which *nephesh* is used demonstrate its importance to the story, suggesting that beneath

[5] Micha Roi, "1 Kings 19: A Departure on a Journey Story," *Journal for the Study of the Old Testament* 37, no. 1 (2012): 25.

[6] Roi, "1 Kings 19," 26-27.

the surface of Elijah's desire to forgo his prophetic ministry are the larger issues of life and death.[7]

The very real possibility of Elijah's death, foretold by the messenger, prompts a quick and frenzied response on Elijah's part, demonstrated in a rapid succession of Hebrew verbs stacked on top of one another.[8] The last three of the four main verbs in 1 Kings 19:3 indicate a rapidity of action—"he arose and he went for his life and he went." The first verb, *wayyar*, is less clear, with some translations identifying the root as *raah*, thus Elijah "saw" what Jezebel planned and began his journey. Other translations opt for the root *yara*, indicating that Elijah "feared," and this explicit fear prompted Elijah's flight. The Septuagint, Peshitta, and a number of Masoretic Text manuscripts prefer *yara*, heightening the sense of apprehension and dread that characterizes journey stories. The Masoretic Text prefers *raah*, which indicates Elijah perceived his circumstances and took action—"he got up and set forth."[9]

Whether fear is explicitly referenced in the writer's choice of verbal root or not, Elijah's actions clearly suggest it. Like Jacob's journey to the Jabbok River, in which he sends his traveling companions ahead of him, Elijah leaves his servant in Beersheba while Elijah, the Hebrew writer tells us, "went himself a day's journey into the wilderness." Both Jacob and Elijah separate from their traveling companions and are left in isolation to encounter God alone. We are not told, as we are in the Jacob story, that it was night when Jacob encounters God, but we are told twice that Elijah falls asleep (*wayyshkav wayyishan* in 1 Kings 19:5 and *wayyshav wayyishkav* in 1 Kings 19:6).[10] Twice a messenger appears to Elijah, a *malakh* in 1 Kings 19:5 and a *malakh* of the Lord in 1 Kings 19:7. The reappearance of the Hebrew word *malakh* is a reminder that it is a

[7]Jerome T. Walsh, *1 Kings*, Berit Olam Studies in Hebrew Narrative and Poetry (Liturgical Press, 1996), 265.

[8]1 Kings 19:3, *wayyar wayyaqam wayyelek el-napsho wayyabo*, "And he was afraid and he arose and he went for his life and he went."

[9]Roi, "1 Kings 19," 29.

[10]The Jabbok encounter is notoriously complex within the larger Jacob cycle (Gen 25–50). I have written about this odd passage in Gen 32:22-32 in Noel Forlini Burt, *Encounters in the Dark: Identity Formation in the Jacob Story*, Semeia Studies (SBL Press, 2020).

malakh from Jezebel in 1 Kings 19:2 that prompted Elijah's fearful flight to the wilderness in the first place. In the wilderness, however, the previous nefarious message fades into a numinous presence and a nourishing provision, indicated both by the act of feeding itself and the repetition of the particle *hinneh*, indicating surprise. Twice Elijah asks Yahweh to take his life (1 Kings 19:4). Twice Yahweh meets Elijah's need with feeding and provision, the first of which prompts Elijah to eat and to fall asleep again (1 Kings 19:5). The second feeding sustains him on the forty-day and forty-night journey from the wilderness to the mountain of Horeb (1 Kings 19:7).

Walsh notes that Elijah's request to die is nonsensical, given his flight from Jezebel. If he truly wished to die, he should have stayed and allowed Jezebel to kill him, as she had promised. Instead, Walsh points out, Elijah's words reveal a deeper emotional reality—his sense of hopelessness, disillusion, and despair.[11] If we examine Elijah's actions from a different perspective, however, Elijah's sleep prepares him for a deeper knowing. Here—and later at the dark cave at Mount Horeb, the most numinous and holy site in Israel's history—Elijah encounters a numinous presence who will feed and nourish him after his sleep.

For the monastics, sleep was a spiritual practice, one that was part of the rhythm of the Liturgy of the Hours. Sleep was a "little death" that prepared them for a larger death. Compline, night prayer in the Liturgy of the Hours, begins in this way: "May Almighty God grant us a peaceful night and a happy death." Night prayer prepares monastics for death, both the daily dying to self that is part of the life of every Christian and the physical death that awaits us all. Compline is a prayer of trust in which "we place ourselves in divine hands."[12]

Like many of us, Elijah is reticent to place himself in the divine hands, proclaiming that his life is "too much" (1 Kings 19:4). The angel of the Lord responds by using the same language of "too much" in the context

---

[11]Walsh, *1 Kings*, 267.

[12]Wiederkehr, *Seven Sacred Pauses*, 166.

of provisional feeding: ("And he said, 'Get up, eat, lest the journey be too much for you'"; 1 Kings 19:7). The interplay between the angel of the Lord and Elijah in this scene harks back to the provision of sustenance in the wilderness in 1 Kings 17:2-6. There the Lord instructs ravens to feed Elijah. Elijah receives bread and meat in the morning and in the evening, which fortifies him to provide miraculously for the widow at Zarephath and her son (1 Kings 17:24).

Walsh refers to the "unmistakable echo" between these two scenes in Elijah's life, particularly the Hebrew writer's use of the words *ugah* ("round flat loaf, bread cake") and *tsappakhath* ("pitcher; jar") in 1 Kings 17:13-14 and 1 Kings 19:6. Given the rarity of the word *tsappakhath* in particular (occurring elsewhere only in 1 Sam 26), Walsh contends that these links may be, like the ravens and the widow of 1 Kings 17, "another manifestation of Yahweh's providence toward his prophet."[13] Alan J. Hauser and Russell Gregory point to the intimacy of the provision: "The scene is very domestic and intimate, as when a member of the household touches the sleeping person to arouse him to a meal. Thus, the messenger asserts that Yahweh is the God of life simply by performing an everyday task that is necessary if life is to continue."[14] This providential provision is not merely for the sake of nourishment. Rather, it deepens Elijah's spiritual formation and allows him to persevere in ministry, as the next scene conveys. Indeed, the angel of the Lord seems to acknowledge the difficulty of Elijah's journey so far, tending to him physically so that he can meet Elijah in a deeper way at Mount Horeb.

The depth of this later encounter is signified even in the geographical movement from the wilderness to Mount Horeb, to the darkness of the cave, a symbol of unknowing and spiritual rebirth. Elijah's experience also takes on deeper meaning when we recall that Mount Horeb is another name for Mount Sinai, the site of Moses' first encounter with Yahweh (Ex 3) and the subsequent theophany in which Yahweh gave the

[13]Walsh, *1 Kings*, 269.

[14]Alan J. Hauser and Russell Gregory, *From Carmel to Horeb: Elijah in Crisis* (Sheffield Academic Press, 1990), 64.

Law to all Israel (Ex 19). The sacred sites of wilderness, mountain, and cave all differ geographically. Nevertheless, they are all thin spaces, both spiritually and ancestrally. They connect Elijah to all those who have come before him.[15]

The Great Silence

Where Elijah's movement in 1 Kings 19:1-8 was frenetic, fleeing from Jezebel and her machinations, here the action slows. Time and geography both change—"And he went there to the cave and he spent the night there" (1 Kings 19:9). The sojourn in the cave and at the mountain function as a sacred pause in Elijah's departure-on-a-journey story. The temporality of the night and the darkness of the cave signify competing realities in Elijah's experience: uncertainty and newness; death and rebirth; and danger, protection, and trust. These realities, symbolized in the geographical movement from desert to darkened cave, suggest a movement inward. Elijah is invited to reflect more deeply on his ministry and on his own life with God. As with the Divine Office, words precede the silence: ("And behold, the word of the LORD came to him and he said to him, 'What are you doing here, Elijah?'"; 1 Kings 19:9). The question is not, of course, a geographical one. Rather, the word of the Lord acts as a spiritual director. The best spiritual directors do not declaim or define—they pose questions that allow people to sit in silence, to reflect, and to name their own experience, as I discussed in chapter five. The word of the Lord poses a question, refrains from naming Elijah's problem (and its attendant solution), and allows Elijah to name his own experience.

While Elijah describes his experience as he understands it, he does not give an accurate reporting of the facts: He alone has been zealous for the Lord, while the children of Israel have forsaken the covenant of the Lord, torn down the Lord's sacrifices, and slain the Lord's prophets

---

[15]Elijah's connections to Moses are well-attested by scholars, with some even proclaiming Elijah to be a second Moses. These intertextual connections and innerbiblical allusions are beyond the scope of this chapter.

with the sword. Elijah is left alone, his life being sought (1 Kings 19:10). In Elijah's exhaustion and disillusionment, his understanding of these events is clearly at odds with the events themselves. Just one chapter before, Obadiah, the servant of the Lord, had hidden one hundred prophets of Yahweh in caves (1 Kings 18:1-15). Even after hearing this, Elijah proclaims, "I am the only one of the LORD's prophets left" (1 Kings 18:22), the same line he repeats in 1 Kings 19:10. Regardless of what is actually true, Elijah feels alone in his service to the Lord. Even after Elijah's successful battle against the Baals convinced the people that the Lord was God (1 Kings 18:16-46), he claims that the children of Israel have flouted the Lord's commands (1 Kings 19:10).

Elijah's spiritual malaise and misconstruing of the truth lead Hauser and Gregory to call Elijah a prophet "in crisis." They differentiate between a courageous picture of Elijah, who tells the widow at Zarephath, "Fear not" (1 Kings 17:13), and Elijah who successfully humiliates and slaughters the prophets of Baal (1 Kings 18:40), with a limp picture of a prophet too fearful to stay and fight Jezebel. The food provided by the messenger of the Lord does not sustain him for future action, Hauser and Gregory claim. Rather, this meal gives him just enough strength to utter his "self-pitying complaints."[16] Yet the Lord does not reprimand Elijah. Like a good spiritual director, the Lord invites Elijah to shift his perspective—"Go out and stand on the mountain before the face of the LORD" (1 Kings 19:11).

Elijah moves out of the darkness of the cave, where he has believed one thing, and stands on the mountain, where he is invited to consider his life from a different vantage point. What follows is an experience that reminds us not to expect the Lord always to act in the same way. Elijah stands at Horeb, arguably the most sacred site in Israel's spiritual biography. At Horeb, Moses first encountered the Lord (Ex 3) and later received the Ten Words (Ex 19–20). It is this second experience of Moses, what scholars refer to as "The Standing at Sinai," that most closely

---

[16]Hauser and Gregory, *From Carmel to Horeb*, 61.

correlates to Elijah's initial experience of the Lord after he is invited to exit the cave and stand before the face of the Lord. At Sinai, Moses experienced God through thunder and lightning, thick cloud, trumpet blast, fire and smoke, and earthquake (Ex 19:16-25). However numinous the presence of God might have been for Moses, the narrator makes it clear—"Moses spoke and the voice of God answered him" (Ex 19:19). God was decidedly *present* in these things. While 1 Kings 19:11-12 lists many of the same events as Exodus 19:16-25—wind, earthquake, and fire—the narrator makes it plain here too: The Lord is *not* in any of them, the repetition of the particle *lo* ("no, not") attached to each noun. This negation is a grammatical element that reveals the negative theology inherent in the narrative.

In his discussion about hearing the voice of God, Robert Mulholland describes the difficulty of piercing through "the noise of your own understanding" to hear God.[17] The noise of Elijah's own understanding is, much like the wind, the earthquake, and the fire, loud and distracting. It is not until these things die down that Elijah can move from what he feels is the certainty of his situation into the unknowing necessary to hear the Lord.

Elijah's experience outside the dark cave at Mount Horeb is a contemplative experience in which he discovers all *the Lord is not*. There is an *unsaying*—what scholars call an apophatic discourse—in which language negates and unsays itself.[18] This philosophy is pre-Christian, originating in the Greek philosophies of Plato yet intersecting Christianity through the Neoplatonic school. Developed by later thinkers such as Dionysius (or Denys), negative theology embraces silence as the way in which God can be (un)known: "The fact is that the more we take the flight upward, the more our words are confined to the ideas we are capable of forming; so that now as we plunge into that darkness which is beyond intellect, we

---

[17]M. Robert Mulholland, *Shaped by the Word: The Power of Scripture in Spiritual Formation*, rev. ed. (Upper Room, 2001), 58.

[18]William Franke, ed., *On What Cannot Be Said: Apophatic Discourses in Philosophy, Religion, Literature, and the Arts* (University of Notre Dame Press, 2007), 1:9.

shall find ourselves not simply running short [*syntellein*] of words but actually speechless [*athentos*] and unknowing."[19] As William Franke puts it, the actual encounter with God must take place in a silence beyond words.[20] While Greek philosophy is famously associated with metaphysical discussions such as these, as Noam Reisner says,

> The story of ineffability in Western thought must begin, if anywhere, with the Hebrew Bible and its portrayal of a mysterious, omnipotent paternal deity. The God portrayed in the Bible, enigmatically alluded to as Yahweh, is a deity of radical contradictions. On the one hand the Bible portrays Yahweh as a being infinitely beyond the comprehension of man but on the other hand as susceptible to a wide array of distinctly human emotions.[21]

Part of Yahweh's so-called radical contradictions lies in the use of these natural forces that display Yahweh's power but do not define him. As Nahum M. Waldman says, monotheistic religion does not identify these forces of nature with God. They are separate from God and serve as God's tools and messengers (Ps 104:4). Waldman notes, "God in His essence is unknowable and in His manifestation ineffable, inexpressible, something awesome and totally other with respect to ordinary perceptions of reality."[22] Indeed, Elijah discovers that the Lord is understood more fully in silence. The Lord is *not* in the wind. The Lord is *not* in the earthquake. The Lord is *not* in the fire. When these noises have subsided and the last fire has died down, the narrator tells us, there is the voice of a soft whisper.

In his groundbreaking monograph on the theological implications of silence in the Hebrew Bible, John Kessler argues that Elijah comes to a deeper understanding of the Lord's character and purpose through the dialectic of speech *and* silence. Kessler examines Elijah's story in

[19]Pseudo-Dionysius, *Pseudo-Dionysius: The Complete Works*, trans. Colm Luibheid (Paulist Press, 1987), 1033B-C.

[20]Franke, *On What Cannot Be Said*, 1:17.

[21]Noam Reisner, "Silence and Presence: Ineffability in Ancient and Medieval Western Thought," in *Milton and the Ineffable*, Oxford English Monographs (Oxford University Press, 2009), 14.

[22]Nahum M. Waldman, "Sound and Silence," *Jewish Bible Quarterly* 22, no. 3 (1994): 228.

conjunction with Abraham in Genesis 22 and Job in the whirlwind, noting: "The silence of God spoken of in these texts relates *not to God's inaction, but to human wrestling with the incomprehensibility of the purposes of God.* All three texts present the reader with an individual caught up in a confusing wasteland." Kessler's use of the word *wasteland* is an apt description of wilderness, one the Prophets use to describe the exile (Is 34:11; Jer 4:23). For Kessler, Abraham, Elijah, and Job are "called to inhabit *a space between speech and silence.* God is not absent, but inscrutable."[23]

Like Elijah's experience itself, the meaning of the key word *demamah* is mysterious. Scholars are divided about what exactly what, if anything, Elijah hears. As Waldman notes, *demamah* is interpreted by some as "silence" and by other ancient texts as "murmur," a kind of sound.[24] Some modern translations, citing evidence from comparable Semitic languages, likewise translate *demamah* as "murmur."[25] For Waldman, the mystical implications of translating the word as "murmur" are linked to a theology of creation as evidenced by the psalmist: "Day to day makes utterance, night to night speaks out; there is no utterance, there are no words, their sound is not heard; their voice carries throughout the earth, their words to the end of the world" (Ps 19:3-5). Pre-Hebraic theology also understands God as communicating through the cosmos, such as the Ugaritic tablets: "I have a word I would tell you, a speech I would utter to you: speech of tree and whisper of stone, conversation of heaven and earth, even of the deeps with the stars." Waldman also points to mystical Jewish texts such as that of Meir Ibn Gabbay, whose book *Avodat ha-Kodesh* compares the communication between God and Israel to that between two violins. When the string of one violin is

[23]John Kessler, *Between Hearing and Silence: A Study in Old Testament Theology* (Baylor University Press, 2021), 131, emphases original.

[24]The Greek version renders *phōnē auras leptēs* as "the sound of a gentle breeze." The Vulgate translates *sibilus aurae tenuis* similarly, "the whistling of a light breeze." The German version is based on Luther's translation, *ein stilles sanftes Sausen* ("a still, soft whistling"). The Targum on Kings translates *kol dimesabehin bahasaï* as "the sound of those praising God (silently)." The Syriac offers the translation "a word spoken softly."

[25]The New English Bible, "a lowing murmuring sound." NAB renders the word "a tiny whispering sound."

activated, the corresponding string on the other also resounds. Thus, the human being activates God. If we translate *demamah* as some kind of sound, Waldman claims, then the powers of nature or the voice heard in this text are instruments God uses and not to be identified with God, whose communication is "garbed in otherness."[26]

Translating *demamah* as "silence" is only complicated by the grammar—*demamah* is in a construct relationship with *qol.* A construct-noun relationship means that these two nouns are stitched together in an "of" relationship. The grammar suggests that what Elijah hears is the "sound/voice *of* silence." What does this mean, then? Does Elijah first hear silence and then a voice? For Waldman, the grammatical relationship between the two words strengthens the impression that we are faced with a paradox, one in which silence is not an absence or a void but a "concrete fullness, an experience conveying there is a presence."[27] This fullness of presence spills out over the narrative and invites awe, wonder, and humility. Waldman summarizes it this way:

> We suggest, then, that the purpose and lesson of the non-verbal phenomenon in 1 Kings 19 is to drive home concretely the idea of the otherness and mystery of God, but not of His isolation and indifference. Just as God is not in the wind, the earthquake, or the fire, He is also not in His word and not limited to it, for the word, too, is a tool used by the ineffable God. The prophets are granted the word or burdened with it; they do not possess it. Even the prophets who hear and transmit the divine word must remember their limitations and that the reality of God is beyond their grasp.[28]

Thus, it is not just that the word of the Lord is ineffable—the Lord is ineffable in his quiddity, in his being. His words are inscrutable, and he is beyond being. Likewise, Kessler points to the lexical field of silence represented by *demamah*, *qol*, and *daqqah* as pointing to the elusive nature of both the experience itself and Yahweh. This final term, *daqqah*,

[26]Waldman, "Sound and Silence," 230-32.
[27]Waldman, "Sound and Silence," 232.
[28]Waldman, "Sound and Silence," 235.

designates the grinding of a substance into fine powder (Ex 30:36; 32:20; 2 Sam 22:43; Is 28:28). Kessler states, "It seems most likely that *qol demamah daqqah* is a phrase deliberately constructed to stand in opposition to the intensely soniferous and physical manifestations described in 19:11-12, yet describe a phenomenon *sufficiently perceptible so as to draw Elijah's attention to it*." Kessler notes that a rendering bringing together the concepts of "sound," "stillness," and "reduction to fine particles (dust)" yields a translation of "A sound of finely ground stillness."[29]

Kessler points to this sound of finely ground stillness as the motivating factor that compels Elijah to leave the cave, where he hears the voice of the Lord. As demonstrated by the covering of his face, Kessler argues, Elijah is aware that he is entering sacred space. Only then is Yahweh's voice heard.[30] Building on Kessler as well as the apophatic tradition, it seems apparent that it is only when we divest ourselves of our own words that we can enter into the dark caverns of our own unknowing and emerge, as Elijah does, with humility and a clearer picture of our own lives. We quiet the noise of our own understanding and see, as Elijah does, that things are not quite what we think.

When Elijah stands at the opening of the cave, he hears the same question the Lord posed to him earlier ("And behold, a voice came to him and said, 'What are you doing here, Elijah?'"; 1 Kings 19:13). It is only when we are quiet and stilled, when we enter the Great Silence, that our perspective can change and we can discover, as Elijah does, that we are not alone. Rather, we are, as Plotinus puts it, "alone with the Alone."[31] And it is the Alone who, like a good spiritual director, asks the very questions that will help us reframe our own narratives. Elijah looks up to discover there are seven thousand who have not bowed to Baal (1 Kings 19:18), and he is sent on his way to anoint Elisha, who will go on to fight for Yahweh and experience Yahweh in his own way.

---

[29]Kessler, *Between Hearing and Silence*, 142, emphasis original.

[30]Kessler, *Between Hearing and Silence*, 143.

[31]As quoted in Annie Dillard, *Teaching a Stone to Talk: Expeditions and Encounters* (Harper Perennial, 2013), 60.

Silence as Spiritual Practice

Among the monastics, silence was a spiritual practice that cultivated awareness. As Martin Laird puts it, "Silence and awareness are in fact one thing."[32] We cultivate silence not for the purpose of vocal absence, silence for silence's sake, but so we can attune ourselves to the God who loves us. When do we do so, we may discover, along with the monastics, what Laird calls "the wild hawk of the mind," the scattering of our thoughts with its making of grocery lists, its replaying of past grievances, and its preoccupation with anything other than prayer.[33] Like anything else, the cultivation of silence is a muscle that must be developed over time. We trust that, in the cultivation of silence, just as Yahweh does not condemn Elijah for his imperfections, neither does God condemn us for our inability to keep the practice perfectly.

Decades ago, Henri Nouwen diagnosed part of our inability to keep silence as arising from fear: "One of our main problems is that in this chatty society, silence has become a very fearful thing. For most people, silence creates itchiness and nervousness. Many experience silence not as full and rich, but as empty and hollow. For them silence is like a gaping abyss that can swallow them up."[34]

The fear of being swallowed up by the silence is, I would add, a fear that the word we may hear from God will be anything but nourishing. In short, we fear condemnation, something the Johannine literature assures our hearts against: "There is no fear in love. But perfect love drives out fear, because fear has to do with punishment. The one who fears is not made perfect in love" (1 Jn 4:18 NIV). The God we encounter in silence is the God who loves us. Simply put, God loves what God has made. We can be assured that God is our Advocate in the quiet silence where we replay the tapes of all we have done and left undone. Again,

---

[32]Martin Laird, *A Sunlit Absence: Silence, Awareness, and Contemplation* (Oxford University Press, 2011), 44.

[33]Martin Laird, *Into the Silent Land: A Guide to the Christian Practice of Contemplation* (Oxford University Press, 2006).

[34]Henri J. M. Nouwen, *The Way of the Heart: Connecting with God Through Prayer, Wisdom, and Silence* (Ballantine Books, 1981), 52.

the writer of 1 John helps us: "This is how we know that we belong to the truth and how we set our hearts at rest in his presence: If our hearts condemn us, we know that God is greater than our hearts, and he knows everything" (1 Jn 3:19-20 NIV). As Nouwen says about the ministry of silence, "But isn't the purpose of all ministry to reveal that God is not a God of fear but a God of love?"[35]

Keeping silence is also a radical act of trust, one Richard Foster claims we bristle against: "One reason we can hardly bear to remain silent is that it makes us feel so helpless. We are so accustomed to relying on words to manage and control others. If we are silent, who will take control? God will take control, but we will never let him take control until we trust him. Silence is intimately related to trust." In this way, keeping silent is like the death depicted in Compline—keeping silence demonstrates our trust that God will *keep our lives*. We also trust that God will be, as Foster puts it, our justifier when others misconstrue our motivations. We need not "straighten others out," Foster claims, but we allow God to preserve our reputations.[36] We can trust that God will sort things out in God's own way, however that looks.

When we rest secure in that love, "befriending the silence," we give ourselves over both to God and to the ministry God has for us.[37] Elijah's ministry beyond the cave of silence is a demonstration of this (1 Kings 19:19-21). As Nouwen says, "Silence is the home of the word," one that makes us pilgrims, guards the fire within us, and teaches us to speak.[38] Foster agrees—"Under the Discipline of silence and solitude we learn when to speak and when to refrain from speaking."[39] Entering the interior silence gives our words generative power, as the lives of desert fathers and desert mothers demonstrated. The silence and the solitude that necessitates it create in us a greater compassion in our ministries. Thomas

---

[35]Nouwen, *Way of the Heart*, 52.

[36]Richard J. Foster, *Celebration of Discipline: The Path to Spiritual Growth*, 25th anniversary ed. (HarperSanFrancisco, 1998), 100-101.

[37]Nouwen, *Way of the Heart*, 53.

[38]Nouwen, *Way of the Heart*, 41-42.

[39]Foster, *Celebration of Discipline*, 98-99.

Merton says as much in *The Sign of Jonas*: "It is in deep solitude that I find the gentleness with which I can truly love my brothers. The more solitary I am the more affection I have for them. . . . Solitude and silence teach me to love my brothers for what they are, not for what they say."[40]

Thus the fruit of silence is a life in which we attune ourselves to the God who loves us, in which we are able to bear one another's burdens with greater compassion and in which we trust God is the keeper of our lives. Keeping silence as a spiritual practice, an inner desert into which we can enter, is also one way we keep in step with Christians who walk the darkness of Compline.

Walking in the Dark

Wiederkehr reminds us that Compline is an invitation to walk the path of darkness and silence. Early monastic communities prayed Compline in the dark, symbolizing their own entrance into darkness. This embodied approach to prayer was a reminder that God alone protects us from dangers within and without. Dark in his own inscrutability, God is within Godself a holy darkness and a reminder that darkness need not always be associated with evil. Wiederkehr writes, "This darkness is not one we need protection from, but rather is a darkness we are invited to enter. It is a bit like standing before the hidden face of the divine, longing for entrance yet fully aware that we know so little about the one we call God."[41] And yet walk the path we must, like Elijah, entering and exiting caves of our own knowing and unknowing.

The important thing is that we keep on walking that dark walk, that we keep on entering and exiting caves of knowing and unknowing. It is in the searching for God, the almost-finding God, and the experience we have of missing God that keep us pausing sacredly, if even just for one night. As Frederick Buechner says, "Part of the inner world of everyone is the sense of emptiness, unease, incompleteness, and I believe

---

[40] Thomas Merton, *The Sign of Jonas* (Harcourt, Brace, 1953), 261.
[41] Wiederkehr, *Seven Sacred Pauses*, 163, 160.

that this in itself is a word from God, that this is the sound that God's voice makes in a world that has explained him away. In such a world, I suspect that maybe God speaks to us most clearly through his silence, his absence, so that we know him best through our missing him."[42] In trust, we pray our last prayer. As we enter into the darkness and the silence, we trust that whether we are awake or we are asleep, we are with God. We learn through the continued walking in the dark that we can trust God. We can trust ourselves. And we can let go. As Merton says, "My life is a listening, His is a speaking. My salvation is to hear and respond. For this, my life must be silent. Hence, my silence is my salvation."[43]

As the prophet Hosea will demonstrate in chapter seven, in the wilderness, the love of God is demonstrated not only in silence but also in prophetic speech.

Questions for Reflection and Discussion

1. What role does silence play in your life? How often do you intentionally position yourself to hear it?
2. Richard Foster says that keeping silence is a "radical act of trust." What do you think he means by that?
3. What does Elijah's story reveal about God's provision in ministry?

---

[42]Frederick Buechner, *Secrets in the Dark: A Life in Sermons* (HarperOne, 2006), 19.
[43]Thomas Merton, *Thoughts in Solitude* (Farrar, Straus & Giroux, 1956), 69.

7

PURGATION AND BELOVEDNESS IN THE SPIRITUAL LIFE

Yahweh and Israel in Hosea's Metaphorical Desert (Hosea 2)

Nudos amat eremos.
[The desert loves to strip bare.]

Jerome

Desert apatheia has a child whose name is love.

Evagrius Ponticus

But Love has pitched his mansion in the place of excrement;
For nothing can be sole or whole that has not been rent.

William Butler Yeats, "Crazy Jane Talks with the Bishop"

Jerome, *Select Letters*, trans. F. A. Wright, Loeb Classical Library (Harvard University Press, 1933).
Evagrius Ponticus, *The Praktikos and Chapters on Prayer* (Cistercian Publications, 1981), 14.

We could skip hell if we wanted to, and I always did.

As a teenager, I didn't know much about hell, but others who had been there told me about it. Before the advent of cellphones to light up even the remotest corners of modern life, the room was completely dark, with walls painted black. It was also made to be as hot as possible, the nineties precursor, I suppose, to hot yoga rooms today. Rather than sweating out toxins, people were made to sweat about their sins as they envisioned eternal life separated from God.

Heaven was well-lit, with walls painted white. Invariably, a man with sandy blond hair and piercing blue eyes stood in the center of the room. Whatever church deacon who happened to be portraying Jesus that year always looked more like Brad Pitt than the historical Jesus of Nazareth, a Middle Eastern Jew. Weeping, Brad Pitt Jesus held out his hands to the preacher's kid who had been bribed into playing the faithful son or daughter who met Jesus in death. They hugged as the lights grew brighter, symbolizing admittance into eternal life.

Even though I only visited heaven, I dreaded going there every year.

But because I was a church kid in the nineties, social pressure dictated I pile in the church van and go to Judgment House each October.

I'm sure they were well-intentioned, but I'd like to send my therapy bill to every architect, literal and theological, who put Judgment House together. Looking back on it with (theologically trained) adult eyes, what I find most problematic about Judgment House is the image of God it presented. Or, perhaps, I'm more correct to say the *images*, plural, of God it presented. On the one hand, God seemed willing to give you only so many chances before sending a car with your name on it to mow you down, transporting you straight to hell. The more violent the death, the better for dramatic effect. This was a God who couldn't wait to get you, a God too angry to love you. On the other hand, the God in heaven seemed to be just the opposite—this was a God too saccharine to take seriously, a Hallmark greeting-card God lacking any real substance or depth. This God conveyed nothing about the real commitment and life of obedience required to be a follower of Jesus. This was a God who could guarantee you a spot in heaven but had no idea what to do with you once you got there. The love of this God was as bland as the Communion wafers we ate after the service ended, a God too shallow to love you.

Neither depiction of God said anything *biblical* about judgment or love, instead promoting only fear on the one hand or tepid, teabag-water intellectual assent on the other. Judgment existed on one side, love on the other.

In the prophetic books, however, love and judgment often go together. In particular, the book of Hosea uses what J. Andrew Dearman calls the "metaphorical geography" of the wilderness to demonstrate the intertwining of Yahweh's love and judgment.[1] Of the five times where *midbar* ("wilderness" or "desert") is used in Hosea (Hos 2:3, 14; 9:10; 13:5, 15), three instances refer to Israel's original wilderness sojourn. In each instance, *midbar* is used in positive contexts that underscore both Yahweh's provision for his people and their own commitment to him following the exodus from Egypt.[2] However, even a cursory reading of the original wilderness sojourn demonstrates that Israel's commitment to Yahweh does not last long. The initial gratitude and jubilation captured by the songs of both Moses (Ex 15:1-19) and Miriam (Ex 15:20-21) quickly give way to a cacophony of complaints regarding that same provision. Famously, the Israelites murmur that they want to return to the life they knew in Egypt (Ex 17:3; Num 11:1-6; 14:1-4), a reality I explored in the chapter "Feasting on the Word." Given the lackluster way in which Yahweh's new bride responds in the original wilderness sojourn, it is surprising that Hosea uses the metaphor of wilderness so frequently and to such rhetorical effect.

Yet Hosea is a desert text, one in which Yahweh's own desire to return to the desert is at the heart of what Louis Stulman and Hyun Chul Paul

---

[1]J. Andrew Dearman, *The Book of Hosea*, New International Commentary on the Old Testament (Eerdmans, 2010), 121.

[2]Cooper Smith, "The 'Wilderness' in Hosea and Deuteronomy: A Case of Thematic Reappropriation," *Bulletin for Biblical Research* 28, no. 2 (2018): 249.

Kim refer to as the "divine pathos." In Hosea 2, Yahweh becomes a "vulnerable family member," one who is deserted by his family as they pursue other lovers.[3] Left in the metaphorical geography of the desert where they first met, Yahweh vows to lead the Israelites there too, using the desert in two ways—as a site of didactic and divine denuding (Hos 2:3) and as a site of divine alluring (Hos 2:14). In every way, Yahweh not only takes Israel to the metaphorical desert—but *Yahweh is himself like the desert Israel encounters*. At times, Yahweh appears stark and fearful, a picture of the risk of death involved in this desiccated place. At other times, Yahweh is like an oasis in the desert, succoring and slaking thirst.

This God of the desert is complex precisely because this God is personal, inviting Israel not to experience a place but a person. This person takes on all the qualities of the stark and fearful desert space (Hos 2:1-13), yet at the same time vows to allure Israel to the wilderness to speak to her heart (Hos 2:14-23). Yahweh's cry is that of a plaintive lover who longs for the nubile bride he first met and married there. Rooted once again in his own pathos, Yahweh *is* the desert Israel encounters: the person who kindled their love, cut the initial covenant, and longs to renew it once more. The two pictures of wilderness in Hosea 2 represent judgment and love. The two pictures also represent two sides of the same divine face, for Yahweh's love fuels Yahweh's judgment.

Taken together, Hosea 2:1-13 and Hosea 2:14-23 are teachers in the spiritual life. Hosea 2:1-13 is a picture of the mystical stages of purgation, illumination, and union, while Hosea 2:14-23 highlights belovedness as a core reality in the life of the believer. Both realities have the capacity to shape the metaphorical geography of the believer's heart.

The Desert Who Strips Bare

Before my explorative exegesis of Hosea 2:1-13, it is important to acknowledge that this is a spiritually startling text, one that raises difficult

[3]Louis Stulman and Hyun Chul Paul Kim, *You Are My People: An Introduction to the Prophetic Literature* (Abingdon, 2010), 190.

questions both about God and about how abusive interpretations might lead to actual abuse. The crux of the challenge begins with Hosea's first of five references to *midbar*. In a staggering statement, Yahweh vows to "strip [Israel] naked and expose her like the day she was born," making her like a parched desert, slaying her with thirst. This opening line makes it clear that Hosea's portrayal of the God of the desert will be complex and not easily categorized, forcing us to examine God's involvement in the wilderness narratives of our own lives. Our own spiritually upending experiences invite us to decide what we believe about God. Do we believe the God who leads us into the wilderness is good—tender and loving and kind—or not? When God assumes the qualities of the wilderness in our lives—silent, stark, seemingly indifferent—do we believe God still loves us even when haven't yet encountered Hosea 2:14 in our own narrative? When God behaves in ways that jar us and run counter to our previous experiences of God, do we reexamine the theological systems we have constructed, or do we abandon God instead?

Spiritually speaking, we are able to believe in God's love for us by building a personal history or friendship with God. We build a friendship with God in much the same way we build a friendship with another person. In friendship, we slowly offer our trust, we share our secrets, we engage in misunderstandings with one another and resolve those misunderstandings by talking things out, and we pay attention to a person's character and temperament as it reveals itself over time. We do much the same with God. We build a history with God *first*, and we construct a theological system based on that history *second*. Our experiences with God are just one source of information, certainly. Wesleyan tradition, for example, lists four sources: Scripture, reason, and tradition, along with experience. But our experiences are an important source.

Even our best theological systems may fail us, but God never will. Our shared history with God allows us to trust the absolute power God wields over our lives, to rest in God's love for us even when things don't make sense, and to listen again when we don't understand or even agree with the things God says. This also means that we can engage a text with which we disagree and read it again, wrestling with it but doing so with grace. It is only in the context of a personal relationship with the Word that we can trust the words that are written. We learn to believe in God's love for us even when God's message to us through a particular text is a painful one.

Such a belief would have been imperative for Hosea's audience, who heard the sobering opening lines in Hosea 2. The initial warning begins with the Hebrew particle *pen* ("lest"), indicating the surety of the action taking place if the unfaithful wife does not repent. Several key elements, both exegetically and tonally, indicate the severity of this divine purging. The two main verbs in the clause, for example (*aphshitennah*, "I will strip her," and *hitsagtiha*, "I will expose her"), indicate that Yahweh is the one who will cause this to happen.[4] Second, the semantic range and the intertexts, which use the key verb *pashat*, are much like the metaphorical desert in which Yahweh situates his wife—stark and frightening. The verb *pashat* is variously nuanced elsewhere in the Old Testament as having to do with stripping off, undressing, cutting loose, or even making a raid. Several references in Samuel and Chronicles deal with stripping the land in battle, raiding it, and leaving nothing behind, or stripping the clothes off the dead after the devastation of battle (e.g., 1 Sam 23:27; 27:10; 1 Chron 10:9; 2 Chron 35:11). Elsewhere in Hosea, *pashat* is also nuanced in this way—Ephraim and Samaria's deeds are exposed, and a bandit breaks in and raids outside (Hos 7:1).

Hosea 2:3 depicts Israel as utterly vulnerable—exposed, naked, and gasping for life like a newborn baby. Yahweh will raid the land, acting as Israel's enemy, unless his unfaithful wife repents. Through this purging experience, Yahweh exposes what Israel, his unfaithful wife, has done and left undone. She chased other lovers, taking the gifts of Yahweh—grain, new wine, fresh oil, and silver and gold—and offered them to Baal as trysting trinkets. In all this, Hosea contends that she has acted shamefully

---

[4]Both verbs appear as first-person singulars in the *hiphil* verbal stem, indicating that the agency of the fulfillment of these actions belongs to Yahweh alone.

(Hos 2:5). About this very shame, Yahweh promises to "uncover her immodesty" (Hos 2:10). A version of the wilderness imagery from Hosea 2:3 is picked up again in Hosea 2:12, where Yahweh promises to destroy Israel's vine and fig trees. Yahweh will turn her into a "forest" whose produce is devoured by the beasts of the field. Here again, Yahweh vows to strip her bare—taking away everything on which she has relied and served rather than Yahweh. In Hosea 2:1-13, various forms of the participle *meahavim* ("lovers") are used no fewer than five times (Hos 2:5, 7, 10, 12-13), demonstrating the pervasive and deep entrenchment of her adultery.[5] In the pursuit of other lovers, Hosea notes, Israel forgot Yahweh (Hos 2:13).

Throughout Hosea, the forgetfulness of the people is a repeated theme (Hos 4:6; 8:14; 13:6), one in which the entire community is implicated. In each instance, Yahweh either promises direct retribution or acknowledges simply that destruction is the natural result of their forgetfulness.

Reading Hosea 2:1-13 in the Era of #Metoo

While it would be tempting in the era of #metoo and #churchtoo to read Hosea's depiction of God as an angry, avenging spouse, two points help us not make such a knee-jerk theological interpretation. First, it is important to contextualize Hosea's rhetoric in light of his social location. Renita Weems offers a helpful cultural contextualization, noting that three things stood at the center of the prophetic mindset: the political fate of the land, the history of the relationship between Israel and God, and an explanation for Israel's demise as a nation. Therefore, "Women, sex, and marriage were politicized in prophetic speeches and provided a means by which the prophets could integrate three separate but interrelated commentaries on Israelite society: the social world of Israel, the political fortunes of Israel, and the religious life of Israel."[6] Using the

[5]The Hebrew vacillates between Israel's own thoughts, in which she speaks of "my lovers" (*meahabay*), and Yahweh's speech, in which a third-person feminine singular pronominal suffix is added (*meahabeha*, "her lovers").

[6]Renita J. Weems, *Battered Love: Marriage, Sex, and Violence in the Hebrew Prophets* (Fortress, 1995), 5.

metaphor of marriage allowed Hosea to arrest the attention of his audience, who viewed it as a central and inviolable institution. The violation of covenant between Yahweh and Israel, Hosea suggests, is as serious and as shocking as the rupture caused when a wife, the subordinate party in the relationship in that patriarchal world, violates the terms of marriage.

Second, we err when we map contemporary egalitarian relationships onto the social world of Hosea and then draw theological conclusions based on that mapping. As the dominant party, Yahweh uses his power to protect and care for the tiny nation of Israel, the subordinate party. This hierarchical structure was inherent to Hosea's social context, in which a wife was subordinate to a husband. As such, she would have expected a similar provision and nurture from her husband, whose societal power could protect her vulnerability.

Weems notes that it was possible for a tiny nation such as Israel to experience a modicum of fame due to its special status with Yahweh, even making a unique claim on Yahweh. The only condition for sustained protection and nurture was obedience on the part of the weaker party to the dominant party. This meant that Yahweh could exercise his power to protect and to punish if Israel did not keep the covenant. Weems states, "God, then, is not a harsh, cruel, vindictive husband who threatens and beats his wife simply because he has the power to do so. He is himself a victim, because he has been driven to extreme measures by a wife who has again and again dishonored him and has disregarded the norms governing marriage relations."[7] The payoff for Weems's argument is this: Yahweh has power but does not abuse that power. Yahweh is in fact the beleaguered party whose right it is to punish—or, as I argue, purge.

Socially speaking, we stand at a great distance from Hosea's worldview. Modern relationships among spouses differ greatly from Hosea's social dynamic. In healthy relationships, both parties have power, experience vulnerability, and mutually submit to each other. Any relationship in

---

[7]Weems, *Battered Love*, 20, 19.

which one party exerts dominance over another, whether verbally, physically, emotionally, psychologically, or spiritually, is abuse, plain and simple. Likewise, any interpretation that uses this text to justify abuse of any kind has also performed an act of *exegetical abuse.* Nothing in this text justifies abuse. Hosea's original audience would not have understood it that way, nor should we. Theologically speaking, the one key point we share in common with Hosea is that we submit ourselves to a God who uses his power to protect, to provide, and to punish, but never to abuse. God has absolute power, and God is absolutely trustworthy to wield that power with justice, righteousness, and mercy, to temper judgment with unfailing love. This is the way Yahweh related to Israel, it is the way God relates to us, and it is in this familial way we that ought to relate to one another.

Yahweh's Beloved Family

The familial nature of Yahweh's relationship to Israel makes their forgetfulness of Yahweh's covenant even more devastating. That Israel's forgetfulness can take place in the context of such an intimate, familial relationship is at the core of Yahweh's own devastation, as is his own commitment never to forget his love for Israel. Outside Hosea, both the Pentateuch and the Prophets affirm Yahweh's own character and his promise never to forget his covenant with Israel. At one of the most vulnerable moments in their own history together, Yahweh assures the people: "Can a woman forget her nursing child, or show no compassion for the child of her womb? Even these may forget, yet I will not forget you. See, I have inscribed you on the palms of my hands; your walls are continually before me" (Is 49:15-16 NRSV). It is within Yahweh's own nature to remember—he never slumbers nor sleeps (Ps 121:4). He has not forgotten his covenant, maintaining it for a thousand generations (Deut 7:9).

Nevertheless, the forgetfulness of the unfaithful wife is highlighted in Hosea and demonstrated not only in actions prior to Hosea's prophetic ministry (e.g., Ex 32) but also in Moses' warning to the people not to forget the Lord in times of prosperity (Deut 8:11-20). The consequences for forgetting Yahweh are spelled out clearly in the Pentateuch—Israel will be destroyed (e.g., Deut 8:20). This forgetting of Yahweh in the form of adulterous worship of other gods is a violation of the original covenant between Yahweh and Israel, which was first ratified in the wilderness (Ex 20:1-6). To forget is to negate the terms of that covenant, one Israel exuberantly agreed to keep: "Everything that the Lord has spoken we will do" (Ex 19:8 NRSV).

While the Israelites' story before and after Hosea's ministry demonstrates her penchant for forgetfulness, it is in Yahweh's own nature to remember the covenant. Indeed, it is this recollection of the covenant and the desire for the purified love of his wife that drives Yahweh's purgative action. His threat to purge, denude, and desiccate her "like a wilderness" and "like a forest" (Hos 2:3, 12) is for the purpose of alluring her back into the wilderness where they first met (Hos 2:14). If the purging occurs in the wilderness, the rekindling of their love will also occur there. Before such a renewal can take place, however, Israel must understand her own desertion of Yahweh. Through her pursuit of other lovers and the perversion of the original marriage contract with Yahweh, Israel has effectively abandoned Yahweh in the desert where they first met. It is she who has abandoned Yahweh, not the other way around.

This ironic recollection of her own forgetfulness is a necessary humbling, one that can lead to a deeper love for the God she met in the wilderness long ago. Such is the nature of the purgative way. As Belden C. Lane puts it: "Mountain and desert experience is 'wintry' phenomenon, more kenotic than pleromic, more given to being emptied than to being filled. It is harsh, lean in imagery, beggarly in its gifts of love. Yet, as Hosea and Jeremiah knew well, no love is deeper and more honest than desert love."[8] It is only in stripping everything else away in the desert and in denying all other loves that true love for God can be kindled. This

---

[8]Belden C. Lane, *The Solace of Fierce Landscapes: Exploring Desert and Mountain Spirituality* (Oxford University Press, 1998), 37. The terms *kenotic* and *pleromic* are both Greek in origin and are theological antonyms. *Kenotic* refers to an emptying, those things that sap our strength, while *pleromic* refers to a filling, those things that give us strength.

purgative action is certainly painful for Israel, who must experience the consequences of all they have done and left undone. It is also painful for Yahweh, whose abandonment by his family has rendered him *pathetic*. *Pathetic* is derived from the term *pathos*, and readers are meant to feel pity, sorrow, and grief for Yahweh, who is deserted by Israel and left to wander a metaphorical desert of his own. Yahweh's rhetoric is rooted in anger, a secondary emotion that cannot mask the deep pain underneath this rupture in his family.

As Stulman and Kim put it, "Family imagery in Hosea is significant because here God becomes a vulnerable family member. In this broken family, God is dependent upon the other members, just as the family members are dependent upon God."[9] In the process of purgation, Israel is vulnerable to Yahweh, who has made himself like a desert—impassible and fierce. Yet Yahweh is also vulnerable precisely because of his deep love for his family. The pathos of Yahweh, while perhaps startling in the context of the Old Testament, should not surprise those of us who maintain a trinitarian theology. Yahweh's "dependence" and "vulnerability," as Stulman and Kim phrase it, are qualities readily recognizable in the Christ of the Gospels. What Hosea does is to pull us in closer to the God who suffers when his family rejects him, reminding us of the pathos ever-present in the Godhead. Like the Christ of the Gospels, Hosea's Yahweh is not *only* "Other," *only* sovereign, *only* transcendent, or *only* capable of exercising his anger at Israel's desertion by making himself like a desert. Hosea's Yahweh is *also* lowly, vulnerable, near and not far, and *passive*—able to feel emotions, including the pain of rejection. If Yahweh and Jesus are truly one, as trinitarian theology attests, then Yahweh can express the pain of abandonment and rejection as easily as Jesus in the garden prior to his arrest and crucifixion (Mt 26:36-46; Mk 14:32-42; Lk 22:39-46). Just as Jesus both wanted *and* needed the support of his friends, Yahweh appears to want *and* need the family who has deserted him. This rejection is all the more *pathetic*—capable of arousing

[9]Stulman and Kim, *You Are My People*, 190.

our pity and sadness—when we consider the deep love Yahweh expresses for his family in Hosea.

Hosea envisions Yahweh's deep love for his family as emerging out of his own womb. Hosea 2 begins by naming two of Hosea's children, this time removing the negations before their names in the previous chapter (Hos 1:4-9). In particular, Hosea's reference to *rukhamah* (literally, "she was pitied") in Hosea 2:1 highlights the depth and intimacy of Yahweh's love for his estranged family. The semantic range of the verb includes showing love for, having compassion on, or offering pitying love. Its grammatical usage in Hosea 2:1 demonstrates that these particular children are on the receiving end of Yahweh's loving compassion.[10] Cognate forms of the triradical root *rkhm* underscore that this pitying compassion arises as out of Yahweh's own womb—these are the children Yahweh has borne himself.[11] Elsewhere, this motherly imagery is reflected in Yahweh's tender words to Israel in their release from Babylonian exile: "Can a mother forget her nursing child, or show no compassion for the child of her womb?" (Is 49:15 NRSV).

Set within the context of children in the desert of exile whom Yahweh promises to bring home, Yahweh's is a "womby" love, one rooted deeply in the imagery of family. In Deuteronomy, Yahweh's compassionate, womby love is again associated with his desire for a family whose love is purged from other interests: "Do not let anything devoted to destruction stick to your hand, so that the Lord may turn from his fierce anger and show you compassion, and in his compassion multiply you, as he swore to your ancestors" (Deut 13:17 NRSVUE). Here two different forms of the verb are used, both of which indicate Israel is the recipient of Yahweh's love.[12] These two forms are linked to the multiplication

---

[10]Here the verb appears in the third-person feminine singular of the *pual* verbal stem, which underscores its passive nuance.

[11]The segholate nouns *rakham* and *rekhem*, and the verb *rakham*, all carry the nuance of the "womb."

[12]*Rakhamim* (an adjectival form) and *rikhamka* (a *piel* perfect with a second-person pronominal suffix).

promised "to your ancestors" (literally, "to your fathers") and are therefore rooted in the original Abrahamic covenant (Gen 12:1-3).

Moreover, womby love is not only something Yahweh shows—it is an action he performs. In Exodus, Yahweh's womby love is part of his quiddity, the very self out of which he operates: "And he said, 'I will make all my goodness pass before you, and will proclaim before you the name, 'The LORD'; and I will be gracious to whom I will be gracious, and will show mercy on who I will show mercy" (Ex 33:19 NRSV). In Hosea, *rakham* and its various cognates are used repeatedly (Hos 1:6-8; 2:1, 4, 23; 9:14; 14:3), in each case connected to familial language. That Yahweh plays various roles in his own nuclear family—husband to an unfaithful wife and parent to piteous children—underscores the nuanced and vulnerable way in which Yahweh's womby love plays out in Hosea 2. Notably, it is Israel's spurning of Yahweh's love that is the occasion for the prophetic work of Hosea as a whole and the lawsuit (*riv*) Yahweh drags out into the rhetorical public square. Through his lawsuit and near divorce of his wayward wife, Yahweh's purpose is in keeping with the mystical aim of purgation—to open her heart to his own love.

Purgation in Christian Tradition

Purgation is not relegated to the prophetic literature or to the writings of the medieval mystics—it is the modus operandi of God in every believer's life. Indeed, conformity to the image of the God *requires it.* "Being conformed," M. Robert Mulholland says,

> goes totally, radically against the ingrained objectification perspective of our culture. Graspers powerfully resist being grasped by God. Manipulators strongly reject being shaped by God. Controllers are inherently incapable of yielding control to God. Spiritual formation is the great reversal: from being the subject who controls all other things to being a person who is shaped by the presence, purpose and power of God in all things.[13]

[13]M. Robert Mulholland, *Invitation to a Journey: A Road Map for Spiritual Formation* (InterVarsity Press, 1993), 27.

Thus, conformity necessitates confrontation at the very places where we are least like God. Conformity also requires us to willingly submit ourselves to the one who has made us for himself in the first place. In trust, we submit ourselves to the wilderness of purgation, because that is where God speaks to our hearts.

As I have demonstrated throughout this book, Christian tradition has long acknowledged the desert experience as vital for spiritual formation. Yahweh's threat to "strip [Israel] naked and expose her as in the day she was born, and make her like a wilderness" (Hos 2:3 NRSVUE) resembles the mystical "purgative way." Part of a threefold pattern that also includes illumination and union, the purgative way strips believers of besetting sins, habits, passions, idols, and ways of thinking contrary to the gospel. In short, anything standing in the way of the spiritual formation of believers is cast under the loving gaze of Christ and his cross. This threefold pattern evolved over the centuries, beginning with Origen and Origen's student Evagrius Ponticus, continuing through the writings of Dionysius the Areopagite, and finding fullest expression through the writings of mystics such as Bernard of Clairvaux and Bonaventure.[14]

Writing in the thirteenth century, Bonaventure explained the threefold way as follows:

> God himself rests in these three things [the sleep of peace, the splendor of truth, and the sweetness of charity], dwelling in them as in his proper throne. Therefore, it is also necessary to ascend to each of these three through three steps according to the threefold way—through the purgative, which consists of getting rid of sin; through the illuminative, which consists in the imitation of Christ; and through the unitive, which consists in receiving the Bridegroom. And thus each way has its different steps through which we begin from the bottom and move toward the top.[15]

The purgative way is therefore the painful way, in which believers come face-to-face with everything in their lives that is contrary to the love of

---

[14]Bernard McGinn, ed., *The Essential Writings of Christian Mysticism* (Random House, 2006), 150.
[15]McGinn, *Essential Writings of Christian Mysticism*, 150-51.

God. As Lane puts it, "The way of purgation involves an entry into what is unnerving, even grotesque in our lives, into what quickly reveals our limits. It seems at first, like most beginnings in the spiritual life, a mistake, a false start, an imperfection in God's planning, a regression in our own growth. Only through hindsight do we recognize it for the unexpected gift that it is."[16]

There is no other fierce landscape more appropriate for this purging to take place than the desert. With its stark landscape, its barrenness, its indifference to whether a person lives or dies, the desert is where all other things on which people rely are removed. In Yahweh's lawsuit against his wayward spouse, Israel, he not only envisions stripping Israel bare like a wilderness—but he takes on those same qualities himself. As in the Christian tradition of purgation, however, this stripping bare was purposeful—a divine deprivation or divine denuding intended to kindle desire in the heart of his wayward spouse.

The Desert Who Allures

Indeed, Hosea's second use of *midbar* ("desert") hinges on this very notion—now that she is attentive and stripped of the lovers on which she had relied, Yahweh can speak to Israel's heart (Hos 2:14). At the heart of this alluring is Yahweh's own heart—his own longings to return to the desert where he first committed himself to Israel. These longings are apparent in his daydream about Israel's commitment to him in the wilderness immediately after their release from slavery: "There she shall respond as in the days of her youth, as at the time when she came out of the land of Egypt" (Hos 2:15 NRSVUE). Francis Landy puts it intriguingly:

> God's fantasy is romance, a play of lovers in a wilderness that affords freedom from social constraints and cares, and prying eyes. The wilderness is liminal, both in time and space, and hence initiatory. At the threshold between child and adulthood (hence "as in the days of her

[16] Lane, *Solace of Fierce Landscapes*, 27.

> youth") it effects a conjunction of sexual awakening and death, and hence the full range of human experience.[17]

For Yahweh, the desert was the site of initiation into relationship with Israel. In the desert, the romance developed, and Yahweh became Israel's sole husband and provider, the one who protected Israel from the abusive Pharaoh. The gratitude expressed immediately following Israel's release from slavery was reflected in song, both through Moses and all the people (Ex 15:1-19) and through Miriam, who invited the women to sing and dance (Ex 15:20-21). While the jubilant celebration of Yahweh's deeds gave way to marital spats around bitter water, manna, and the uncertainty of this new life together, Hosea envisions the desert as the place where love was first kindled. The desert, for Yahweh and fledging Israel, was a place of play, one in which Yahweh's longings for relationship were met.

For Lane, Yahweh's love for Israel exists somewhere in the dialectic between the *Deus absconditus* (the "hidden God") and the *Deus ludens* (the "playful God"). His comments about the playful nature of Yahweh provide a useful overlay through which to explore the implications for spiritual formation present in the desert metaphor of Hosea 2:14-23. About the longing of Yahweh, Lane offers the following:

> This is a difficult truth that desert and mountain paths readily teach. Hosea evokes, in his own tragic experience of unrequited love, Israel's memory of walking hand-in-hand with Yahweh like young lovers in the cool desert evening (Hos. 2:14-15). The desert is the place where God hides, where love at times seems almost cruel, but it's also the place where deep intimacy and trust are learned. There in the long, haunting stretches of Sinai, the people of God discover how often desert terror gives way to desert love. In the wilderness the people of Israel experienced, more than they might have liked, the rough play of God's deep longing for them.[18]

---

[17]Francis Landy, "In the Wilderness of Speech: Problems of Metaphor in Hosea," *Biblical Interpretation* 3, no. 1 (1995): 49-50.

[18]Lane, *Solace of Fierce Landscapes*, 178.

That Lane connects Hosea back to Israel's experience at Sinai is apropos—Hosea 2:15 invites Israel to recall the excitement and terror of her status as a new bride in the desert following her release from slavery in Egypt. It is this initial desert experience that forms and stretches Israel's nascent faith and solidifies her nubile status. What appears at times as divine hiddenness is rooted in Yahweh's own deep longing for Israel, the bride of his own narrative youth. The original wilderness sojourn, as recalled by Hosea, was a kind of trysting space in which new love demonstrated itself, at times in shy and playful ways. Lane notes that this playful aspect of Yahweh's character is often mistaken for aloofness or cruelty. Recapturing playfulness as part of Yahweh's essential nature is vital for knowing him rightly. Lane states: "God's elusiveness serves her [*sic*] longing for relationship. Hiding, therefore, can become an act of playful teasing—a blithe form of seduction, God's way of inviting us to the place of surprised encounter. . . . God as *Deus absconditus* is never far removed from God as *Deus ludens*, a God revealed in playfulness."[19]

Of course, it is often our experience of God as *Deus absconditus* ("the hidden God") that most tests our understanding of God's love for us. Here Tish Harrison Warren offers a helpful word:

> We cannot hold together human vulnerability and God's trustworthiness at the same time unless there is some certain sign that God loves us, that he isn't an absentee landlord, or, worse, a monster. But we cannot divine such a sign from the circumstances of our lives or of the world. We have to decide what we believe about who God is and what he is like. We have to decide if anyone keeps watch with us.[20]

Herein lies the important point—*we have to decide*. We decide whether we will believe God loves us only in those textual and theological spaces that make sense—or whether we will choose to believe the best about God in the hard textual and theological spaces too. Do

---

[19]Lane, *Solace of Fierce Landscapes*, 179.

[20]Tish Harrison Warren, *Prayer in the Night: For Those Who Work or Watch or Weep* (InterVarsity Press, 2021), 28.

we abandon God, or do we abandon ourselves to God? We *choose* God again in the hard and confusing spaces in the same way that we choose God in the spaces where everything makes sense—by believing in God's love, no matter what. We do so by tracing our own history with God, looking to the character God has displayed in our lives and in the lives of those we love. Sometimes this clarity comes only through the broader perspective of looking back. What we see at a specific moment may not make sense in the present—only in the future.

In moments like these, I take a line from my pastor to be instructive—"Faith precedes clarity."[21] We decide to trust God before we have the clarity we'd like in the moment to do so. We learn to believe God's love also by examining the stories of Christians in ages past, who experienced God's hiddenness and who believed that God's hiddenness was not God's negligence. When we befriend these ancient Christians, they become our prayer partners in much the same way as the actual friends whose prayers on our behalf we rely. Ultimately, however, we must do what Warren suggests—*decide* that God loves us. In the words of Lane, we also decide that God's hiddenness is sometimes rooted in play, in God's own desire to seduce us into a deeper relationship with Godself.

The so-called blithe seduction Lane references is captured in the first phrase of the second pericope in Hosea 2: "Therefore, behold, I will seduce her" (Hos 2:14). Taken together, the Hebrew term *patah* with the later use of the phrase "speak to her heart," particularly when paired with the imagery of wilderness, underscores the intimacy of the encounter. This is an invitation to the heart of the unfaithful wife from the heart of Yahweh himself. Intriguingly, one pentateuchal intertext warns the Israelites not to be "seduced" by worship of other gods (Deut 11:16), the precise reason Yahweh must seduce them and bring them metaphorically back to the desert in the first place.

The semantic range of *patah* is broad and can deal with being simple, being persuaded, seduced, enticed, and even deceived. Given its

[21]Eric Spivey, sermon, Vestavia Hills Baptist Church, Birmingham, AL, May 2025.

association with the seduction of virgins in Exodus (Ex 22:16), it is no surprise that Hosea's use of the term has proved off-putting for commentators. Nevertheless, Bo H. Lim and Daniel Castelo rely on canonical intertexts not only to disabuse readers about any divine spousal abuse implied but also to sanitize any trace of eroticism from Hosea's literary wilderness. Drawing largely on the comfort oracle of Isaiah 40, Lim and Castelo note that the similarities both in language and in metaphorical geography effectively exonerate Yahweh from anything untoward:

> Like Hosea 2:16-25, Isa. 40–54 announces salvation oracles to a capital city in the wilderness by addressing it as a bride, virgin daughter, and mother. In Isaiah, God's speech is certainly intimate and impassioned, yet no eroticism is implied. In Isaiah and Hosea, the prophetic announcement that God will "speak tenderly" signifies that judgment has come to an end and the era of salvation has begun.[22]

While it is true that, like the transition from First Isaiah (Is 1–39) to Second Isaiah (Is 40–55), Yahweh's tone shifts from one of castigation to one of comfort, signaling salvation on the heels of purgation, the language, setting, and cultural background all suggest a certain seductive romance at the heart of Yahweh's enticement. The romantic undertones in Hosea 2:14-23 are not the whole of the prophet's message, but they are inescapably bound to the divine pathos at the heart of it. Here Dearman's comments on *patah* help underscore the important link to the romance of the desert. For Dearman, Yahweh's use of persuasion is not a depiction of "self-centered seduction" but an appeal based on personal commitment. Yahweh's appeal centers on rekindling the love he established with the Israelites in the wilderness following their release from slavery in Egypt. As the place of "marital beginnings," Yahweh's seduction of Israel, speaking to her heart, and bringing her to the

[22]Bo H. Lim and Daniel Castelo, *Hosea*, Two Horizons Old Testament Commentary (Eerdmans, 2015), 73. In Is 40:2, the phrase *dabberu al-lev* ("speak to her heart") mirrors the phrase in Hos 2:14, *wedibbarti al-libbah* ("speak to her heart"). Isaiah refers to Jerusalem specifically at the time of her exile, while Hosea refers to Israel as a whole in the context of the eighth century.

wilderness are, as Dearman states, a way to "reprise the national identity as a second bridal period."[23]

Indeed, identity—both the identity of Yahweh and the identity of the people—is at the heart of the matter, as the German mystic Meister Eckhart long recognized. Following Eckhart, who claims that God's innermost being is a "solitary wilderness" and a "vast wasteland," Lane says that the desert in which Yahweh invites Israel to meet in Hosea 2:14 is Yahweh himself. Following Eckhart, Lane states, "Only as I have 'desertified' myself, as it were—making myself a desert, stripped of everything but the spark of the soul within—am I fit to meet that Desert which is God."[24] Here Lane captures the dual understanding of desert in Eckhart's mystical thought—the desert is both hidden divinity and the ground of the soul.[25] Indeed, it is Hosea 2:14 that Bernard McGinn refers to as Eckhart's "signature text" for the desert motif.[26] Eckhart's sermon "The Book of 'Benedictus': Of the Nobleman," best captures his thinking on the subject:

> Who is then nobler than he who on one side is born of the highest and the best among created things, and on the other side from the inmost ground of the divine nature and its desert? "I," says our Lord through the prophet Osee, "will lead the noble soul out into a desert and there I will speak to her heart" (Os. 2:14), one with One, one from One, one in One, and in One, one everlastingly. Amen.[27]

For Eckhart, it is the solitariness of the soul with God and absorption into God that renders it "just and noble." Here Eckhart highlights what McGinn calls the "essential meaning of the desert theme," namely, the union of indistinction that the noble soul achieves with "the inmost ground of the divine nature."[28] Both the soul and God are desert, as

---

[23]Dearman, *Book of Hosea*, 121.

[24]Meister Eckhart, *The Essential Sermons, Commentaries, Treatises, and Defense* (Paulist Press, 1981), 265; Lane, *Solace of Fierce Landscapes*, 70.

[25]Bernard McGinn, "Ocean and Desert as Symbols of Mystical Absorption in the Christian Tradition," *The Journal of Religion* 74, no. 2 (1994): 167.

[26]McGinn, "Ocean and Desert," 168.

[27]Eckhart, *Essential Sermons, Commentaries, Treatises*, 247.

[28]McGinn, "Ocean and Desert," 168.

Eckhart explores in *Sermon 10*: "I have spoken of a power in the soul which in its first outpouring does not take God as he is good and does not take him as he is truth. It seeks the ground, continuing to search, and takes God in his oneness and in his solitary wilderness [*einoede*], and in his vast wasteland [*wüestunge*], and in his own ground."[29]

It is into this vast spiritual hinterland that is the very heart of Yahweh's own being to which Israel is invited in Hosea 2:14. And what Israel will find in that invitation is a God very much like the desert—a person of paradox, a desert of dialectics—both abundant and austere, purging and playful, seductive and strident, fulsome and fierce. The "solitary wilderness" and the "vast wasteland" is the person Israel meets in the desiccation of their own soul—and that person must be received with emptied hands and hearts rent asunder. Israel must find solace—they must lie down in safety (literally, "in trust"; Hos 2:18)—in the fierceness that is Yahweh's own desert. Everything else must be deserted in order to receive Yahweh as *Desert*, for Yahweh invites Israel not to a place but to a person—to his (own) grounded Self, asking whether Self and Self alone is enough. It is this same question that the Desert who is God asks us all—does the knowledge of this God of fierce love provide enough solace, or are other lovers required?

That this God of abundance and austerity addresses Israel at all—and by extension us as readers—is a surprise akin to water in the wilderness. It is a grace that Yahweh desires his people in the desert, and grace is always like the God who offers it—surprising. When Israel might expect judgment, the prophet pivots with the surprising and hopeful word of Hosea 2:14. In what follows, the geography grows forward beyond the desert—straining ahead to an eschatological vision in which the bow, sword, and warfare are abolished—and also leans back to the creative vision of Genesis 1, in which the wild animals, creeping things, and birds of the air are part of Yahweh's covenant and submit to it (Hos 2:18-20). Like Isaiah's vision in which Yahweh will judge between the nations and

[29]Meister Eckhart, *Predigt 10*, in *Meister Eckhart: Teacher and Preacher*, ed. Bernard McGinn (Paulist Press, 1986), 265.

arbitrate for the people, so "they shall beat their swords into plowshares and their spears into pruning hooks; nation shall not lift up sword against nation, neither shall they learn war any more" (Is 2:4 NRSVUE), Hosea understands that once the covenant is reestablished between Yahweh and Israel, the people will lie down in safety (Hos 2:18).

The creative outcome in which even the wild animals, creeping things, and birds of the air submit to Yahweh's covenant and therefore cause no trouble for Israel is predicated on the renewed marriage contract between Yahweh and Israel. This renewed relationship begins with the removal of the Baals and the agreement to take Yahweh once again as husband (Hos 2:16). As H. D. Beeby says, the change of appellation from *Baal* to *husband* involves more than removing the names of the Baals from Israel's mouth. The Hebrew *ish* ("husband") and the corresponding *ishah* ("wife") speak to "an enduring mutuality, a truly personal relationship" rather than the connotation of *boss* and the sexual implications of Baal's origins related to the word *fructifier*.[30]

The agreement to reenter into this personal relationship results in Yahweh's promise to betroth Israel to him forever, offering wedding gifts of his own righteousness, justice, covenant lovingkindness, womby love, and faithfulness (Hos 2:19-20). Yahweh's promise to betroth involves the ancient custom of engagement to a virgin and the bride price paid to the virgin's father.[31] Yet Israel is not a blushing, virginal bride. Time and again, she has played the harlot, as Hosea's earlier accusations suggest (Hos 2:1-13). This makes Yahweh's choice to pay a bride price out of his own righteousness all the more striking, yet in keeping with what we know canonically of his character. As Beeby helpfully says,

> Israel with her virginity restored can be expected shyly and demurely to say "I will" at the new wedding ceremony (v. 15). Yet Israel's "I will" to God is predicated wholly on the reiterated "I will" of God. Israel has said

---

[30]H. D. Beeby, *Hosea: Grace Abounding; A Commentary on the Book of Hosea*, International Theological Commentary (Eerdmans, 1989), 29.

[31]Relevant intertexts from the Pentateuch include Ex 22:16; Deut 20:7, 28:30. These all deal with various issues related to a woman's virginity and/or marriage.

> "I will" so often; she is an expert at it, a professional in fact. She has said "I will" to all and sundry. What is being offered her is the opportunity to say "I will" with utter sincerity and singleness of heart to her true husband. But how can he believe her? Has he not learned his lesson and finally admitted his wife's total inability to keep her promise? The answer is that the lesson has indeed been learned. He is not deceived. He knows that Israel's "I will" is anchored in his own constant "willing."[32]

In short, Yahweh's commitment to his wayward wife is rooted in his own grace and his desire that Israel know him.

Knowledge of Yahweh—or the lack of it—is a repeated theme in Hosea. In particular, failure to know Yahweh is linked frequently with devastation (e.g., Hos 4:1-6; 5:4). Israel's refusal to know the Lord, choosing spiritual fornication instead, once again highlights Yahweh's own pathos in *wanting* Israel to know him, as well as his grace in transforming their lack of knowledge into a deeper knowledge of himself. Historically, the verb *yada* ("to know") in Hosea 2:20 functions as a technical term signifying mutual legal acknowledgment between a suzerain and a vassal. Lim and Castelo note that Israel's future is dependent not on political strategizing with other nations during times of national stress but on loyalty to Yahweh.[33] However helpful the insights of Lim and Castelo are for situating Hosea's message in its historical place and time, *yada* is more semantically flexible than their interpretation suggests. Included in the semantic range of the verb is the kind of intimacy found only in a marriage relationship. Such is the kind of knowledge indicated by the narrator in Genesis 4:1. It is this kind of intense, intimate knowledge that opens the possibility for rekindled love. As Landy eloquently puts it, "The knowledge carried by the speech and its tone constructs and grows out of the play space, the liminal and primordial wilderness; the lover knows how to talk to the heart. If the wilderness is uncanny, eery, it is also the place of knowledge."[34]

---

[32]Beeby, *Hosea*, 29.

[33]Lim and Castelo, *Hosea*, 76-77.

[34]Landy, "In the Wilderness of Speech," 52.

Only through her entrance into the Desert who is Yahweh himself—at once purgative and seductive—can Israel experience the knowledge necessary for reconciliation. Only through the knowledge of Yahweh can the wayward wife and her children find their way back to the intimacy and the ardor of the original desert wandering. Hosea thus ends his message with a reference to the children who are estranged from both Yahweh and their mother (Hos 2:22-23; cf. Hos 1:4-8). The rekindled romance and the renewed covenant will put the whole family back together again: Jezreel ("God Sows"), from the root word *zara* ("to sow, scatter seed"), will be plentiful once more; Lo-Ruhamah ("Not Pitied") will once again become the object of Yahweh's womby love; and Lo-Ammi ("Not My People") will once again be welcomed back into Yahweh's family. Thus, Yahweh's vision for his own broken family strains back to the Mosaic and Abrahamic covenants, in which fruitfulness and peoplehood are rooted in the divine will and love (Gen 12:1-3; Deut 7:7-8). God's desire to root his people in the divine will and love is at the heart of the desert experience, both for the original intended audience of Hosea 2 and for people of faith in all times and places.

Reading for Our Belovedness as Spiritual Practice

Because our conformity to the image of Christ is rooted in God's own love for us, God often invites us to enter a barren desert like the one depicted by the prophet Hosea. If we believe that the God who addressed Hosea's audience is the same God who also addresses us today, then we can open our hearts to the ways in which the God of the desert addresses us through Hosea 2. This means that we must be attentive readers. In this case, as an attentive reader, I focus less on the question, How do I read Hosea 2? and more on the question, How does Hosea 2 *read me*? If I find that the God of the desert does address me through this desert text, I may experience any number of emotions based on whatever God reveals. I can trust that whatever I discover about myself, God's loving purpose for me is the same as his loving purpose for

Israel—so God can say, "You are my people" and so I can say, "You are my God" (Hos 2:23).

Such is the nature of conformity to the image of the God who loves me—it is a *process*, one in which I continually put myself under the loving gaze of God. Kenneth Boa offers a helpful reminder:

> The occupational hazard of theologians is to become so engrossed in the development of systematic models of understanding that God becomes an abstract intellectual formulation they discuss and write about instead of a living person they love on bended knees. In the deepest sense, Christianity is not a religion but a relationship that is born out of the trinitarian love of the Father, Son, and Holy Spirit.[35]

Ultimately, our theological systems are argle-bargle, that is to say, nonsense, trustworthy until they are not. We submit ourselves neither to a process nor to a theological system but to a person we have come to trust. We can trust the words we read on a page, whether the biblical text or the words of a creed, only if we have come to know the person hovering over them. This means that our relationship with God must be a very personal one, otherwise we cannot trust the one into whose image we are being formed. If we resist the person, we will resist the process also, pursuing other lovers who will *malform* us. Conformity to the image of Christ, then, begins and ends with our assurance of God's love for us.

Desert father Evagrius Ponticus understood this well, writing that desert *apatheia* has a child whose name is love.[36] Evagrius's use of the term *apatheia* was part of the developing theology of the threefold way, which would later include purgation, illumination, and union. Evagrius understood *apatheia* to be a kind of passionlessness or freedom from destructive "passions." Desert fathers such as Evagrius believed sin had entered the world, distorting our ability to love God, others, and self.

[35]Kenneth Boa, *Conformed to His Image: Biblical and Practical Approaches to Spiritual Formation* (Zondervan, 2001), 31.

[36]Evagrius Ponticus, *The Praktikos and Chapters on Prayer* (Cistercian Publications, 1981), 14.

The passions, as the desert fathers saw them, were the origin of sin for individual believers and included habits of seeing, feeling, thinking, and acting that blinded us from ourselves, from our neighbors, and from God. In short, "the passions distort everything."[37] Evagrius compiled what was a "systematic" list of the passions, which included gluttony, lust "for bodies," avarice, depression, anger, restless boredom, love of praise, and pride.[38]

In contrast to modern English, the desert fathers and the monastic tradition understood *passion* as a negative term only. This meant that "no state of mind or desire, no matter how strong," qualified as a passion unless it destroyed love for God, self, and neighbor.[39] Only in submitting these passions to the loving gaze of God could a person hope to achieve *apatheia*, freedom from their control. When properly freed from passions, desert *apatheia* could lead to greater intimacy and love for God, for self, and for neighbor. Rather than a Stoic ideal of imperturbability or a holy height achievable only for select Christians, *apatheia* was thought to be the normal state of being for *every* Christian.[40]

In the desert text of Hosea 2, a desert God has been deserted by his family and purges them of their passions—their habits, besetting sins, and ways of being in the world contrary to his love for them. It is only through purgation that this desert God can rid them of their other lovers and renew their commitment to love of God alone. This same desert God invites us to enter the desert ourselves and to experience transforming love. Such an invitation begins with our own willingness to reflect on our passions and to grieve them alongside our grieving desert God. This desert God invites us to find him where we have deserted him and to take a lingering and painful look at our other lovers. Therefore, the path of purgation punctures us, exposing the gaping holes

[37]Roberta C. Bondi, *To Pray and to Love: Conversations on Prayer with the Early Church* (Fortress, 1991).

[38]Roberta C. Bondi, *To Pray and to Love*, 34-35.

[39]Bondi, *To Pray and to Love*, 35.

[40]William Harmless, *Desert Christians: An Introduction to the Literature of Early Monasticism* (Oxford University Press, 2004)

inside us that can be filled only with the whole that is God's own self. This puncturing is not divine sadism but emerges from the womb of God's own love for us. Indeed, the prophet Joel knew it well before the poet William Butler Yeats—"Rend your *hearts* and not your clothing," for he is a gracious God of womby love (Joel 2:13).[41] Rending the heart allows God to do what the Lord longs to do in Hosea 2:14—speak to the heart of the one he loves. We are, each of us, the one God loves, and we are, each of us, invited to enter more deeply into the barren desert of God's love.

It is within this desert space itself, in fact, that we learn a grammar of faith that will sustain us there. It is to this grammar of faith that we now turn through an exploration of Psalm 63.

Questions for Reflection and Discussion

1. How does the writer of Hosea 2 use wilderness to different rhetorical ends in the two pericopes I discussed in this chapter?
2. How does the historical context of Hosea 2:1-13 help alleviate some of the emotional tensions evoked by its harsh language? Does that historical background help you feel more comfortable about that language? Why or why not?
3. How have you experienced a *Deus absconditus* (a hidden God) and a *Deus ludens* (a playful God) in your own life?

[41]Here the prophet Joel uses a cognate of the verb *rukhum*, the adjectival form *rukhum*.

8

ALEPH, BET, GIMEL, DALET, HE

Learning Our Letters and Praying with Psalm 63

In all other areas of life our own efforts and activity are crucial and we have to be thoroughly adult; but where the very heart of reality is concerned, where we stand vis-à-vis God, there we are only children. No other state is appropriate or possible.

Ruth Burrows, *Essence of Prayer*

When you pray do not try to express yourself in fancy words, for often it is the simple, repetitious phrases of a little child that our Father in heaven finds most irresistible.

John Climacus

I have taught Hebrew at the seminary and undergraduate level for almost two decades. In some ways, Hebrew is the easiest subject I teach

John Climacus, cited in Henri Nouwen, *The Way of the Heart: Connecting with God Through Prayer, Wisdom, and Silence* (Ballantine Books, 1981), 80.

because learning Hebrew elicits no painful journey of deconstruction and reconstruction of students' faith lives. I'm not teaching the Documentary Hypothesis, disputing beloved Sunday school teachers who have told them that Moses wrote the Pentateuch. I'm not reading Judges 19 with them for the first time, helping them wrestle with the violence in the Old Testament. I'm not pointing out the differences between Joshua and Judges, engaging them with scholarly theories about the Israelites' emergence in the land of Canaan.

Rather than teaching them these very adult topics, I'm helping them learn their letters instead. This means that I get to watch them become children all over again as they learn to read. I tell them that no matter how old we are or how educated we are, we become children again when we learn a new language. We have to learn our letters, struggle to pronounce things correctly, and memorize new words. I tell them all this as I hand out their first assignment—to watch a children's video in which they sing the Hebrew alphabet. They risk looking silly singing a children's song, and I risk not being taken seriously as a teacher for assigning a children's song to seminary students.

In the video, a cartoon teacher begins singing the Hebrew alphabet very slowly to cartoon students: "*Aleph*, *bet* (*vet*), *gimel*, *dalet*, *he*, *vav*, *zayin*, *khet*, *tet*," all the way through the twenty-two letters of the Hebrew alphabet. It's a silly little video that in my experience helps the Hebrew letters stick better than any other pedagogy I've tried. I still sing it in my mind whenever I flip through a Hebrew dictionary looking for a word, much in the same way we sing our ABCs to remember where a letter falls in our English alphabet.

At the beginning of the semester, before I've really proved to them that I have what it takes to teach them Hebrew, I make one more pedagogical choice that risks my being taken seriously, and that it is to include a quote from Mr. Rogers at the top of my syllabus, which I frame by saying, "About life in general, Mr. Rogers gave us this sage advice through the characters on his show":

Daniel Striped Tiger: B is for Buck, and D is for Duck.

Harriet Elizabeth Cow: Very good.

Ana Platypus: And C is for Kangaroo!

Harriet Elizabeth Cow: Um, not quite, Ana. It sounds like it might be a C, but K is for Kangaroo.

Ana Platypus: Oh! Why did I have to make that mistake?

Harriet Elizabeth Cow: *Because you're learning, dear. Everyone makes mistakes while they're learning something. In fact, everyone makes mistakes sometimes.*

We read the quote aloud in class, and I explain to them that we are going to cultivate a joyful, nonshaming environment in which we are free to learn and to make mistakes along the way. The hope is that we attach ourselves securely to one another, to the language we are learning, and, yes, to God, so that when Hebrew gets really hard (*which it does, very quickly*), we can trust the process, we can trust one another, and we can trust that the same God we encounter in our prayer closet is the God of the Hebrew language too.

Time and again, I have watched my Hebrew students learn their letters and learn to pray at the same time. The difficulty of Hebrew grammar forces students into a posture of prayer. They develop a grammar of faith as they progress through difficult intellectual terrain.

This is what the psalmists do too. And when we pray the prayers they prayed, particularly the prayers of lament, those prayers also teach us to become children again.

The Letters of Lament

Eugene Peterson describes the texture of the Psalms as both literary and sacred: "The Psalms are poetry and the Psalms are prayer: this is the texture of the text."[1] It is this very texture that allows them to be a medium of serious dialogue with God:

[1]Eugene Peterson, *Answering God: The Psalms as Tools for Prayer* (HarperOne, 1991), 11.

> This texture, the poetry and the prayer, accounts for both the excitement and difficulty in dealing with this text. The poetry requires that we deal with our actual humanity—these words dive beneath the surfaces of prose and pretense, straight into the depths. We are more comfortable with prose, the laid-back language of our arms-length discourse. The prayer requires that we deal with God—this God who is determined on nothing less than the total renovation of our lives.[2]

If we allow ourselves to participate with the work God is wanting to do in us, nowhere is this total renovation of our lives more possible than in wilderness. Indeed, when the psalmists encounter wilderness, they offer poetic prayers in the form of lament. It is in wilderness indeed that we learn our letters again, composing a grammar of faith that cultivates secure attachment to the God who loves us. Peterson notes that we learn this language within lamentation itself: "The language of prayer is forged in the crucible of trouble. When we can't help ourselves and call for help, when we don't like where we are and want out, when we don't like who we are and want a change, we use primal language, and this language becomes the root language of prayer." Peterson draws on the imagery of children and childbirth to describe how we learn to pray. Language itself "gets its start under the pressure of pain," as our first sound is a wail.[3] Our first words are not eloquent—our first words are instead a desperate cry to have our needs met.

Indeed, a child whose first language consists of nonsensical syllables and wails learns to trust a parent when that parent responds to their needs. Peterson writes:

> Language 1 is the language of personal intimacy and relationship. It is the first language we learn. At first it is not articulate speech. The sounds that pass between parent and infant are incredibly rich in meaning, but less impressive in content. The coos and cries of the infant do not parse. The nonsense syllables of the answering parent have no dictionary entries. But

[2]Peterson, *Answering God*, 12.

[3]Peterson, *Answering God*, 35.

> in the exchange of gurgles and out-of-tune hums, trust develops. Parent whispers transmute infant screams into grunts of hope. The cornerstone words in this language are names, or pet names: mama, papa. For all its limited vocabulary and butchered syntax, it is more than adequate to express complex and profound love, and to develop that basic trust foundational to human existence. Language 1 is our primary language, the language we use to express and develop our human condition.[4]

Peterson describes language two as the language of information, in which things are named and we find our place in a world of objects. Language three is the language of motivation, in which we discover that language has the power to make things happen. This is the language of advertising and politics, in which we use our words to move others. Our culture prizes these two languages, Peterson says, because these types of languages get us what we want. However, "This is fatal to prayer. Informational language is not prayer language. Motivational language is not prayer language. To pray in these languages is, in effect, not to pray. We must let the Psalms train us in prayer language—the language of intimacy, of relationship, of 'I and Thou,' of personal love."[5] Just as children learn individual words slowly over time, building their grammar, so through prayer to the God who loves us, we build a grammar of faith. The Psalter is a school that teaches us to build our own prayer grammar.

Grammar of Faith

Molly T. Marshall explains: "The psalms offer us a grammar to speak our faith. Our faith is formed by praying these searching texts. They introduced us to the One before whom all hearts are open; they offer us a way to share life more fully with God."[6] Scholars before and after Peterson describe the Psalms as a grammar of faith. Bill Bellinger provides a useful survey of scholars who have articulated the Psalms in this way.

---

[4]Peterson, *Answering God*, 37.

[5]Peterson, *Answering God*, 37-40.

[6]Molly T. Marshall, "Plowing the Soil of the Heart: The Psalter and Spirituality," *American Baptist Quarterly* 21, no. 2 (2002): 506.

Bellinger draws on Ludwig Wittgenstein's notion of theology as grammar, which suggests that grammar articulates an understanding of God. For Wittgenstein (and Bellinger), theology as grammar deals with the faith formation of persons and how they live. While this grammar forms the building blocks of our own spiritual formation, Peter Candler suggests that texts in general (and the Psalms in particular) function like maps or itineraries through a journey in which readers are invited to participate, what Candler labels a "grammar of participation." There the reader engages the text in conversation. As Bellinger explains it, "The Psalter as grammar of faith and the language of life engage each other. The grammar forms life."[7] The form this life takes is prayer, a dialogical conversation with God in which we learn to trust the God in whose image we are made. In particular, Peterson draws on the parent-child relationship to describe how this grammar prepares us for prayer:

> We learn to pray not with a grammar, but with parents. The same way we learn language. Our first professors of English, our parents, do not first teach us nouns, then verbs, and follow these up with training in adjectives and adverbs, after which we learn imperatives and subjunctives. We get language as it comes to us, a tumble and tangle of words. We swim out of the silent womb into a noisy cataract, all the parts of speech crashing noisily into our ears in seeming disorder. Gradually the morphemes find an ordered place in our mind and phonemes a coherent reproduction in our larynx and lips. The psalms are our parents, not our professors, in prayer.[8]

It is indeed training in prayer that is the purpose of the Psalms, as Bellinger attests: "So I take the opening of the book [the Psalter] to affirm that, central to its grammar of faith, the Psalter is a school of prayer."[9]

Within this school of prayer, no curriculum teaches perseverance and trust more deeply than lament. No part of the curriculum is more deeply

---

[7]W. H. Bellinger, *Psalms as a Grammar for Faith: Prayer and Praise* (Baylor University Press, 2019), 6-7.

[8]Peterson, *Answering God*, 107.

[9]Bellinger, *Psalms as a Grammar*, 24.

felt and more prevalent than the literature of lament. Indeed, there are more individual laments in the book of Psalms than any other psalm type, so much so that Bellinger and others label lament "the backbone of the Psalter." Structurally, lament psalms follow a fairly typical pattern with four moves: an address to God, a portrayal of crisis, a petition to God, and a positive conclusion. This positive conclusion comes, it seems, irrespective of whether the psalmist's situation has actually changed. Indeed, Bellinger offers that "in most cases, it appears that the crisis itself has not passed, but what has changed is the perspective of the one praying."[10]

Bellinger provides a helpful differentiation between our contemporary context and the context of the lamenting psalmist, one worth quoting in its entirety:

> The world of prayer these texts commend is rather different from the culture in which we find ourselves. We live in a culture that seeks to deny pain and death. The Psalms, in contrast, saw long before there were therapists the way to hope is through fear; the way to real joy is through depression; the way to loving one's enemies is through hostility. Not around these realities but through them. Denial leads to holding grudges, fear, and festering wounds. That is not faith. Rather, speaking boldly to the One who can act, asking God to embrace pain—that is the vision of faith in these texts. The hallmark cry of these prayers is the probing question, "How long?" It is more than venting, a cry out; it is a cry to the One who can transform life. This God is the one who accepts these raw and utterly honest prayers. What defines the people of faith—in line with the name Israel—is speaking to God, struggling with God, no matter what. The community never moves beyond the possibility of addressing this God. So, I take these prayers to be bold, liberating, frightening acts.[11]

Such acts are "frightening," to use Bellinger's word, in part because lament invites conflict into the relationship. Rather than going along as things are, pretending that we feel fine when we do not, lamentation is a type of prayer in which we protest. We protest our circumstances, we protest the length

---

[10]Bellinger, *Psalms as a Grammar*, 24, 26.

[11]Bellinger, *Psalms as a Grammar*, 47-48.

of time it is taking to hear a response from God, and at times we question whether God is with us at all. Even in a human relationship, this is a risky move, one that only pays off only if the other party is loving, trustworthy, and willing to engage our feelings honestly. As we know, sometimes this type of risk in our human relationships is not worth it; thus we maintain a status quo because the relationship cannot withstand the genuine intimacy required by conflict. To take this chance with the God of the universe is, in the context of the ancient Near East, perhaps to risk one's very life. Yet lament, or wrestling with God, is built into the grammar of Hebrew faith from its narrative founding (e.g., Gen 32:22-32). While the relational push/pull between Israel and God is there from the beginning, the psalmist still takes a fearful risk, one in which he must be certain of God's goodness irrespective of how he feels in the moment. If the psalmist could not trust God, he could not voice his lament. True lamentation—having it out with God—demonstrates both trust and attachment.

Attaching to God

Beginning in the 1940s, the field of psychology began to explore the effects on children when they experienced sustained physical or emotional separation from their primary caregivers. In particular, John Bowlby's empirical studies with children revealed that prolonged separation from parents led to protest, despair, and detachment. Bowlby's work demonstrated the necessity of relational bonds for a healthy inner and communal life, what we now know to be attachment theory.[12] Today, attachment theory postulates that at least four things are needed in order to keep an infant close to the primary caregiver. First, a child needs a secure base, which refers to the availability of the caregiver to support the child as the child explores the world. Second, a child needs to have the ability for exploration, which allows a child to explore their environment knowing that there is a secure base to which to return.

[12]Joshua J. Knabb and Matthew Y. Emerson, "I Will Be Your God and You Will Be My People: Attachment Theory and the Grand Narrative of Scripture," *Pastoral Psychology* 62, no. 6 (2013): 827.

Third, attachment behaviors refer to how a child behaves when a potentially dangerous situation arises. For example, a child may cry or yell or walk back to the primary caregiver to get their attention. Finally, a safe haven describes the ability of a child to reconnect with a caregiver after exploring their world, experiencing a deep sense of safety, calmness, and protection based on the intimate connection or attachment bond that has been created. This so-called circle of attachment never goes away.[13]

Drawing on the work of attachment theorists, Joshua J. Knabb and Matthew Y. Emerson agree:

> These four attachment components tend to take place in a circular manner, with the child first experiencing the parent as a secure base, which increases his or her confidence as she begins to explore the world, followed by attachment behaviors that seek to reunite the child with his or her secure base during times of distress, which restores the child's sense of safety and protection as he or she re-attaches to the parent.[14]

According to attachment theory, this circle of attachment recurs throughout life. The failure to experience a secure attachment with a primary caregiver can lead to emotional challenges throughout a person's life, causing a child to develop an anxious, avoidant, or shame-filled attachment style. However, in the absence of secure attachment to a primary caregiver, a child may find in God an ideal "substitute attachment figure." Knabb and Emerson argue that the four components of the attachment behavior system are evident in the biblical story of creation, in which an original attachment relationship develops between God and God's people. According to Knabb and Emerson, crying out to God and staying close to God in times of stress is part of the original, God-given design of creation. Viewing God as a "safe haven" to which to return allows us to "regulate distressing emotions and find safety, security, and solace in an unpredictable, dangerous world."[15]

---

[13]Knabb and Emerson, "I Will Be Your God," 828.
[14]Knabb and Emerson, "I Will Be Your God," 828.
[15]Knabb and Emerson, "I Will Be Your God," 828-29, 840.

Their insights provide a useful foundation for examining the relationship between David and God in Psalm 63, particularly given its setting—David in wilderness, or a time of duress.

Intimacy in the Desert in Psalm 63

In the Hebrew, the Psalter is titled Seper Tehillim, the Book of Praises. Its fivefold structure is parallel to the Pentateuch, with its five books of Torah and the five books of psalms in poetic response.[16] Psalm 63 is nestled within Book Two of the Psalter, and it is ascribed to David. Of the seventy-three psalms that are linked to David's story, thirteen refer to specific incidents in his life: Psalms 3; 7; 18; 34; 51–52; 54; 56–57; 59–60; 63; 142.[17] The superscription of Psalm 63 tells us that David is in the wilderness. Moreover, much of the vocabulary in the psalm draws on the imagery of the desert to express David's longing for God. In particular, David's experience of "thirst" amid the "dry and parched land" in which there is no water underscores David's desert location. What is not clear, however, is whether the specific wilderness sojourn refers to David's escape from Saul (1 Sam 23) or from Absalom (2 Sam 15:13-30). Robert Alter argues that David's flight from Saul is the most likely setting for the psalm.[18] Either way, as Willem A. VanGemeren notes, Psalm 63 is part of a collection of psalms that is "bound by a common concern for closeness and fellowship with the Lord."[19]

This closeness is particularly evident in Psalm 63:1-8, in which the psalmist draws on the wilderness setting to highlight his own longing. This is all the more striking when we consider that David is in wilderness because he fears for his own life. Where we might expect fear, we find desire instead. Indeed, when fear fades away, desire remains. The desert is the geographical setting that inspires the psalmist's exploration of his

[16]Bellinger, *Psalms as a Grammar*, 9.

[17]Peterson, *Answering God*, 50-51.

[18]Robert Alter, *The Book of Psalms: A Translation with Commentary* (W. W. Norton, 2009), 216.

[19]Frank E. Gaebelein et al., *The Expositor's Bible Commentary with the NIV: Psalms, Proverbs, Ecclesiastes, Song of Songs* (Zondervan, 1991), 425.

own inner landscape. The psalmist uses the first-person singular form *naphshi* ("my soul") repeatedly in his prayer (Ps 63:1, 5, 8-9), demonstrating that it is his inner life with God that most arrests his attention. While many translate *nephesh* as "soul," this body/soul duality is a Greek idea, not a Hebrew one.[20] Rather, the semantic range for *nephesh* centers on desires, appetites, emotions, and passions—in short, what animates a person and comprises their inner landscape.[21] In Hebrew thought, these realities are not separate from embodied existence but conjoin to create what the writer of Genesis calls a "living being" (Gen 2:7).

In the first usage in Psalm 63:1, the psalmist uses the word to describe the seat of his appetites, with the barren desert landscape depicting his desire for God.[22] The repetition of first-personal pronominal suffixes reveals the desperation of his desire—*naphshi* ("my whole being") and *vesari* ("my flesh"). The first-person pronominal suffix in the first three (Hebrew) words of the poem, "God, you are my God," demonstrates the ownership the psalmist feels in his relationship with God—already they are close, already there is an intimacy between them. Just as deep calls to deep (Ps 42:7), so desire calls to desire. As Henri Nouwen says, we can only seek after things we have in some sense already found.[23] God is already the psalmist's God, and it is this desire that animates the psalmist's very *nephesh*, the hunger and thirst he feels for God in this particular desert space. It is the intimate relationship between them that compels the psalmist to write, "I will seek you early" (Ps 63:1).

The original meaning of the verb *shakhar* and its noun and adjectival cognates refers to blackness, as associated with skin, hair, or, revealingly, the blackness of dawn.[24] The denominative verb used by the psalmist refers to an intense seeking or longing that begins at the darkness of the

---

[20]Such as the ESV, KJV, NASB, NKJV, NLT, NRSVUE, to name a few.

[21]F. Brown et al., *A Hebrew and English Lexicon of the Old Testament* (Oxford University Press, 1962), 659.

[22]Brown et al., *Hebrew and English Lexicon*, 660.

[23]Henri J. M. Nouwen, *The Inner Voice of Love: A Journey Through Anguish to Freedom* (Doubleday, 1996), 111.

[24]Brown et al., *Hebrew and English Lexicon*, 1007.

dawn. In Job 24:5, the author demonstrates the desperation of this seeking by connecting it to the poor who forage for food like animals in the desert: "Like wild donkeys in the desert, the poor go about their labor foraging for food; the wasteland provides food for their children" (NIV). There the barrenness of the desert landscape highlights the desperate search for sustenance, while in Psalm 63 the desert landscape highlights the psalmist's desperate search for God. The intensity of the psalmist's longing is augmented by the grammar itself.[25] The psalmist follows this train of thought, almost breathless in his longing, by saying, "my inner being longs for you," with the *hapax legomenon* best rendered "faint with desire."[26]

That the psalmist is capable of fainting with desire rather than shrinking from fear suggests an intimacy and relationality with God forged earlier in the psalmist's life. Psalm 63:2 implies as much, when he relays his desire is to behold the power and glory of God: "As I have seen you in the sanctuary." This phrasing suggests a relationality built up over time, a rhythm of religious life in which the psalmist has experienced the power and glory of God throughout his life. Though he is faced with the possibility of death, the emotions of the psalmist are regulated when he considers that the "steadfast love" of God is better than even his own life (Ps 63:3). He is able to move to praise because the character and goodness of God have already been established through the *hesed* ("covenant lovingkindness") displayed by God in the context of their covenantal relationship. When the psalmist prays, "your steadfast love is better than life," he does so resting secure in the love he shares with God. Indeed, that is the very fabric of *hesed*—that two are attached to each other.

In Psalm 63:5, the psalmist again returns to the picture of his inner being when he says, "my soul will be satisfied as with marrow and fatness." The phrase is a metaphor for the joy, greatness, and beneficence associated with the love of the Lord.[27] What emerges here is a picture of

[25]Here the Hebrew writer uses the *piel* imperfect form *ashakharekka*.

[26]Gaebelein et al., *Expositor's Bible Commentary*, 426. The Hebrew is rendered *napshi kamah leka*.

[27]Gaebelein et al., *Expositor's Bible Commentary*, 427.

life with God that is rooted not in fear or pacifying an angry deity but a joyfulness in their shared life together. It is a joyfulness expressed by the characters in Fyodor Dostoevsky's novel *The Brothers Karamazov*, in which they discuss Jesus' miracle at Cana in John 2: "Ah yes, I've been missing it and I didn't want to miss it. I love that passage: it's Cana of Galilee, the first miracle. . . . Ah, that miracle, ah that lovely miracle! Not grief, but men's joy Christ visited when he worked his first miracle, he helped men's joy. . . . He who loves men, loves their joy.'"[28] Likewise, the psalmist can offer the praise of "joyful lips" (Ps 63:5) because he rests secure in God's love and in their shared love that is a bountiful table—as the NIV renders it, "the richest of foods."

In Psalm 63:6, the psalmist returns to the theme of longing in the wilderness through the picture of waiting for God in the watches of the night. The rituals of watching in the Old Testament are embedded in the phrase "in the night watches," with the Hebrew root *shamar* dealing with guarding or keeping, suggesting an ongoing activity. According to Old Testament practice, the night was divided into three watches of four hours each (see Judg 7:19; 1 Sam 11:11; Lam 2:19).[29] That this practice was ongoing in the life of the psalmist is suggested both by the root *shamar* and by the two verbs "I will remember you" and "I will meditate on you."[30] The plaintive nature of the psalmist's recollection of God and hope for God's presence is underscored by the semantic range of the verb *hagah*, which refers to moaning, growling, uttering, speaking, or musing. When described of animals, the word is used to convey inarticulate sounds, such as the growl of a lion over its prey or moaning in distress like a dove.[31] The psalmist hides in the wilderness from his enemies, moaning for the God whom he has already learned to trust in the watches of the night.

---

[28]Fyodor Dostoevsky, *The Brothers Karamazov*, bicentennial ed. (Picador, 1990), 382.

[29]Gaebelein et al., *Expositor's Bible Commentary*, 427.

[30]The former is rendered in the *qal* perfect first-person common singular with a second-person masculine singular pronominal suffix (*zekartika*). The latter is in the *qal* imperfect first-person common singular set in relationship to the *bet* preposition with a second-person masculine singular pronominal suffix (*ehgeh bak*).

[31]Brown et al., *Hebrew and English Lexicon*, 211.

In Psalm 63:7, he returns to the theme of joy, and again his joy is rooted in the spiritual history he shares with God: "Because you *have been* my help." Used first in the biblical text in noun form to describe the strong, supporting role of Eve to Adam (Gen 2:18), the Hebrew root *zr* is typically used of the strong succor provided by God for his people. The psalmist can look back on his life with God knowing that God has been a bulwark of protection for him in the past and therefore trust in his protection in his present distress. Beyond the strengthening support of God, in Psalm 63:7 the psalmist also points to the emotional support and closeness of the God who loves him: "And in the shadow of your wings I will sing for joy." In Psalm 63:8, the psalmist again references the inner landscape of his life when he proclaims, "My inner being clings/attaches to you." Taken together, the metaphor of the wing or skirt of God and the psalmist's clinging paints a strong picture of attachment, particularly when considering the wilderness in which the psalm is situated.

Attaching to God in the Wilderness

Peterson describes the Psalms as an example of "the demanding interiorizing of faith."[32] There is no other inner landscape that tests whether we have interiorized the faith more than our experience of wilderness. In this way, wilderness is an inner landscape of grace, one that forms us into children before a divine Parent. Left-brained memorization of Bible verses or mental assent to doctrine, however praiseworthy an endeavor, does not interiorize our faith. Only our experiences of God, built up over time, can do that. When we find security and safety in the God who has loved us well in all seasons of our lives, we activate our right brain, the emotional and affective center of our inner lives. Recalling the story of God's love for us and emotional care for us, and sitting with the feelings that arouses, can help us make it through the wilderness. Doctrine does not securely attach us to God; *affective*, felt experience with

[32]Peterson, *Answering God*, 55.

God alone can do that. This is why exegetical sermons may stimulate us intellectually but leave us emotionally barren. Like the psalmist, we need to feel felt by the God who understands us, loves us, and knows us. That reality alone will sustain us in the wilderness. It is in fact the shaping work of God in wilderness that both tests and strengthens our emotional attachment to God.

As noted above, attachment relationships are ones in which a child looks to a caregiver to provide two primary things: a haven of safety in times of distress and a secure base from which to explore the world. These two aspects of secure attachment create a "cycle of security" that a child can experience throughout their life. The child experiences "increased safety, comfort, and relief from distress and learns through such repeated experiences that she can count on her mother (or other attachment figures) to provide this if she encounters distress."[33] This cycle of security creates a bond, an attachment, that enables a child to rest secure in the physical proximity and emotional attunement of a parent.

Todd W. Hall argues there is significant evidence that Christians become attached to God and experience God as an attachment figure, with attachment researchers noting that God fits the definition of an attachment figure. Highlighting the profoundly relational nature of God, Hall notes that God loves us in all the loving ways articulated in the New Testament: *agapē* (self-emptying and overflowing), *philia* (friendship), *erōs* (longing), and *storgē* (parental affection). Hall claims that the "prototypical expression" of God's love is parental affection or "attachment love."[34]

The spiritual history described by the psalmist—the recollection of beholding God's power and glory in the sanctuary and the meditation of God on the psalmist's bed during the watches of the night—demonstrates that God has been a secure base in times past. As a result, God is a safe haven to which the psalmist returns in the geographical and spiritual wilderness in which he finds himself. It is this cycle of security

[33]Todd W. Hall and M. Elizabeth Lewis Hall, *Relational Spirituality: A Psychological-Theological Paradigm for Transformation* (IVP Academic, 2021), 139.

[34]Hall and Hall, *Relational Spirituality*, 144, 67.

that produces rest for the psalmist, with Psalm 63 labeled "A Psalm of Trust." God is the parental figure to which the psalmist is attached.

Krispin Mayfield describes secure attachment as a "cozy cabin" to which we know we can return again and again. We carry the key in our pocket and know we can return there if we need to. Mayfield writes: "In secure relationships, we know we belong in the cozy cabin, and there's no unease when we're there, no striving or earning our keep. We are delighted in for who we are, not for what we've done—or for who we could be."[35] In Psalm 63, the imagery is not of a cozy cabin but of the sanctuary: "So I have looked upon you in the sanctuary, beholding your power and glory" (Ps 63:2 ESV), the grammar suggesting an action completed in the past but which he can return to in his mind.[36] For the psalmist, God is the deep emotional center that holds him fast in emotional distress, the inner sanctuary to which he can return. The sanctuary serves as the secure base, and God himself is the safe haven in the psalmist's present wilderness.

Writing about another of David's poems, Curt Thompson describes the emotional experience between David and God in this way:

> The poem expresses David's anguish, followed by his deep awareness of God's deliverance. He *feels felt* by God—God has heard his weeping, recognized his cry and responded, so the child feels accepted. . . . This does not happen as a result of the writer's simple assent to a new set of facts; rather he experiences an existential shift that occurs because a need has been met. This exemplifies the psalmist's mentalizing God as one who considers him, who compassionately responds to his distress.[37]

This emotional history between God and the psalmist allows him to experience wilderness differently.

Because the psalmist has cultivated trust in this relational God—indeed, he begins his prayer in this way ("God, you are my God" in

---

[35]Krispin Mayfield, *Attached to God* (Zondervan, 2022), 16.
[36]*Khazitika* is in the *qal* perfect tense.
[37]Curt Thompson, *Anatomy of the Soul* (Tyndale, 2010), 151-52.

Ps 63:1)—where we expect to find fear in the wilderness, we find joy instead. There is a mutual delight between God and the psalmist, a joy present in them both. Prayer itself becomes a place of rest. The psalmist's prayer is not riddled with anxiety, guilt, or fear, nor is it a performance of perfectionistic piety. Prayer is instead a place of desire and joy. The desert of the psalmist's longing is met with bounty, not scarcity, as with "the richest of foods," demonstrating that God really can prepare a table in the desert (Ps 78:19). As a result, the psalm blurs the genre boundary between lament and thanksgiving, containing elements of lamentation but with clear moments of trust, thanksgiving, and praise. Likewise, the wilderness teaches us both to lament and to praise. We learn that God accepts and understands both in equal measure. When the psalmist cries out because of the vagaries of desert life, he can expect to find in God what he has always found—a safe haven and a secure base, an inner sanctuary to which he can return.

Prayer is the grammatical expression of our faith and of our longing, the first language we learn as children. Paradoxically, it is the return to this first language that demonstrates both childlike trust and a growing, mature faith. And it is our experiences of wilderness that most bring these postures into tension with each other—the childlike trust needed for the desert and the maturity to withstand it. We can explore the world and withstand its vagaries, our desert wanderings, because we have attached securely through prayer to the God who loves us. When we rest securely in God's love for us, as the psalmist does, we are free to go out and explore the world—leave home, get on the plane, do the scary and exciting thing—and we are safe to return to our inner sanctuary where God dwells when the wilderness encroaches.

This cycle of safety creates a connective tissue in which we are bound closely to God. It is this very closeness that demonstrates the psalmist as securely attached to God at the moment of his crisis in the wilderness. It is, after all, moments of crisis that test our closeness to God and demonstrate whether our attachment is secure or insecure. It is also in wilderness that God draws especially close, giving the believer a felt sense of his nearness. The psalmist represents what secure attachment to God looks like in wilderness—he is able to rest secure despite the enemies who encroach (Ps 63:9-11). It his experience of God in this very desert, in fact, that causes an overflow of devotion to the God he beseeches.

This overflow of devotion allows him to focalize the "steadfast love" of God, which is better than life (Ps 63:3). The love the psalmist ascribes to God is the same type of love Hall identifies as "attachment love." According to Hall, an attachment bond creates a disposition in a parent who loves a child for no other reason than the bond they share. Attachment love has nothing to do with a child being "likable, loveable, cooperative, or reciprocating." It is this felt sense of God's unconditional love that nurtures the spiritual formation of the believer. Hall puts it this way: "God is a community of love who has existed throughout all eternity, and God invites us to participate in this very love by receiving it and then passing it on to others. As we do this, we are loved into loving." Put another way, secure attachment to God allows us to offer ourselves to others through "the art of loving presence," the cultivation of a heart of empathy and responsiveness to need.[38] When we remember that spiritual formation is the process of being conformed to the image of Christ *for the sake of others*, we remember that God's vision for our transformation is not for us alone—it is for the transformation of the community of which we are a part.[39]

Hesychastic Prayer as Spiritual Practice

It is indeed with the hope of transformation that desert Christians prayed the *hesychasm*, the prayer of rest. Inspired by the prayer of the publican in Luke's Gospel (Lk 18:9-14), the hesychasm is also known as the prayer of the heart. In prayer, we descend from our mind into our

---

[38]Hall and Hall, *Relational Spirituality*, 185-86, 205-24.

[39]M. Robert Mulholland, *Invitation to a Journey: A Road Map for Spiritual Formation* (InterVarsity Press, 1993), 15.

heart and pray, "Lord Jesus Christ, Son of God, have mercy on me, a sinner." A word that means "stillness" or "rest," *hesychasm* is a childlike prayer in which we are invited to, as Henri Nouwen has said of prayer generally, "denounce self-made props and trust that God is enough."[40] The desert fathers and desert mothers prayed the hesychasm when temptations in the desert assailed them. Such a prayer is fundamental to our spiritual formation in the desert—the acknowledgment that we are dependent on the God of the desert to save and to sustain us. Contemporary Christians may likewise find in the prayer of the heart a retreat into an inner desert in which we are nourished, alone, by the God who loves us.

In the end, if there is a purpose to wilderness at all—it is for the sake of spiritual formation.

Questions for Reflection and Discussion

1. What are the elements of secure attachment? Do you understand yourself securely attached to God?
2. How has God invited you to develop your own grammar of faith?
3. What is the tension between joy and lamentation in Psalm 63?

[40]Nouwen, *Inner Voice of Love*, 5.

Conclusion

SPIRITUAL FORMATION IN THE DESERT

Thus says the Lord:
The people who survived the sword
found grace in the wilderness.

Jeremiah 31:2 NRSVUE

How is our spiritual formation, defined by Robert Mulholland as "the process of being conformed to the image of Christ for the sake of others," related to our wilderness experiences?[1] That is the last word I would like to offer in the wilderness, yet it is far from the final word that could be offered there.

I would like to begin with a reflection on Mulholland's final word, *others*. Spiritual formation and wilderness are related in part through our language—how we speak *about* God and *to* other people. We are sometimes unintentionally cruel when we attempt to assuage the pain of people's wilderness experiences. By offering pastoral pablum, such as

[1]M. Robert Mulholland, *Invitation to a Journey: A Road Map for Spiritual Formation* (InterVarsity Press, 1993), 15.

"Everything happens for a reason," a phrase gratefully deconstructed by Kate Bowler, we run the risk of acting like Job's friends, who receive rebuke from God: "You have not spoken of me what is right" (Job 42:7).[2] Such a forthright censure ought to serve as a sober reminder that God takes the suffering of his children seriously and that we ought to take seriously how to speak about God's role in that suffering (and frankly, whether to speak about it at all).

As I understand the book of Job, God does not tolerate well the theological musings of seminarians who have not yet engaged the real world, those for whom dogma is a round peg aggressively wedged into the square hole of people's actual lives. Neither does God brook our own forcing of black-and-white statements onto a gray world. However earnestly it is packaged, theological dogma devoid of human consideration is cruelty. If we love the text more than the Author of that text or the people for whom that text is given, we have not really loved at all. So, we are wise to proceed with caution whenever we attempt to speak about God and the wilderness of people's suffering at all. We are lucky inheritors of a biblical text that does not romanticize wilderness or offer glib reflections on its devastating effects. We need not romanticize the wilderness, because the biblical account does not. The book of Numbers describes it honestly—in the wilderness, just about everybody dies. If I take the biblical text as a whole, the best I can say about it all is that sometimes, there is grace in the wilderness. After all is said and done, I suppose grace is as good a place as any to end. Grace is in fact the beginning and ending point for our spiritual formation in all seasons. In the wilderness, however, grace is another word for Mulholland's penultimate phrase, "to the image of Christ."

Thus, part of our spiritual formation in the wilderness involves taking a good long look at the image of Christ we hold in our hearts and minds. Our exploration in the wilderness, both the biblical text and the text of our own lives, is a reminder that we cannot straitjacket God or the grace

[2]Kate Bowler, *Everything Happens for a Reason: And Other Lies I've Loved* (Random House, 2019).

of God into just one reality. The only thing God appears to be bound by is the particularity of our own lives, and I am not so sure God is even bound by that. I suppose, in fact, that the freeing of God to be Godself is one kind of grace, one we actually give to ourselves. In the wilderness, we are invited to take a good long look at God. I find that this is a lot of what we do in spiritual direction—we begin to relinquish the images of God that can no longer be wedged into the spiritual geography of our lives. Henri Nouwen said as much when he wrote that the Jesus of his youth had died.[3] The truth of the matter is that there *are* certain Jesuses that need to die with us in the wilderness. I cannot name those Jesuses for anyone other than myself and must ask myself every once in a while *which Jesus* I have accepted, as I learned in my growing-up years, "as my personal Lord and Savior."

If the Jesus I have accepted, the Christ to whom I am being conformed, is one who is always fault-finding, always angry with me, always using punishment as the final word in the wilderness, then that Jesus is decidedly *not* the Christ of the gospel. That God is not even the God of the prophets, those mouthpieces for the God of the desert. When the prophets spoke of judgment at the wilderness's edge, they maintained the hope of salvation as the wilderness's redemptive center. If there is anything I have learned as a spiritual director, it is that our theologies and our spiritual anthropologies are intertwined. If I hold on to an image of a God who uses wilderness as corporal punishment, I become a person who feels I must always perform before God or be perfect for God to truly love me. The spiritual disciplines, those very means of grace by which I am positioned to feel God's love, become for me places as dry as the very desert in which I find myself. Rather than ushering me into the presence of the God who loves me in the desert, I am beholden to them and begrudging of them as a means to secure safety before a God I have created in my mind who is always disappointed in me.

[3]Henri Nouwen, *The Inner Voice of Love: A Journey Through Anguish to Freedom* (Doubleday, 1996), 37.

Over time, I become a person who is insecurely attached to a God I cannot possibly love but whom I can only approach with the ambivalence of one who has learned always to be afraid, tentative, walking on eggshells. So I find, try as I might, I can never truly love this God—I can only fear this God. Consequently, I live with a picture of myself that is very small—constricted—always needing to be perfect—and I discover that if I continue to hold on to that picture of myself, I will never be free. And neither will God. Thus, I need to be very sure that the God of the desert to whom I am being conformed is truly the Christ of the gospel. Perhaps, like the Israelites, I will need a Moses, a midwife of the word, who can help me move God from the gnarled edges to the redemptive center of my wilderness story. Someone who can help me see that the spiritual disciplines are the life-giving manna God provides for me there. Or an Isaiah, who can remind me that if I have survived the sword of the wilderness's discipline, I will find grace there too. God lets us decide for ourselves whether the God of the desert can be trusted. This too is an act of grace.

The heart of grace in the wilderness is captured by Mulholland's first phrase, "being conformed." There is something about the wilderness that leads to humility, to the scorching of the earth of the false self. The wilderness teaches us to talk less, because we realize we don't have many answers, and to listen more to the God who has them all. While the book of Numbers recounts the actual deaths of the Israelites in the wilderness, there is a spiritual death we experience there. We know from Mulholland, and perhaps the spiritual biography of our own life, that this being conformed is a process. For this reason, we are wise to heed the words of Teilhard de Chardin:

> Above all, trust in the slow work of God. We are quite naturally impatient in everything to reach the end without delay. We should like to skip the intermediate stages. We are impatient of being on the way to something unknown, something new. And yet it is the law of all progress that it is made by passing through some stages of instability—and that it may take

> a very long time. And so I think it is with you; your ideas mature gradually—let them grow, let them shape themselves, without undue haste. Don't try to force them on, as though you could be today what time (that is to say, grace and circumstances acting on your own good will) will make of you tomorrow. Only God could say what this new spirit gradually forming within you will be. Give Our Lord the benefit of believing that his hand is leading you, and accept the anxiety of feeling yourself in suspense and incomplete.[4]

So many of the key words in de Chardin's humble word are descriptors for wilderness—"something unknown, something new," the new person, the greater Christ in us, the hope of glory, formed out of the crucible of the wilderness; "the intermediate stages," surely a picture of the liminality of the wilderness; "stages of instability," a descriptor of the unmooring we feel there; and the "anxiety" of "feeling yourself in suspense and incomplete," the knowledge that there are many different kinds of wildernesses we will inhabit throughout our lives, each of them disciplining and shaping through their silence. It is an inescapable reality that one of the deep graces of the wilderness is a textured life, and out of the silence of suffering we are given something worthwhile to say. In the end, we find that there is grace in the wilderness of our own *becoming.*

---

[4]Michael Harter, ed., *Hearts on Fire. Praying with Jesuits* (Loyola Press, 2005).

ACKNOWLEDGMENTS

FOR A LONG time now, I have made a habit of writing the date and place where I lived in the front cover of every book I read. To write my own book, I returned to an old literary companion, Thomas Merton's *Thoughts in Solitude*. When I opened it, I read the words I had written on the inside cover, "Wilderness Wandering, 2012." My scribbles inside the front cover reveal, first, that I read that book during the initial years of my doctorate, when I lived in snowy New Jersey, far away from my Alabama home, and, second, that I have been thinking about the topic of wilderness for a long time. In the fourteen years between first reading *Thoughts in Solitude* and the publishing of *God in the Desert*, much has happened in my life. This means that a lot of people have contributed, directly or indirectly, to the writing of this book.

It would be impossible for me to name all those people, so I will acknowledge just a few of them. In spring 2021, my students at Baylor University took a Hebrew class with me in which we translated the wilderness passages of the Old Testament. My students' commitment to the intellectual rigor of the language itself, coupled with their vulnerability and nurture of one another, reminded me that our experiences in higher education can transform us. Two years later, my students at Baptist Seminary of Kentucky acted as guinea pigs for a new elective course, God in the Desert: Spiritual Formation in the Old Testament, which sparked many of the ideas in this book. Those students contributed deeply to my thinking about the subject, and I am grateful.

In 2022, I published a trade book on wilderness through Cascade, *Hope in the Wilderness: Spiritual Reflections for When God Feels Far Away.* That book was my own personal story of six years living in Texas and my subsequent move back to Alabama. The book you hold in your hands would not have been possible without that first book. I offer a hearty and belated thanks to my dear friend and editor, Michael Thomson, who brought that first book into publication.

My own teachers in biblical studies and spiritual formation are the intellectual and spiritual foundation on which I think, write, and pray. They are wise guides, and I would not be here without them. Here are a few of their names: Norfleete Day, my spiritual formation professor in divinity school, to whom this book is dedicated; Robert Smith Jr., who continues to teach me what it looks like to love the Lord; Ken Mathews, who taught my first and most treasured Old Testament classes in divinity school; Danna Nolan Fewell and Kenneth Ngwa, my doctoral professors in Hebrew Bible, whose winsome pedagogy has taught me not only to see the text but to see the persons reading the text; my pastor Gary Furr, who set aside an hour a week to listen to my own wilderness wanderings during my final two years of doctoral work; the many retreat leaders and teachers at the Upper Room Academy for Spiritual Formation, who spent three years helping me integrate biblical studies and spiritual formation; Angela Reed and Ben Simpson, who trained me as a spiritual director; and my own spiritual director, Beth Kilpatrick, who is the kind of person who pulls over on the side of the road on a cross-country trip to do direction with me. Each of these individuals has helped me listen better to God, to other people, and to texts.

My editors at InterVarsity Press agreed to publish this interdisciplinary and admittedly odd little book. Rachel Hastings believed in the worth of the subject and helped me get a green light for the manuscript. She then promptly fired me as her author so that she could, happily, become my boss at IVP instead. Rebecca Carhart-Mader took over as editor of the project and has helped shape it into what it is now. I took one look at her, adored her immediately, and mentally linked arms with her in my mind, confident she would let me be her friend.

Jon Boyd, Zachary Gordon, and Alberto Bonilla-Giovanetti have all contributed to the book in wonderful ways, and I am grateful for their collegiality and especially for their friendship. I am elated to be on the IVP Academic team.

Finally, all my students, past and present, whose insights, friendship, laughter, and prayers have shaped my life and work, thanks for letting me sit with you.

BIBLIOGRAPHY

Allen, William Frances, Charls Pickard Ware, and Lucy McKim Garrison. *Slave Songs of the United States: The Classic 1867 Anthology.* Dover, 1995.

Alter, Robert. *The Book of Psalms: A Translation with Commentary.* W. W. Norton, 2009.

Beeby, H. D. *Hosea: Grace Abounding; A Commentary on the Book of Hosea.* International Theological Commentary. Eerdmans, 1989.

Bellinger, W. H. *Psalms as a Grammar for Faith: Prayer and Praise.* Baylor University Press, 2019.

Boa, Kenneth. *Conformed to His Image: Biblical and Practical Approaches to Spiritual Formation.* Zondervan, 2001.

Boer, Paul A., ed. *The Essential St. John of the Cross: Ascent of Mount Carmel, Dark Night of the Soul, A Spiritual Canticle, Twenty Poems.* Wilder, 2008.

Boersma, Hans. *Pierced by Love: Divine Reading with the Christian Tradition.* Lexham, 2023.

Boersma, Hans. *Scripture as Real Presence: Sacramental Exegesis in the Early Church.* Baker Academic, 2017.

Bondi, Roberta C. *To Pray and to Love: Conversations on Prayer with the Early Church.* Fortress, 1991.

Bowler, Kate. *Everything Happens for a Reason: And Other Lies I've Loved.* Random House, 2019.

Brown, F., S. R. Driver, and C. A. Briggs. *A Hebrew and English Lexicon of the Old Testament.* Oxford University Press, 1962.

Brueggemann, Walter. "The Liturgy of Abundance, the Myth of Scarcity." *The Christian Century*, March 24, 1999.

Brueggemann, Walter. *Spirituality of the Psalms.* Fortress, 2001.

Brueggemann, Walter. *A Wilderness Zone.* Cascade Books, 2021.

Buechner, Frederick. *Beyond Words: Daily Readings in the ABC's of Faith.* HarperOne, 2004.

Buechner, Frederick. *Secrets in the Dark: A Life in Sermons.* HarperOne, 2006.

Buechner, Frederick. *Telling the Truth: The Gospel as Tragedy, Comedy, and Fairy Tale.* Harper & Row, 1977.

Burt, Noel Forlini. *Encounters in the Dark: Identity Formation in the Jacob Story*. Semeia Studies. SBL Press, 2020.

Burt, Noel Forlini. *Hope in the Wilderness: Spiritual Reflections for When God Feels Far Away*. Cascade, 2022.

Burt, Noel Forlini. "To Do You Good in the End: The Wilderness Experience in Israel's Communal Memory (Deut. 8)." In *Biblical and Theological Visions of Resilience: Pastoral and Clinical Insights*, edited by Christopher C. H. Cook and Nathan H. White. Routledge New Critical Thinking in Religion, Theology, and Biblical Studies. Routledge, 2019.

Calhoun, Adele Ahlberg. *Spiritual Disciplines Handbook: Practices That Transform Us*. Rev. and expanded ed. InterVarsity Press, 2015.

Canham, Elizabeth. *Heart Whispers: Benedictine Wisdom for Today*. Upper Room, 1999.

Carr, David. *Holy Resilience: The Bible's Traumatic Origins*. Yale University Press, 2014.

Chesterton, G. K. *Orthodoxy: With Annotations and Guided Reading*. B&H, 2022.

Chryssavgis, John. *In the Heart of the Desert: The Spirituality of the Desert Fathers and Mothers*. Rev. ed. World Wisdom, 2008.

Climacus, John. *The Ladder of Divine Ascent*. The Classics of Western Spirituality. Paulist Press, 1988.

Cohn, Robert L. *The Shape of Sacred Space: Four Biblical Studies*. Scholars Press, 1981.

Dearman, Andrew J. *The Book of Hosea*. New International Commentary on the Old Testament. Eerdmans, 2010.

Dickinson, Emily. *Hope Is the Thing with Feathers: The Complete Poems of Emily Dickinson*. Gibbs Smith, 2019.

Dillard, Annie. *Teaching a Stone to Talk: Expeditions and Encounters*. Harper Perennial, 2013.

Dostoevsky, Fyodor. *The Brothers Karamazov*. Bicentennial ed. Picador, 1990.

Douglass, Frederick. *Narrative of the Life of Frederick Douglass: An American Slave Written by Himself*. Belknap, 1960.

Dozeman, Thomas B. "The Wilderness and Salvation History in the Hagar Story." *Journal of Biblical Literature* 117, no. 1 (1998): 23-43.

Eckhart, Meister. *The Essential Sermons, Commentaries, Treatises, and Defense*. Paulist Press, 1981.

Eckhart, Meister. *Predigt 10. In Meister Eckhart: Teacher and Preacher*. Edited by Bernard McGinn. Paulist Press, 1986.

Exum, Cheryl J. *Fragmented Women: Feminist (Sub)versions of Biblical Narratives*. JSOT Press, 1993.

Felder, Cain Hope, ed. *Stony the Road We Trod: African American Biblical Interpretation*. Fortress, 1991.

Fewell, Danna Nolan. *The Children of Israel: Reading the Bible for the Sake of Our Children.* Abingdon, 2003.

Fewell, Danna Nolan, and David M. Gunn. *Gender, Power, and Promise: The Subject of the Bible's First Story.* Abingdon, 1993.

Foster, Richard J. *Celebration of Discipline: The Path to Spiritual Growth.* 25th anniversary ed. HarperSanFrancisco, 1998.

Franke, William, ed. *On What Cannot Be Said: Apophatic Discourses in Philosophy, Religion, Literature, and the Arts.* Vol. 1. University of Notre Dame Press, 2007.

Gaebelein, Frank E., et al. *The Expositor's Bible Commentary with the NIV: Psalms, Proverbs, Ecclesiastes, Song of Songs.* Zondervan, 1991.

Gossai, Hemchand. *Power and Marginality in the Abraham Narrative.* 2nd ed. Pickwick, 2010.

Gregory of Nyssa. *The Life of Moses.* Translated by A. J. Malherbe and E. Ferguson. The Classics of Western Spirituality: A Library of the Great Spiritual Masters. Paulist Press, 1978.

Guigo II. *The Ladder of Monks.* In *A Letter on the Contemplative Life and Twelve Meditations*, translated by Edmund College and James Walsh. Cistercian Publications, 1981.

Hagberg, Janet O., and Robert A. Guelich. *The Critical Journey: Stages in the Life of Faith.* 2nd ed. Sheffield, 2005.

Hall, Christopher A. *Reading Scripture with the Church Fathers.* InterVarsity Press, 1998.

Hall, Todd W., and M. Elizbeth Lewis Hall. *Relational Spirituality: A Psychological-Theological Paradigm for Transformation.* IVP Academic, 2021.

Harmless, William. *Desert Christians: An Introduction to the Literature of Early Monasticism.* Oxford University Press, 2004.

Harter, Michael, ed. *Hearts on Fire: Praying with Jesuits.* Loyola Press, 2005.

Hauser, Alan J., and Russell Gregory. *From Carmel to Horeb: Elijah in Crisis.* Sheffield Academic Press, 1990.

Hendel, Ronald, Chana Kronfeld, and Ilana Pardes. "Gender and Sexuality." In *Reading Genesis: Ten Methods*, edited by Ronald Hendel. Cambridge University Press, 2010.

Hoare, Liz. *Using the Bible in Spiritual Direction.* Morehouse, 2016.

Holberg, Jennifer L. *Nourishing Narratives: The Power of Story to Shape Our Faith.* IVP Academic, 2023.

Jerome. *Select Letters.* Translated by F. A. Wright. Loeb Classical Library. Harvard University Press, 1933.

John of the Cross. *The Essential St. John of the Cross.* Wilder, 2008.

Johns, Cheryl Bridges. *Re-Enchanting the Text: Discovering the Bible as Sacred, Dangerous, and Mysterious.* Baker Academic, 2023.

Jones, W. Paul. *The Art of Spiritual Direction: Giving and Receiving Spiritual Guidance.* Upper Room Books, 2002.

Kempis, Thomas à. *The Imitation of Christ*. In *The Consolation of Philosophy*. Random House, 1943.

Kessler, John. *Between Hearing and Silence: A Study of Old Testament Theology*. Baylor University Press, 2021.

Knabb, Joshua J., and Matthew Y. Emerson. "I Will Be Your God and You Will Be My People: Attachment Theory and the Grand Narrative of Scripture." *Pastoral Psychology* (2013): 827-41.

Laird, Martin. *Into the Silent Land: A Guide to the Christian Practice of Contemplation*. Oxford University Press, 2006.

Laird, Martin. *A Sunlit Absence: Silence, Awareness, and Contemplation*. Oxford University Press, 2011.

Lamott, Anne. *Bird by Bird: Some Instructions on Writing and Life*. Vintage Books, 1995.

Lamott, Anne. *Dusk Night Dawn: On Revival and Courage*. Riverhead Books, 2021.

Lamott, Anne. *Help, Thanks, Wow*. Riverhead Books, 2012.

Landy, Francis. "In the Wilderness of Speech: Problems of Metaphor in Hosea." *Biblical Interpretation* 3, no. 1 (1995): 35-59.

Lane, Belden C. *The Solace of Fierce Landscapes: Exploring Desert and Mountain Spirituality*. Oxford University Press, 1998.

Leal, Robert Barry. *Wilderness in the Bible: Toward a Theology of Wilderness*. Studies in Biblical Literature 72. Peter Lang, 2004.

Lee, Jerena. "Religious Experience and Journal." In *Spiritual Narratives*, ed. Henry Louis Gates Jr. Oxford University Press, 1988.

L'Engle, Madeleine. *A Stone for a Pillow: Journeys with Jacob*. The Genesis Trilogy. Convergent Books, 2017.

Lim, Bo H., and Daniel Castelo. *Hosea*. Two Horizons Old Testament Commentary. Eerdmans, 2015.

Louth, Andrew. *The Wilderness of God*. Abingdon, 1997.

Lutheran Book of Worship. Augsburg, 1978.

MacDonald, George. *Diary of an Old Soul*. Augsburg, 1975.

Marshall, Molly T. "Plowing the Soil of the Heart: The Psalter and Spirituality." *American Baptist Quarterly* (2003).

Mayfield, Krispin. *Attached to God*. Zondervan, 2022.

McGinn, Bernard, ed. *The Essential Writings of Christian Mysticism*. Random House, 2006.

McGinn, Bernard. "Ocean and Desert as Symbols of Mystical Absorption in the Christian Tradition." *The Journal of Religion* 74, no. 2 (1994): 155-81.

McIntosh, Mark A. *Mystical Theology*. Challenges in Contemporary Theology. Blackwell, 1998.

Merton, Thomas. *Bread in the Wilderness*. New Directions, 1953.

Merton, Thomas. *Collected Poems*. New Directions, 1946.

Merton, Thomas. *The Sign of Jonas*. Harcourt, Brace, 1953.

Merton, Thomas. *Thoughts in Solitude*. Farrar, Straus & Giroux, 1956.

Merton, Thomas. *The Wisdom of the Desert*. New Directions Books, 1960.

Mulholland, M. Robert. *Invitation to a Journey: A Road Map for Spiritual Formation*. InterVarsity Press, 1993.

Mulholland, M. Robert. *Shaped by the Word: The Power of Scripture in Spiritual Formation*. Rev. ed. Upper Room, 2001.

Nault, Jean-Charles, OSB. *The Noonday Devil: Acedia, the Unnamed Evil of Our Times*. Ignatius, 2015.

Nouwen, Henri J. M. *The Inner Voice of Love: A Journey Through Anguish to Freedom*. Doubleday, 1996.

Nouwen, Henri J. M. *Life of the Beloved: Spiritual Living in a Secular World*. Crossroad, 1992.

Nouwen, Henri J. M. *The Road to Daybreak: A Spiritual Journey*. Image Books, 1988.

Nouwen, Henri J. M. *The Way of the Heart: Connecting with God Through Prayer, Wisdom, and Silence*. Ballantine Books, 1981.

Ochs, Carol. *Song of the Self: Biblical Spirituality and Human Holiness*. Trinity Press International, 1994.

Oliver, Mary. *Devotions: The Selected Poems of Mary Oliver*. Penguin Books, 2017.

Otto, Rudolf. *The Idea of the Holy*. Oxford University Press, 1923.

Owens, L. Roger. *Abba, Give Me a Word: The Path of Spiritual Direction*. Paraclete, 2012.

Palmer, Parker J. *Let Your Life Speak: Listening for the Voice of Vocation*. Jossey-Bass, 2000.

Palmer, Parker J. *To Know as We Are Known: Education as Spiritual Journey*. HarperSanFrancisco, 1983.

Peterson, Eugene H. *Answering God: The Psalms as Tools for Prayer*. HarperOne, 1991.

Peterson, Eugene H. *Eat This Book: A Conversation in the Art of Spiritual Reading*. Eerdmans, 2009.

Ponticus, Evagrius. *The Praktikos and Chapters on Prayer*. Cistercian Publications, 1981.

Pseudo-Dionysius. *Pseudo-Dionysius: The Complete Works*. Translated by Colm Luibheid. Paulist Press, 1987.

Reed, Angela H., Richard R. Osmer, and Marcus G. Smucker. *Spiritual Companioning: A Guide to Protestant Theology and Practice*. Baker Academic, 2015.

Reisner, Noam. "Silence and Presence: Ineffability in Ancient and Medieval Western Thought." In *Milton and the Ineffable*. Oxford English Monographs. Oxford University Press, 2009.

Ringgren, Helmer. *Israelite Religion*. Translated by David E. Green. Fortress, 1966.

Rohr, Richard. *Everything Belongs: The Gift of Contemplative Prayer*. Crossroad, 2003.

Rohr, Richard. *Falling Upward: A Spirituality for the Two Halves of Life*. Rev. and updated ed. Jossey-Bass, 2024.

Rohr, Richard. *Things Hidden: Scripture as Spirituality.* Franciscan Media, 2008.

Roi, Micha. "1 Kings 19: A Departure on a Journey Story." *Journal for the Study of the Old Testament* 37, no. 1 (2012): 25-44.

Sadler, Rodney S. "Genesis." In *The Africana Bible: Reading Israel's Scriptures From Africa and the African Diaspora*, edited by Hugh R. Page Jr. Fortress, 2010.

Simopoulos, Nicole M. "Who Was Hagar? Mistress, Divorcee, Exile, or Exploited Worker: An Analysis of Contemporary Grassroots Readings of Genesis 16 by Caucasian, Latina, and Black South African Women." In *Reading Other-Wise: Socially Engaged Biblical Scholars Reading with Their Local Communities*, edited by Gerald O. West, 63-72. Society of Biblical Literature, 2007.

Smith, Cooper. "The 'Wilderness' in Hosea and Deuteronomy: A Case of Thematic Reappropriation." *Bulletin for Biblical Research* 28, no. 2 (2018): 240-60.

Smith, James K. A. *Desiring the Kingdom: Worship, Worldview, and Cultural Formation.* Cultural Liturgies. Baker Academic, 2009.

Spitzer, Esther. "A Jungian Midrash on Jacob's Dream." *Reconstructionist* (October 1976): 22-23.

Steere, Douglas. *On Beginning from Within.* Harper & Brothers, 1943.

Stulman, Louis, and Hyun Chul Paul Kim. *You Are My People: An Introduction to the Prophetic Literature.* Abingdon, 2010.

Sweeney, Jon M., and Mark S. Burrows, eds. *Meister Eckhart's Book of Darkness and Light: Meditations on the Path of the Wayless Way.* Hampton Roads, 2023.

Tamez, Elsa. "The Woman Who Complicated the History of Salvation." In *New Eyes for Reading: Biblical and Theological Reflections by Women from the Third World*, edited by John S. Potter and Barbel Von Wartenberg-Potter. Meyer Stone, 1987.

Taylor, Barbara Brown. *An Altar in the World: A Geography of Faith.* HarperOne, 2009.

Thompson, Curt. *Anatomy of the Soul.* Tyndale, 2010.

Thornton, John F., and Susan B. Varenne, eds. *Mortal Beauty, God's Grace: Major Poems and Spiritual Writings of Gerard Manley Hopkins.* Vintage Books, 2003.

Tickle, Phyllis. *The Divine Hours: Prayers for Autumn and Wintertime.* Doubleday, 2000.

Trible, Phyllis. *Texts of Terror: Literary-Feminist Readings of Biblical Narratives.* Overtures to Biblical Theology. Fortress, 2009.

Trible, Phyllis, and Letty M. Russell, eds. *Hagar, Sarah, and Their Children: Jewish, Christian, and Muslim Perspectives.* Westminster John Knox, 2006.

Turner, Denys. *The Darkness of God: Negativity in Christian Mysticism.* Cambridge University Press, 1995.

Waldman, Nahum M. "Sound and Silence." *Jewish Biblical Quarterly* 22, no. 3 (1994): 228-36.

Walsh, Jerome T. *1 Kings.* Berit Olam Studies in Hebrew Narrative and Poetry. Liturgical Press, 1996.

Walton, Kevin. *Thou Traveller Unknown: The Presence and Absence of God in the Jacob Narrative*. Paternoster, 2003.

Ward, Benedicta, trans. *The Sayings of the Desert Fathers: The Alphabetical Collection*. Rev. ed. Mowbray, 1981.

Warren, Tish Harrison. *Prayer in the Night: For Those Who Work or Watch or Weep*. InterVarsity Press, 2021.

Waters, John W. "Who Was Hagar?" In *Stony the Road We Trod: African American Biblical Interpretation*, edited by Cain Hope Felder, 187-205. Fortress, 1991.

Webster, John. *The Domain of the Word: Scripture and Theological Reason*. T&T Clark, 2012.

Weems, Renita J. *Battered Love: Marriage, Sex, and Violence in the Hebrew Prophets*. Fortress, 1995.

West, Gerald O., ed. *Reading Otherwise: Socially Engaged Biblical Scholars Reading with Their Local Communities*. Society of Biblical Literature, 2007.

Whyte, Alexander. *Lord, Teach Us to Pray*. Harper & Brothers, n.d.

Wiederkehr, Macrina. *Abide: Keeping Vigil with the Word of God*. Liturgical Press, 2011.

Wiederkehr, Macrina. *Seven Sacred Pauses: Living Mindfully Through the Hours of the Day*. Sorin Books, 2008.

Wiederkehr, Macrina. *A Tree Full of Angels: Seeing the Holy in the Ordinary*. HarperOne, 1988.

Willard, Dallas. *Hearing God: Developing a Conversational Relationship with God*. InterVarsity Press, 1984.

Willard, Dallas. *Renovation of the Heart: Putting on the Character of Christ*. 20th anniversary ed. NavPress, 2021.

Willard, Dallas. *The Spirit of the Disciplines: Understanding How God Changes Lives*. HarperOne, 1988.

Williams, Delores. *Sisters in the Wilderness: The Challenge of Womanist God-Talk*. Orbis Books, 1993.

Yeats, William Butler. *The Poems of W. B. Yeats: A New Edition*. Macmillan, 1989.

Zakovitch, Yair. *Jacob: Unexpected Patriarch*. Yale University Press, 2012.

Zornberg, Avivah. *The Beginning of Desire: Reflections on Genesis*. Schocken Books, 2011.

Zornberg, Avivah. *Bewilderments: Reflections on the Book of Numbers*. Schocken Books, 2017.

Zornberg, Avivah. *The Particularities of Rapture: Reflections on Exodus*. Schocken Books, 2001.

SCRIPTURE INDEX

www.ingramcontent.com/pod-product-compliance
Lightning Source LLC
LaVergne TN
LVHW091140080826
845145LV00008B/2207
* 9 7 8 1 5 1 4 0 1 0 3 0 3 *